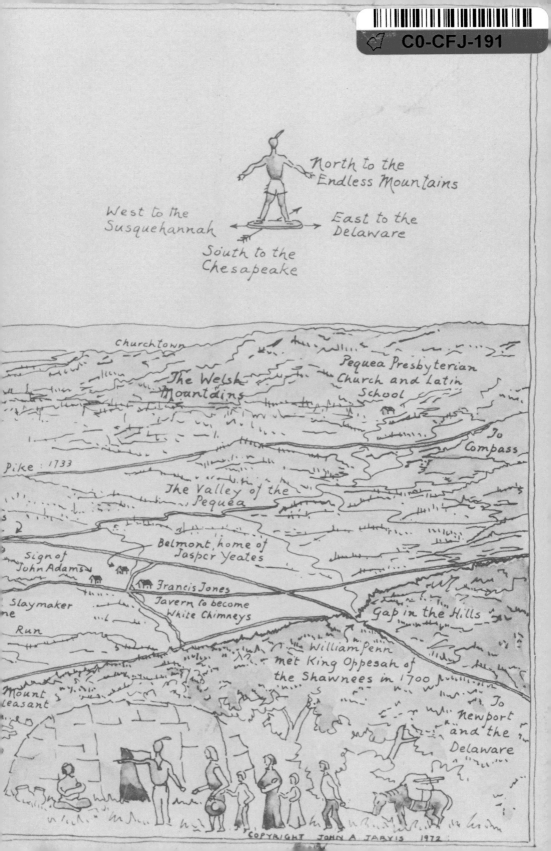

North to the
Endless Mountains

West to the
Susquehannah

East to the
Delaware

South to the
Chesapeake

Churchtown

The Welsh
Mountains

Pequea Presbyterian
Church and Latin
School

To
Compass

Pike 1733

The Valley of the
Pequea

Belmont, home of
Jasper Yeates

Sign of
John Adams

Francis Jones

Slaymaker
ne

Tavern to become
White Chimneys

Gap in the Hills

Run

Mount
leasant

William Penn
met King Oppesah of
the Shawnees in 1700

To
Newport
and the
Delaware

Captives' Mansion

S. R. Maypmaker II

Also by S. R. Slaymaker II

SIMPLIFIED FLY FISHING

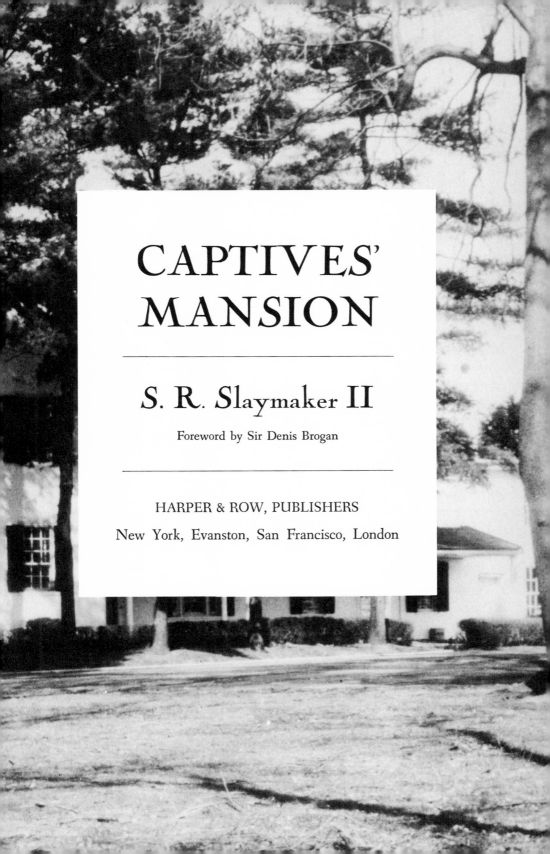

CAPTIVES' MANSION

S. R. Slaymaker II

Foreword by Sir Denis Brogan

HARPER & ROW, PUBLISHERS

New York, Evanston, San Francisco, London

Photographs of the paintings on pages 1, 41 and 126 are reproduced by courtesy of the Frick Art Reference Library. Photographs on pages 177, 202 and 203 are by Donald W. Eckert.

FIRST EDITION

Designed by Patricia Dunbar

Library of Congress Cataloging in Publication Data

Slaymaker, S.
  Captives' mansion.
    1. White Chimneys, Pa.   2. Slaymaker family.
3. Lancaster Co., Pa.—History.   I. Title.
F157.L2S52   917.48'15   72-9155
ISBN 0-06-013923-4

Contents

Dedicated to the memory of the first "S.R."

Illustrations

Acknowledgments

WEBSTER'S SEVENTH NEW COLLEGIATE DICTIONARY defines history as "a chronological record of significant events (as affecting a nation, institution) usu. including an explanation of their causes." By this definition my book is a history—a history of an American home. But historians generally exclude from their field works not possessed of supportive data to undergird significant events, explanations of their causes and the conclusions to which they give rise. Such works require footnotes and bibliographic references, which don't make for easy reading. And since my book comprises a story within a story (mine and the home's), a purist historian's treatment somehow seemed as unnatural as it did redundant. It is, however, factual, being based almost entirely on the personal papers of the home's inhabitants, area historical information, and, in several instances, long-accepted local legends.

As a Cambridge undergraduate in 1946–47 I had the privilege of attending Sir Denis Brogan's American history lectures. In great measure they contributed to making this book possible by stimulating my interest in and appreciation of the subject. Thank you, Professor Brogan.

I'm most grateful to Jack Ward Willson Loose, BS, MA, a distinguished economic historian whose specialty is Pennsylvania history in all its facets. His extensive efforts in verifying the validity of my research have been very helpful. Should unknown data turn up somewhere and render invalid anything that I've written, Mr. Loose cannot be blamed. He worked painstakingly with resources available.

The same applies to that true Renaissance man, John Rengier, Esq., who mixes the practice of law with the writing of plays. Mr. Rengier's counsel with respect to my treatment of the Boyd case is deeply appreciated.

Many thanks are due a longtime and dear friend, the novelist Shirley Watkins Steinman, whose reading of my manuscript led to many helpful suggestions. I'm indebted, too, to Gerald Lestz, a journalist with Lancaster Newspapers, Inc., and a specialist in Pennsylvania folk life, for his critique of the manuscript.

For his longtime interest in my writing and his encouragement in this particular project, I tender sincere thanks to Arnold Gingrich, publisher of *Esquire*. To my editor at Harper & Row, M. S. Wyeth, Jr., for his conviction that this was a story that needed telling, and for his valued guidance, I owe a deep debt of gratitude. I would also like to thank his able colleague, Henry Reath, and the book's production editor, Richard E. Passmore, who faithfully saw it through to the end.

I appreciate greatly the map-making expertise evidenced in John Jarvis's splendid renditions of the Pequea Valley, past and present. My business colleague and close friend, Francis C. Markert, is deserving of especial commendations for his excellent progressive floor plans of White Chimneys.

The research of Lancaster genealogist Clyde L. Groff and the proofreading of my secretary, Thistle Rupp, and Julianne Clarke Swanger were very helpful.

The person deserving of more thanks than I'm capable of putting into words is my wife, Sal, who typed three complete drafts of the book in one year, all the while caring for two children, running our home (with precious little help), and putting up with her high-strung businessman–gentleman farmer–writer husband. Top kudos to you, Sal!

S. R. SLAYMAKER II

White Chimneys
Gap, Pennsylvania
March 11, 1973

Foreword

It is a grievance of a great many Anglo-Saxons in the United States of America that the oldest human artifacts inside its territory are the work of various sophisticated tribes of Indians, of Spaniards, and of formidable nomad Indians like the Sioux and the Iroquois. Sympathy for the wrongs done the Indians who made the extremely interesting constructions of New Mexico or on the frontier of what is now Mexico has come to represent a sense of guilt, so that a frontier hero as portrayed by John Wayne has come to be regarded as, at the very best, a rather dangerous and murderous type.

Perhaps because of this natural and justifiable reaction there has been a writing down of the later European settlers in the United States. Furthermore, very few artifacts of the seventeenth century survive, even in Virginia or in New England. It is not until the last years of the century that something we can call an American civilization can be identified. Nevertheless, that civilization did come into existence and has some remarkable monuments to its credit.

Mount Vernon is a very attractive set of buildings, if not as perfect an example of country house architecture as Mr. Jefferson's Monticello. And, of course, there are some very pleasing plantation houses in Virginia, as well as the elegant city of Charleston, South Carolina.

One of the drawbacks to the exaggeration of the architectual merits of Colonial building is that attention has been concentrated largely on such historically and aesthetically impressive structures as Mount Vernon and Monticello. This has led to a neglect of buildings which, if not historically or even aesthetically so important, are yet of great interest and often of great charm.

White Chimneys, the Slaymaker family mansion at Gap, in Pennsylvania, near the attractive county seat of Lancaster, is not to be compared with any of the country houses of the Virginia gentry or with the urban elegance of either Charleston, Philadelphia or Boston, but it has one very great advantage which not many of the houses of those modern cities possess: it has been continuously inhabited by the Slaymaker family for almost two hundred years and is in itself a museum piece of American architecture.

It is not merely a question of architecture. It is a question of human history or, if you like, of ecological history. Since the late eighteenth century the Slaymaker family have been the local squires of Gap and are also, in their own dramatic family history, an illustration of the vicissitudes of settlement in Pennsylvania. This family's saga is not one reflecting ever-waxing success, for there were many ups and downs in the history of the Slaymakers. These ups and downs and the story of the Slaymaker estate itself are part of the social history of the great colony of Pennsylvania.

Mr. Slaymaker's book reminds us that it was not merely the Quakers who played a great part in the creation of the colony: German Calvinists and the very interesting groups of German Pietist sectarians, principally Mennonites and Amish, also played their parts. The Slaymaker family were, from an economic point of view, much more successful settlers, more worthy of the patronage of the Penn family, than were these German Pietists. Even today the rigorous rules of, say, the Amish, as well as their way of dressing, of worship, indeed of farming, recall religious settlements at least as unique as any known in New England.

This book has, among its many grounds of interest, that of showing the symbiotic relationship between the present-day Slaymakers and the highly disciplined Amish Pietists who are their tenant farmers. It is true there are signs today in Lancaster County that this austerity (indeed, the acceptance of what seem to the modern way of life irrelevant taboos) permits of some sophistry, that its practitioners may better adjust to the technical superiority of modern rural life; but it is the fidelity rather than the occasional backsliding of the Amish which is more impressive than any adoption of modern ways of life either in the use of farm machinery, of modern dress or of modern educational standards. The relationship between the Slaymaker family and their Amish tenant farmers has been, on the whole, one of instructive collaboration.

One of the chief grounds of interest in White Chimneys is singular. Mount Vernon and Monticello and some less celebrated Virginia and Carolina plantations have been either kept up or restored, regardless of expense, in honor of General Washington and Mr. Jefferson and other leading figures of the Southern gentry. But the Slaymaker mansion has an interest which, from many points of view, is greater than either Mount Vernon or Monticello. Since White Chimneys has been inhabited continuously by the Slaymaker family from the time of its Colonial beginnings, the home is *not* a model of symmetry, of the harmony that is so much admired and imitated all over the South—indeed, over a great part of the United States. (For example, I know a very elegant, very expensive, very modern imitation of an eighteenth-century manor house which is about six years old but already has all the necessary appearance of antiquity which is so much admired in, let us say, California.)

Slaymaker generations have continuously altered their house, expanded it, improved it, and sometimes—if the Irish bull may be accepted—improved it for the worse. But what is interesting and what is impressive is the continuity of life of White Chimneys and the degree to which the various parts of the house have withstood alterations, most of which have turned out to be harmonious—even if not regular—in the fashion that modern architects favor. I know few houses in the American States which have the charm of continuous habitation that White Chimneys has. I can remember, for example, great friends of mine who had been living on the same site in Maryland since the early seventeenth century, and I used to cite them as an example of the fact that America is not always changing and of the fact that some parts of the Atlantic states boast as good specimens of architectural history as any in England. But just as I know another very rich family which has ignored its duties to its own very great properties, so I learned, with distress, that the Maryland family I allude to have very recently abandoned their commitment to their Maryland home site and are now settled in Manhattan.

It is perhaps one of the great virtues of White Chimneys that it does not look as if it had been designed by an interior or exterior decorator as a museum piece or a brand-new Elizabethan, Classical, Colonial or other artificial construction. Indeed, one of the most interesting achievements of Mr. Slaymaker's book is his story of the degree to which it has been possible to reconstruct the ancestral house so that, even when the results are not aesthetically of the first order, they are historically of the greatest interest.

The historical role of the Slaymaker family and of their houses is one of the charms of the family assets. It is true that the military record during the War of the Revolution, for example, was not particularly brilliant, but it was at any rate a war record—and it was repeated in the War of 1812.

It is not very common in the United States to have family assets like those of the Slaymaker family, or family businesses like their investments in Lancaster, and part of the charm and part of the academic accomplishment of Mr. Slaymaker's book is the revelation of American business from the period of Andrew Jackson right down to the present day. The dramatic ups and downs in the Slaymaker family fortunes are highly educational.

Mr. Slaymaker's account of how he was won over and charmed by the not very solvent assets he inherited from his grandmother is a success story of a kind we do not usually associate with American business. To salvage White Chimneys, to continue to play the role of squire which had almost ruined some predecessors, Mr. Slaymaker had to give up a great deal of the agreeable social activities common to the prosperous, landed exploiter of tax losses which he was not. It is obvious from his book that Mr. Slaymaker has found that the sacrifices he made to salvage the assets were well worth the price. In this respect he became a real squire. So this *is* a success story in a very deep sense—not only in the dramatic discoveries that Mr. Slaymaker made about the many hidden treasures of his family inheritance, but of the role he could play in perpetuating it.

There is a sense in which this is a Virgilian story: the salvation of a family inheritance which might otherwise have been broken up, sacrificed to real estate speculation or—what would have been almost worse —to the creation of a bogus architectural novelty which would not have had anything like the estate's present sacred character, one that justifies the trust of the Penns when they launched their Holy Experiment.

Sir Denis Brogan

1 Hedgerley Close
Cambridge, England

Prologue

MY STATE was reminiscent of a boyhood ether sleep: a slight numbness in limbs, dryness of mouth, stomach churnings that lessened as anxiety gave way to gathering weariness and resignation to the fact that the inevitable was finally happening.

I had inherited a village, its mansion house, and one hundred acres of farmland in Pennsylvania's southeastern Lancaster County, the so-called Pennsylvania Dutch Country and Garden Spot of the U.S.A.

It was August 15, 1955, and I was driving to the property for my first visit as its new squire. The previous owner, my aged grandmother, had died two weeks before.

It wasn't as if there had been no warning. My grandfather, who died in 1940, wanted me to have the plantation. If his wife survived him, it was to come to me on her death. So I had fifteen years to plan for its future. But as a young and impecunious minor functionary in a family business, I had scant means with which to plan. And it was not looking a gift horse in the mouth to state that an overflowing cup should have accompanied the bequest. For the mansion house, White Chimneys, had not been lived in for ten years. My grandmother moved to Lancaster in 1945, leaving the place under the care of a farm manager, a tenant farmer, and a caretaker. Led to believe that their stewardship would be judged by the balance sheet, they feared repairs like the plague. Decay had set in.

Immediate rehabilitation was out of the question. Should I heed the lawyers and sell, or should I try to hang on in hopes of an eventual windfall? If only this were possible! Deep down I had a gnawing desire not to represent the last of six successive generations that had inhabited White Chimneys more than 175 years.

As I drove from Lancaster on U.S. Route 30 toward my village,

Slaymakertown, I could only hope that the inevitable would be for the best. On rounding the bend on Salisbury Hill's summit, I looked down into the hollow where the village lay, the large Federal-fronted mansion on the left with its green roofing and many white chimneys, girded about with wide lawns dappled by the shadows of giant beech trees. The barn, tobacco sheds, and outbuildings, too, glistened snow white in bright sunlight. On the right side of Route 30, facing the mansion, were three tenant houses. Farther to the east on the mansion's side were two more.

Slaymakertown looked picture neat, as indeed it was meant to appear to passers-by. But the paint deceived. As always when approaching the place, I thought of white elephants. This time, though, there could be no passing by. I had done so in recent years, to avoid being reminded of what one day had to be faced up to. This was to be my first meeting with tenant farmer Don Ranck, who had been there for four years.

He was a six-footer of about 180 pounds, in his late twenties, with curly brown hair, an open, placid face, and a peaches-and-cream complexion. The plain cut of his Sunday best bespoke the Mennonite faith. We shook hands as he smilingly noted that I'd inherited him, too.

Don wanted to tour the farm, so we drove out the lane to the highest hilltop. Fields sloped away toward the blue-green Welsh Mountains on the north and the Mine Hill Ridge to the south. To the east was the small town of Gap and to the west, down the lane in the hollow, lay the mansion, farm buildings, and village, beyond which the rising ribbon of Route 30 West ascended Salisbury Hill. The historic and bucolic Pequea Valley seemed more strikingly lovely than I had known it before, bathed now in sunshine, now in shadow owing to a scudding overcast spanked by gusts that foretold a storm.

We studied badly eroded slopes. Fields of corn, hay, and tobacco were cut through, top to bottom, by ugly brown gashes or "washes." Don said a tractor could not cross some of them. He talked about the ways soil erosion could be licked at little expense to farmers by the Department of Agriculture's Soil Conservation Service and about his crop rotation plan for the coming year. I found myself nodding in agreement. I told him that I would be in touch with him. As we drove back to the mansion the storm broke.

I ran to the side porch entrance and into caretaker Lloyd Homsher, who was waiting with the key and a warm welcome. We had been friends for years. His father had been the caretaker before him. As a young man he lost his right arm in a factory accident. He then understudied his father at gardening and had been at White Chimneys for twenty years. Now at forty-five he was, as always, shy, calm of mien, and possessed of a quiet wit. He did not ask about my plans but earnestly noted that he was handy in more than gardening. I was amazed to learn that caretaker Lloyd was a carpenter, plumber, electrician, and, as he laughingly added, "a one-armed paperhanger." When I repeated my remark about staying in touch, he seemed pleased. We then parted, and I went inside.

The house was musty and full of sheet-shrouded furniture, trunks, and packing boxes. I picked my way from the colonial farmhouse in the rear into the Federal mansion and stood in the hallway where Lafayette had been received by my great-great-great-grandfather in 1825. On the walls of the two front rooms hung portraits of the earliest inhabitants. Large, Sargent-like renditions of later generations were in the 1923 ballroom wing. Looking back after fifteen years I'm tempted to credit the commanding stares of these likenesses with dictating my eventual decision. But I must admit that the portraits exerted little influence at the time. However, the old family papers did.

I found the musty manuscript collection in the garret in tin boxes, piled amid cobwebbed homemaking paraphernalia of bygone days: yarn winders, spinning wheels, dough trays, a butchering table, and bundles of flax. The papers had not been examined since the 1920s. Then my grandfather had permitted a history professor to search for "important" signatures. Several were found, including a letter from George Washington. These were framed and hung. The rest—letters, deeds, agreements, and business correspondence spanning two centuries—were sealed in the tin boxes and stored in the garret.

I sat on a steamer trunk and stared at the boxes as rain beat on shingles overhead and thunder rattled drenched windows. It occurred to me for the first time that my grandfather might have feared skeletons. The papers could reveal a tale of White Chimneys' evolution differing from that given to historical and patriotic-genealogical societies. These musings came naturally. For as a history major at college I had pondered researching the papers for a master's degree. The idea had been shelved when I went to work. Perhaps, I thought, the proper time had come. What could be more apropos than developing the story behind the home's evolution while rehabilitating it—or at least trying to—so that the story might be ongoing?

My thought train was broken by waxing sunlight. It illuminated the boxes, highlighting a spiderweb hanging between them and a yarn winder. A dead house fly was stuck in its gossamer folds. I can see it as clearly as if it were yesterday and don't know why because it signified nothing at the time. Had I been of a more imaginative bent, a portent might have been sensed. For my impulse was to lead to ensnarement. I would become the mansion's captive, no more able to escape it than were my predecessors.

I decided to disappoint the lawyers in the morning by telling them that there would be no sale.

PART I

Colonial

Judge Henry Slaymaker
Painting by John Hesselius

His wife, Faithful Richardson Slaymaker
Painting by Gustavus Hesselius

He recognized on the sign, however, the ruby face of King George, under which he had smoked so many a peaceful pipe; but even this was singularly metamorphosed. The red coat was changed for one of blue and buff; a sword was held in the hand instead of a sceptre; the head was decorated with a cocked hat, and underneath was painted in large characters, "General Washington"!

WASHINGTON IRVING, "Rip Van Winkle"

Slaymaker Family Tree

Mathias Schleiermacher (Slaymaker) (?–1763)

- Lawrence (?–1747)
- Mary (1757–1797)
- Margaret (?–?)
- Henry, Jr. (1762–1826)
- Mathias II (1728–1804)
  - Hannah (1764–1847)
  - Faithful (1767–1847)
  - Lydia (1769–1794)
- Henry (1734–1785) m. Faithful Jones Richardson
  - James Fleming (1781–d. "in youth")
  - Isabella (1784–1834)
  - Faithful (1783–?)
  - Elizabeth (1785–1851)
  - Isabella Angelica (1819–1891)
  - Jasper (1787–1827)
  - Amos (1755–1837) m. Isabella Fleming
    - Sarah (1771–1804)
    - Samuel (1774–1830)
  - Henry Fleming (1789–1860) m. Rebecca Slaymaker Cochran
    - Amos Henderson (1791–1856)
    - Jean (1793–d. "in youth")
- John (1733–1798)
  - Sophia (1) (1776–1777)
  - Sophia (2) (1779–1856)
  - William Daniel (1797–1856)
  - John R. (1799–1815)
- Daniel (1740–1801)
- Barbara (1758–1831)
  - Hannah (1801–1860)

Samuel Cochran I m. Jane Cameron Redsecker (1828–1894)

- Hannah Cecelia (1817–1859)
- Isabella Angelica (1819–1891)
- Beckie Ann (1821–1843)
- Amos Fleming (1823–1892)

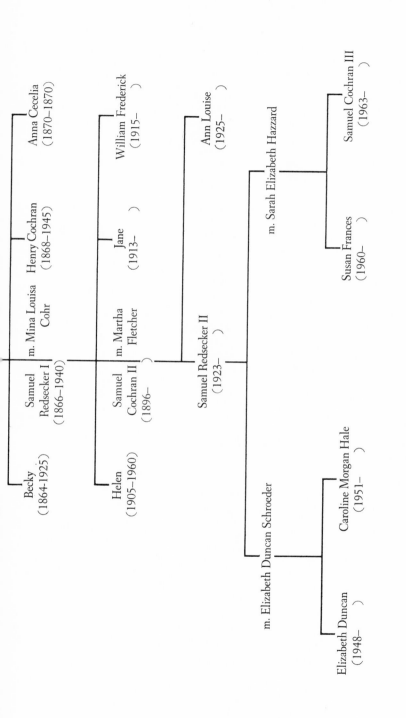

Becky
(1864-1925)

Samuel
Redsecker I
(1866–1940)

m. Mina Louisa
Cohr

Henry Cochran
(1868–1945)

Anna Cecelia
(1870–1870)

Helen
(1905–1960)

Samuel
Cochran II
(1896–)

m. Martha
Fletcher

Jane
(1913–)

William Frederick
(1915–)

Samuel Redsecker II
(1923–)

Ann Louise
(1925–)

m. Sarah Elizabeth Hazzard

Susan Frances
(1960–)

Samuel Cochran III
(1963–)

m. Elizabeth Duncan Schroeder

Caroline Morgan Hale
(1951–)

Elizabeth Duncan
(1948–)

1

I MOVED INTO White Chimneys on a Saturday morning in early May, 1956. The mansion and outbuildings reflected faint tints of orange from the sun peeping through the "Gap in the Hills." Snorts from a large yellow bulldozer reverberated on cool, still air. It gouged a curving, choco-late-colored gash through verdant hay far out on the south slope. An erosion-resistant waterway was in the making.

"Welcome home!" grinned caretaker Lloyd Homsher as he helped me unload the car. Farmer Don Ranck, his wife, and two small daughters joined us and offered a shoofly pie for my first dinner. They said that it would bring good luck.

Across the highway one of the tenants was washing his car. He was unshaven and rough-looking and sported a blue silk jacket with "Smokie's Motors" imprinted in red. He glanced suspiciously at us. I greeted him with a wave. He smiled weakly and turned back to his bucket and hose. I felt a fleeting moment of unease. The tenants were sure to be my biggest headache because of their houses' state of disrepair.

Directly on taking the reins in the preceding August I became totally absorbed in starting farm improvements. Priority was given to the land. The Department of Agriculture's Soil Conservation Service was called in. Air photos were taken from which a plan was drawn for contour farming facilitated by erosion-resistant diversion terraces and waterways. Thanks to the beneficence of the U.S. government, my out-lay was smaller than anticipated but sufficient to necessitate a call on the bank. The loan was padded to permit minimal repairs to the tenant houses.

Most Lancaster County tenant farming agreements from time im-memorial have required a landowner to provide his farmer with a rent-free house, fertilizer, one-half of the yearly seed bill, taxes, insurance, and the cost of major repairs. A tenant farmer is responsible for labor, half the yearly seed bill, and light repairs. Income is divided between both. This was the arrangement I inherited.

The caretaker's house was also rent-free. Both dwellings naturally had been kept in good repair, but not the rental properties, thanks to the paucity of information supplied to my ailing grandmother by the farm manager. He salved his conscience, however, by recommending that rents be kept low—specifically, where government controls left them at the end of World War II—all of which left me in the difficult position of having to raise rents while being unable to justify the move until extensive repairs were made. The bank loan could provide only a start. So I mulled over alternatives for a decision come spring, when I planned moving in. There was too much else to do during that first fall and winter of 1955–56.

I was going through divorce proceedings. They were not calculated to enhance my outlook, either financially or morale-wise. My daughters, Libby, seven, and Caroline, four, enlivened some weekends, most of which were devoted to house cleaning, inventory taking, and minor alterations to the kitchen, the better to facilitate bachelor homemaking.

As a boy I spent little time in the kitchen. It was always amply staffed with longtime help and was thought of in purely utilitarian terms. On moving back, though, I saw it through the eyes of a history buff and wondered about its original appearance. Over the years it had become an aesthete's nightmare, a study in tacky, nondescript modernity.

For years my grandmother had an old-maid companion, a onetime high school art teacher, whose asserted responsibility every few years was to pick colors for the painting of the kitchen. Her last effort during World War II was the most nauseous. Plaster walls were coated a bilious yellow and woodwork a shocking green, all in high gloss.

The floor was covered entirely by licoricelike linoleum of pre-1914 vintage. It was scarred by imprints from chair legs. Hard against the room's northern extremity stood a huge, misanthropic-looking cast-iron coal range, flanked on the right by a Grand Rapids cupboard. To the left of the stove, in the northwest corner, was a pantry with a sink and gas stove. In the center of the west wall was a door to the cellar stairs. A serving pantry comprised the southwest corner. In the south wall beside it was a portal through which food was passed to the dining room. In the center of the kitchen's south end a floor-to-ceiling cupboard had been built, flush with the wall. Bordering it, in the southeast corner, a door led to the dining room. In the middle of the east wall, flanked by two windows, was the door opening on the lane.

Once the kitchen was cleaned and I had time to settle into it, previously unnoticed hints of its original appearance became evident. The wavy window glass had obviously been blown. An overabundance of paint coatings could not disguise long, wrought-iron strap hinges on the door and the rough, hand-hewn texture of the large wall cupboard.

These hallmarks of early days inspired a thorough examination. So after my first dinner of fried chicken—topped off with Don's shoofly pie —I sat over coffee at a white-enameled steel table and stared at the coal range. Evidently, there had been a fireplace behind it, for the top of a rough wooden mantel was visible, and above it was a chimney. I had never heard of a fireplace and guessed that it had been filled in or boarded over.

I crawled on the range and peered behind it. Boarding covered the wall. Its oyster-gray hue bespoke moldering whitewash. Anxiously, I caught Don in the lane after milking. We could not budge the range. Don called Lloyd, and we moved it sufficiently to permit the ripping away of the boarding with a claw hammer.

We ogled in silence at a massive Early American fireplace. The whitewashed brick back wall was fire-blackened. Primitive cast-iron andirons and a large iron pot were heavily encrusted by dirt and cobwebs. Two crane holders were built into the west wall, but the crane was missing. In the center of the wall, to the right of the fireplace, we found a warming closet where cooked food was kept warm by heat from the fireplace.

After preparing coffee for my helpers, I phoned my father in Lancaster (he had grown up at White Chimneys), described our finds, and asked what he knew about them. He had never heard of the fireplace or warming closet. For as long as he could remember the range had been there. He guessed that it had been installed during an extensive renovation in Civil War times, which his grandmother described when he was a boy.

After Don and Lloyd left, I poured another cup of coffee and examined the walls. How many were the layers of paint? Might their composition lend clues as to their dates? If so, the kitchen could be restored to something like its original state! I put down the cup and rose to turn out the lights. A warping in the linoleum where it met the hearth caught my eye. I moved to rip it back and was overjoyed to see five-inch-wide board flooring. There was no doubt now that a superb restoration was possible.

I had decided to use my boyhood bedroom directly at the head of the stairs from the dining room in the rear house. Perhaps it was the effects of coffee as much as excited musings over restoration that kept me tossing there most of the night. Through the window overlooking the flower garden came liquid murmurs from the waterfalls in the west lawn's stream. Now and again there was a rustling of breeze-tossed leaves and distant creaks in woodwork. I remember thinking that the house was settling down contentedly now that it finally had an occupant. Lloyd had said that "it isn't good for a place like this not to be lived in."

Ghosts, about which a few Gap old-timers talked, did not intrude. I fell asleep feeling very much at home.

The prototype of a country squire is a doughty individual who at once dominates and patronizes his tenants. Beyond not having the wherewithal to play the part properly, I found it constitutionally impossible to do so. For I was possessed of that occupational failing of most salesmen, a Willy Loman-like desire to be liked. Thus the guarded glance of the car-washing tenant was, to quote Arthur Miller's *Death of a Salesman*, like getting "yourself a couple of spots on your hat" and "being finished."

Earlier, I had decided to buy materials and paint for those tenants willing and able to renovate on their own. Now, in a fit of good will, I decided to offer to help them myself. As jobs were completed I would raise rents, but they would be kept well below going rates. During the week following my arrival I called on the tenants and posed the proposition. All had at least one family member who could help. They were visibly delighted, and we parted on a first-name basis.

After commuting from the office during spring evenings in 1956 I cooked dinners on the gas stove in the kitchen pantry. Then Lloyd and Don joined me for coffee and farm talk. After they retired, I pursued with great care the removal of paint samples from the kitchen's walls.

Samuel Redsecker Slaymaker II, in garret with family papers

According to family legend the original house, comprising kitchen and dining room, was built in 1720 by a well-to-do Welsh Quaker immigrant named Francis Jones. His home, my grandfather used to say, descended to his lovely grandniece, Faithful Richardson, who presented it as her dowery when she married our direct forebear, Henry Slaymaker, in 1754. Given the fact that before her marriage Faithful had been painted by the noted artist Gustavus Hesselius, the tale seemed plausible.

And it evidenced pleasingly genteel beginnings. More's the pity that it wasn't true.

Throughout the preceding winter's evenings at my parents' home in Lancaster I researched the earliest family papers and read extensively on area history. Courthouse and cemetery records were studied. A genealogist was retained to investigate the lineage of Francis Jones. The story that emerged reflected the home's unpretentious origins in the primeval beauty of the Pequea Valley.

2

A LEGEND OF Lancaster County has it that William Penn first viewed the valley beyond the Gap in the Hills in the spring of 1700. By then his "Holy Experiment" in religious and ethnic toleration—made possible by King Charles II's large middle Atlantic land grant in repayment of a loan from Penn's father—was firmly established in Philadelphia and had extended west to the Welsh Quaker villages of Bryn Mawr, Bala Cynwyd, and Haverford. Beyond these tiny villages the road dwindled to an Indian path that wound through fragrant woodland of oak, maple, cedar, and dogwood full of wild turkey, grouse, and deer, eventually fording the sparkling waters of the Brandywine Creek. From the Brandywine almost imperceptibly the terrain's elevation rises to a plateau. In Penn's time it combined woods and natural pastures of knee-deep grass, prime potential grazing land.

Beyond, the plateau land rises again into a wall of timber dented by a single gap—the Gap in the Hills—from whose summit Penn could see a lush verdant valley beyond. To Penn it must have seemed a passageway to the west through which his utopia was ordained to extend. Here was a transit whose fertile limestone soil would ensure permanent settlement, thus securing it to the seacoast behind.

He had heard of this valley from Swedish settlers who lived in the Delaware River area earlier. His informants spoke of an opening through the hills which led to the valley's floor. This "Gap in the Hills" was situated on a north–south trail from New Castle on the Delaware over which the Swedes had traded with Indians of the interior.

The natives were Shawnees, Delawares, Conestogas, and Pequeas—all related to the Susquehannas, who were under the suzerainty of the Iroquois confederacy of the Five Nations. The Indians posed no threat to William Penn. Word of his fair dealings with them had surely preceded him.

The legend continues to the effect that during Penn's first visit his packhorses were unloaded near a large rock by a spring on the hillside. With evening's first shadows Indians emerged from the woods. King Opessah of the Shawnees was greeted by Penn and an interpreter. Braves produced a deer carcass. Wood was piled high. A fire was lit and ale flowed from the voyagers' casks. While the spitted deer roasted, the red men danced for Penn's party. Later, the proprietor himself is said to have danced with an Indian maiden. An understanding about future settlement was arrived at.

The next day the travelers returned to Philadelphia. It only remained for Penn's agents in the British Isles and Western Europe to sell Opessah's land to potential settlers so that the "Holy Experiment" could move westward.

A decade elapsed between Penn's visit to the Pequea Valley and its settlement by the Ferrée and Schleiermacher families in 1710.

The Ferrées had been French Huguenot silk manufacturers and members of lower Normandy's lesser nobility since 1255. Mathias Schleiermacher, a young civil servant in Hesse-Cassel, Germany, of the Reformed faith, feared for his family's safety when France's King Louis XIV in 1685 revoked the instrument of religious toleration that was the Edict of Nantes. French armies ravaged the Palatinate. Twelve hundred German towns went up in flames. Mathias, his wife, Catherine, and two small children, Lawrence and Margaret, fled this cockpit of desolation "in the darkness of the night," as their families' chronicle says, for Strasbourg on the left bank of the Rhine in the province of Alsace. Here they were befriended by the widowed Mary Ferrée, who had moved there earlier.

Seeking greater security, both families moved to Lindau, Bavaria, where they heard of a new Moses, William Penn, who was selling cheaply his rich land in the New World, title to which would ensure owners political asylum and freedom of opportunity and religion.

On March 10, 1708, the Ferrée-Schleiermachers were passported by the Bavarian Civil Service to emigrate "via Holland and England to the Island of Pennsylvania to reside there." Final clearance came on May 10 from the pastor and deacons of the Reformed Walloon Church, who described them as professors of "the Pure Reformed Religion . . . without having given cause for scandal that has come to our knowledge."

The little band traversed the Palatinate's burned-out landscape toward the riot of spires and masts that marked the burgeoning maritime metropolis of Rotterdam. After sailing on a bark to London, they settled in a Palatine colony in Spitalfields.

Being people of substance, the Ferrée-Schleiermachers formed the nucleus around which poorer transients gathered. Through Penn agents, Madame Ferrée was their spokesman to, and dickerer with, William Penn. He asked that she be brought to his London residence for an interview. The cultured and indomitable widow so impressed the proprietor that he petitioned the sovereign herself for an audience. This occurred on August 27, 1708.

That England's Queen Anne took pleasure in the company of women of accomplishment was soon obvious, for after one sitting she granted Madame Ferrée a patent of naturalization, covering all fifty-four of the persons in the Ferrée-Schleiermacher entourage. Permission for the group to colonize in America was granted in the same instrument.

Mathias Schleiermacher and Mary Ferrée's holdings comprised roughly four thousand acres from agent Martin Kendig's large share of Penn's 1710 land grant in the Pequea Valley. Possession could not be effected until the surveyor general of the province finished subdividing. Payment was then to be made to agent Kendig.

Martin Kendig, like other Penn agent-servants, was a middleman for the proprietor. Penn dispensed with the work of getting settlers by allowing agents to take a commission on any portions of their own grants sold. The only injunctions laid down were those that could be expected; customers had to be "Godly" and able to come across with the money.

Since surveying would take two years, it was decided that the

Ferrée-Schleiermacher group would cross the Atlantic and proceed up the Hudson River to a Huguenot colony at Esopus. When surveying was completed in Pennsylvania, they could descend to their Promised Lands.

In early September, 1708, the Pool of London, with its forest of masts, slipped back into the city's sooty mists, behind the Ferrée-Schleiermachers and their band. The encircling horizon now became green-blue ocean for six weeks of hard biscuits, salted fish, pickled pork, scents of pitch and brine, squeaks and groans of straining rigging.

So the haven signaled by the Hudson's approaches brought on deeply felt emotions of thanksgiving. After the Reverend Josiah Kochesthal led the group in prayer, they embraced. With laughs and tears they probably commented on the familiar Rhine-like appearance of the Hudson's steep wooded hills. They must have been thankful that they made it to Esopus before the river froze and rejoiced to settle down in the log cabins of their hosts before the first snow fell.

For two years these immigrants waited at Esopus. In 1710 word reached them that their Pequea Valley lands had been surveyed. When ice was out in early spring, they set sail downriver to the ocean, but this time only to coast along the shoreline to the mouth of the Delaware and up the river to Philadelphia.

When Mary Ferrée and her friends put into Philadelphia, they found bustling markets with dairy cattle, sheep, oxen, and horses—descendants of the original Swedish stock. From full-to-the-rafters stores they bought hardware, smoked meat, and flour. Maps of their holdings were prepared in the office of Penn's secretary, James Logan.

The Pequea Valley comprised the western extremity of Chester County and was referred to as Conestoga township. The valley was watered by two small, southwesterly-flowing rivers, the Pequea and, a few miles to its west, the Conestoga. Both emptied into the Susquehanna River. Penn's west road had been extended through Chester County to the Gap in the Hills. Here it crossed the trading road running south to New Castle. By 1710 the west road from Philadelphia was being pushed southwesterly to the Susquehanna. It was called the Great Conestoga Road.

It was over this dirt path that the Ferrée-Schleiermacher caravan of wagons bumped west on a summer's day in 1710. Reports of the settlers' arrival have it that Madame Ferrée stepped in front of the others to meet the first deerskin-clad native, who muttered that he would take them "to Beaver." They followed the guide to one of several streamside shacks of bark-covered sapling poles. There was Beaver, who not only graciously grunted a welcome but provided huts for the party for the night.

In the morning Beaver bade them follow him westward a few miles to a point known as the Great Flats of the Pequea. Here, where the stream widened, lay the main encampment of Conestoga Indians under King Tanawa.

The king's welcome was said to have been a royal one with day-long feasting and dancing. The travelers were asked to remain at the camp until their building sites had been picked. They accepted supplies of smoked fish, meat, and dried corn.

The Schleiermachers built by a spring in a glen formed by the base of a steep hill. Mathias had been given suggested building instructions by James Logan's office. He followed them faithfully. They called for a log cabin "thirty foot long and eighteen foot broad . . . with a partition near the middle and another to divide one end of the house into two small rooms . . . with loft overall . . . the lower floor is the ground . . . this may seem a mean way of building but 'tis sufficient and safest for ordinary beginners."

During the autumn of 1710 the ring of axes against tall walnuts was heard around the hill as these ordinary beginners set about to bring civilization to the valley before the flying of the first snow.

In the years following the Ferrée-Schleiermacher settlement, increasing numbers of immigrants entered the Pequea Valley. Among them was a Welsh Quaker named Francis Jones who had settled in Bristol, near Philadelphia, where he prospered as a soapmaker. That Francis had not moved west mainly to acquire farming land was manifest in the size of his purchase: only three hundred acres. A Quaker of means could have bought more heavily. Nor did he wish to continue in the soap business. Rather, he saw in the Gap crossroads an ideal location for a tavern. With waxing immigrant traffic, Francis Jones would never want for customers.

The Jones settlement could not have been as fraught with such hardships as that of the Ferrée-Schleiermachers. Jones's first home in

Bristol was only forty miles from the Gap. The building of the tavern home probably posed few problems, thanks to adequate indentured help. Indeed, it is likely that building proceeded while Francis, wife Hannah, and their seven children remained in Bristol.

Francis chose a comely site: a mile northwest of the Gap, in a half-saucerlike declivity, bounded to the north and west by gently rising hillocks—open on a southeast plain facing the Gap. He built between a spring and a northerly-flowing brook. Francis eschewed James Logan's log house building plans, possibly considering such houses too crude, fit only for Germans, who—it was common knowledge—built more substantially for their prized animals than for themselves.

The Jones tavern house, like those in Wales, was built to endure. It measured 15 by 15 feet and had 21-inch-thick limestone walls. A few hundred feet to the north was a limestone escarpment. His help quarried the rock and, as was the custom, moved it on horse-drawn sleds to the building site.

The building comprised a one-room first floor, connected with a second floor and garret by a stairway on the left of a large open fireplace. This covered more than half of the room's north end. Wide oak floor boards were pegged to supporting beams under which was a cellar. There, beneath the fireplace, was a huge vault. This, and a smaller vault in the west wall, could store prodigious amounts of preserves, potatoes, apples, and meats. In the cellar's south wall were bunklike alcoves, possible sleeping quarters for indentured help.

In keeping with the building customs of rural British cottagers, Francis's walls were plaster-coated. Roofing was probably thatched straw. The door opened on a two-mile road which Francis laid out to connect the Great Conestoga Road to the south with the Newport Road in the northwest. Jones's road drew travelers from both thoroughfares.

The exigencies of tavernkeeping could hardly have precluded the need for farming, since the family needed food grains to be self-sufficient. With the rich soil, a substantial excess was available to be carted south to Newport, there to be sold and shipped to England. Fields of wheat, barley, and oats were probably tended by Francis's sons from outbuildings a few feet to the north of the tavern.

The Jones Tavern was built between 1710 and 1720. During this

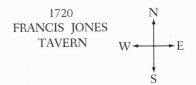

1720
FRANCIS JONES
TAVERN

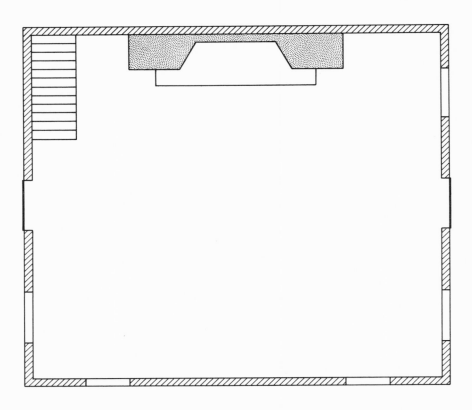

▨▨▨▨▨▨▨▨▨▨ Permanent Wall or Partition

▨▨▨   ▨▨▨ Door

▨▨▨ ___ ▨▨▨ Open Passageway

▨▨▨ ▭ ▨▨▨ Window

Rear view of White Chimneys, showing original Jones Tavern

decade and the one following, the immigrant tide continued to swell as William Penn opened land to the west of the Pequea Valley across the majestic sweep of the Susquehanna River. Many settlers were Swiss-German Mennonites, pietistic sectarians whose sixteenth-century founder was Menno Simons. Penn favored them, for as the supply of his British coreligionists dwindled, he saw the Mennonites as their German counterparts whose pacifism would sit well with the Indians, thus ensuring felicitous expansion of his Holy Experiment. There was a sprinkling of German Lutherans and Calvinists (like the Schleiermachers), and increasing numbers of Scots-Irish Presbyterians from the North of Ireland who fled the oppressive Test Act of the Established Church of England.

Thus the clientele of Francis Jones's tavern represented in microcosm the melting pot that was Colonial Pennsylvania. The tavern's size was sufficient to board only a few travelers, but its single, large kitchen–living room was surely beehive-active, night and day.

The interior walls of plaster were whitewashed and girded about by a rough-hewn plate rail, two feet below the raftered ceiling. Plates of pewter and possibly Delft china could have graced the rail; mugs of pewter and silver the mantel. Dining tables, in all probability, were rough stretcher types—possibly set against the west wall so as to provide space at the room's center. Such tables were usually set with benches, but Francis could have afforded Philadelphia-built Windsor chairs—perhaps a deacon's bench or even a Hepplewhite sofa.

Jones Tavern on a busy summer evening must have presented a colorful tableau. In the ruddy afterglow of sunset, packhorses and wagons jostled for space at hitching trees. Mennonites in dusty, drab homespuns crowded the spirit barrels at the doorway. Inside, by the hearth, food was served by Hannah Jones's ubiquitous children. There was corn bread and porridge for youngsters, while grownups sat at a center table piled high with smoked ham, apple butter, bread, pumpkin pies, and sugar cakes.

It was clear to the Muse of History—if not to a practical-minded businessman like Francis Jones—that this kaleidoscopic color represented more than his paying guests; these were also the bits and pieces of the keystone evolving in the ramshackle structure that was Georgian England's American colonies in the mid-eighteenth century.

3

IN THE SPRING OF 1956 my late grandmother's kitchen resembled the galley of a superannuated tramp steamer complete with iron range, black floor covering, porcelain-skirted light bulb, and sickening yellow and green in high gloss. All of which made the place increasingly unlivable, but income-producing facilities had to be given priority over the kitchen.

Since soil conservation was off to a good start, the tenant houses came next. They would occupy most of my free hours, and I had promised to help Don on the farm during a three-week vacation in August. So leaves would fall before Francis Jones's room could be resurrected.

On a Saturday morning in early June, Lloyd and I tackled our first house. The tenants joined us in stripping dirty and curling strips of old wallpaper and scraping dull, scuffed woodwork paint. Sandwiches were prepared by the family for an on-the-job meal at noon. I ordered beer and soft drinks.

An air of euphoria and high resolve prevailed. I castigated the ex-overseer for permitting the house to decay. The tenants swore eternal fealty; they would stay on always, pay rent promptly, and take scrupulous care of the house. After fifteen years I can't help noting our similarity to mainland Chinese, purposefully slaving at a commune project. There were exaggerated pronouncements and merciless self-criticism, together with effusive adulation of Slaymakertown's facsimile of Chairman Mao. As I had often been the recipient of the slings and arrows loosed by heartless buyers at cub salesmen, the adulation was easy to take. Misgivings about my new status faded. I became suffused with good feelings. Slowly—well, as I must admit now, not so slowly—the role of country squire began to be fun.

Lloyd kept working on the house during weekdays. He replaced rotten windows, repaired roofing and flooring, and finally wallpapered rooms. The tenant family head and I took over when we returned from work. We puttied, plastered, and painted. By the beginning of my vacation in August, the effort was topped off with an outside painting party. Relatives of the tenants joined in the job for two days.

Like a rose amid tumbleweed, the trim, gray frame dwelling with dark green shutters stood off the mansion's east lawn in glaring contrast to the other tenant house. Throughout the project the neighboring house's curtains were in constant agitation. Occasionally its tenants loitered in porch shadows, staring at us. They came and went between their house and the one facing the mansion across the highway. Soon neither family "was speaking" to the one renovating. Even though we told them that precedence was determined by the flip of a coin, they were evidently suspicious about my intentions. But to me they were friendly, in a nervous sort of way (probably wondering whether their allotment of the landlord's time and substance would fall short of their lucky neighbors'). Might I spend too heavily and be forced to retrench at their expense? Perhaps the initial recipients of my largess would turn me against them. Would their renovations really start in the fall, as promised?

I could not blame them. For new brooms do sweep clean and after heavy duty soon wear out. So I reassured them repeatedly and—I hate to admit it—rather breezily, for their dependence on my whims was somehow gratifying. Squiring had become that enjoyable!

During August I spent full time with Don and his hired boy in the fields. As a youngster I had helped the farmer make hay with mule-powered mowers, rakes, and wagons. With pitchforks we loaded wagons in the fields and unloaded in the barn's haymow. Now, Don's tractor and mower cut the hay. After drying, it was gathered by his automatic baler into easy-to-load-and-unload bundles. Haymaking was a warmup for heavy work in the tobacco fields.

Since cigar tobacco was first introduced into Lancaster County more than a century ago, no method of automating its care and harvesting has been devised. In early spring seed is planted in beds which are covered with muslin to protect seedlings from frost. In late May plants are removed and replanted in fields. Throughout the summer they are cultivated, "suckered," and "topped" (the removal of worthless excess growth). Harvesting begins in mid to late August and is completed before the first frost, which is traditionally determined by the arrival of full moon.

Plants are cut manually with long-handled clippers. Stalks are then "speared" onto "laths" (four or five plants to a wooden strip) with a hollow, bayonetlike attachment which is placed on the lath and removed when stalks are in place. Laths of tobacco plants are hung on railed wagons and taken to curing sheds, where they are rehung on rafters. The crop cures during the fall. In early winter the laths are removed to an earthen dampening cellar (beneath the shed). Here leaves become damp, so that they can be stripped by hand from stalks.

Most of a tobacco farmer's winter days are spent in his stripping room, which is partitioned from the dampening cellar and warmed by a space heater. Leaves are sized: the largest for outside cigar wrappers and the smaller for inside fillers. Tobacco leaves are then compressed and baled in paper bundles in manually operated presses. From January to March, tobacco buyers "are out" purchasing crops. By the time the farmer makes his sale and delivers his tobacco it's time to prepare the seed bed for next year's crop.

As a teenager I labored in White Chimneys' tobacco fields to train for my prep school cross-country team. At age thirty-three, again stripped to the waist, with sweat-stung eyes, I leaned over the hand cutters, clipping along the seemingly endless rows of pungent green leaves. The stakes were higher now. Don had no built-in family help: just two little girls. Hired hands came high. I could save him money and thus undergird the farm operation. Its success depended on holding a good farmer. And Don was that.

I begged off from only one chore. At seventeen I ran a tobacco spear into the palm of my left hand. My grandparents' aged doctor in Gap stanched blood after much was lost. I should have gone back to spearing right after the accident. Now, even after a sixteen-year absence from the fields, and some gory wartime vignettes, I could not manage spearing. Don was most understanding.

All the while bulldozers chugged in the west pasture where a one-acre farm pond was being built. The Department of Agriculture's handbook encouraged the building of farm ponds for "irrigation, stock watering, and recreation." The government paid a large share of construction costs and stocked bass and bluegills. As an avid fisherman, I was all for a pond. Don enthused over the irrigation possibilities, and the tenants about prospects of swimming and skating. So everything in the government's handbook of cut-rate goodies was applied for, even partial payment for soil tests and lime and hay seed mixtures for the now completed waterways.

Francis Jones's old quarry had become an eyesore. Even before it became a nocturnal dumping place for a sloppy minority of natives, the quarry at the top of the hill served no useful, let alone aesthetic, purpose. It remained only because in prebulldozer days it was too expensive to fill. It had become a rat harbor, and Don feared an infestation of the farm buildings. So one balmy August morning a dozer closed Francis's quarry while Don, Lloyd, and I crouched downhill with 22-caliber rifles and picked off fleeing rats.

My communing that summer with other areas of the Pequea Valley's first settlers was on a more aesthetic plane. On lazy Sunday afternoons I ambled about ancestor Mathias Schleiermacher's original cabin, William Penn's spring, Madame Ferrée's graveyard, and high ground overlooking Pennsylvania's first gateway to the west, the Gap in the Hills.

Another direct descendant of Mathias—a distant cousin, William Slaymaker Kinzer—lived in the original Slaymaker log home. Bill, a contemporary of my father, and his family used to exchange Sunday afternoon calls when I was a boy. His rambling home (it has been added to a couple of times) made no particular impression then. But after my research, I found it exciting to sit with Bill in the original room before its immense fireplace over which hangs Penn's deed. I closed my eyes and saw Mathias, tall, in dark linsey-woolsey, seated on a stool by the hearth, reading from a German almanac while Catherine baked bread in embers.

Mary Ferrée's home no longer stands. The small stone-walled Ferrée graveyard, however, is a well-known Lancaster County landmark which I had passed often but never entered. I did so that summer.

Mind pictures of the Penn party meeting with King Opessah on the west slope of Gap Hill were difficult to come by, for the spring is contained now in a concrete reservoir behind the hardware store. Still, the spot evoked excited musings on its importance to Penn's expanding venture.

With White Chimneys came a tract of nineteen acres of woodland on Gap Hill. It had not been lumbered for many years. I mulled over the possibilities of timbering the largest trees so as to garner funds for tenant house repairs. Selective cutting would prevent an eyesore and ensure lumber on an ongoing basis.

One Saturday afternoon in late August I hiked through the lot to examine timber. From a promontory I could see the valley below as Penn first viewed it in 1700. A barely perceptible nip of autumn was in the air. Thin, intermittent wisps of haze, the results of farmers burning brush, wafted through treetops and across fallow fields. Green swatches

Mathias Schleiermacher's homestead, with original log walls

Mary Ferrée's grave, with original tombstone behind contemporary marker

of corn inset with thick stands of hardwood in heavy leaf blended serenely with green-ocher carpets of grass. Houses and barns and traffic-strewn Route 30 were blinked away. I imagined more woodland on the valley's floor. Indians burned off only enough timber to provide garden plots. Over the years these were abandoned when they became less fertile. Hence, those natural pastures which Penn noticed. Conjured, too, were visions of an occasional deer rather than the omnipresent Jersey cows.

Those atavistically inspired musings in the Jones and Schleiermacher cabins, the sudden thrill experienced at Madame Ferrée's grave and the vision of Penn's vista—not to mention my delight in being a bona-fide country squire—provided me impetus sufficient to continue the rehabilitation. If I had to exist on cheese in the garret, I'd carry on.

Work on the Francis Jones room began in September, 1956. After the second tenant house renovation was under way, Lloyd's lawn work had tapered off. So he spent full time working with the tenants. I helped, the better to dampen a rumor to the effect that my interest was flagging. My remaining time was spent in the tediously slow job of paint removal in the Jones room.

Specialists in Early American architecture from Pennsylvania's Historical and Museum Commission confirmed what I had suspected from my research. The lie was given that handed-down yarn about the original house comprising both a kitchen and dining room. No one would have built a wall 21 inches thick between two rooms. Plainly, the dining room was added later. Thus, Francis's entire home had been the 15-by-15-foot stone cabin—the contemporary kitchen. Nor was this primitive dwelling the dowery of Francis's grandniece, Faithful Jones Richardson, when she married Mathias Schleiermacher's son Henry Slaymaker. In fact, she was an orphan and very likely penniless.

After being made a justice of the peace, Francis Jones died in 1737. He willed the tavern to his son Joseph, who later sold it to another family.

In 1779, through an odd quirk of fate, the house was acquired by Henry Slaymaker. It ceased to be a tavern and became simply a country home.

The kitchen room, I felt, would be more felicitously restored as a home. As such, a more comfortable idiom would surely prevail. So I envisioned the place as a living room, with the two pantries serving as a working kitchen.

By way of speeding the job, I hit upon a variant of the tenant house "work-ins." Friends from Lancaster were invited to an all-day paint removal party. The mansion was a local landmark, and with the rising interest in Americana, I guessed that such an outing would be considered an "in" sort of affair. It was. More than a dozen volunteers showed up on the first Saturday in October. At day's end a keg of beer was tapped, and Chincoteague oysters were served before a dinner of spaghetti and meatballs. Willing hands with scrapers and paint-removing fluid had stripped the walls and woodwork clean. The black floor covering was removed. So was the stove, which later was sold for scrap iron. It could have been kept as a Victorian antique, but it was barely movable, and there was no place to store it.

I debated about rubbing the woodwork to what was probably its original and natural state. This would have been a long job. Since the Museum Commission experts assured me that paint had been used on woodwork in rural homes of the period, I decided to match the color of the first layer, a light gray. This original coat had been made from sour milk and pigment imported from England. Possibly it was applied when the first Slaymakers moved in. The plaster walls of such homes were often whitewashed. An eggshell wall paint seemed a good match.

Before painting was begun, I studied plate rails of the period. A facsimile, primitively rough-hewn, was prepared by a cabinetmaker. Lloyd and I mounted it on markings left by the original.

After I finished painting, the garret was searched for period artifacts. The extent of my find was proof enough of my forebears' proclivity for never throwing anything away. An Early American stretcher table, eight Windsor chairs, and a deacon's bench were brought down. So was a spinning wheel, a yarn winder, and a dough tray—not to mention pewter plates, brass candlesticks, a coffee grinder, and butter molds. A percussion cap rifle and powder horn were hung below the mantel, over the hearth.

One summer afternoon when I was a teenager a heavy rain had stopped field work, and I had killed time by exploring the back garret. Against the forward wall was a large chest of drawers. My flashlight's beam fell on a filthy carpet pinched between the wall and the chest. I moved the chest and found behind the carpet a crude passageway connecting the 1720 garret with that of the Federal addition. I had never known this aperture existed. On crawling through, I touched a ceiling beam and something moved. My light revealed the rifle and powder horn, heavily layered in dust. Excitedly I brought them out. They were in excellent condition. I was surprised to note that the horn still contained powder.

Unfortunately, the rifle's mechanism was of mid-nineteenth-century vintage. This was the only nonperiod piece in the restored kitchen room. I consoled myself with the thought that the rifle could have been converted from an earlier flintlock type to a percussion gun (as many were), and that it could have been the property of the earliest inhabitants.

With artifacts placed and varicolored hook throw rugs scattered on the sanded and waxed pine floor boards, the room became a striking study in Early Americana, a fair replica of what it had once been; fair, because the architectural aberrations of later years made a more exacting effort unrealistic. One Civil War period pantry had replaced the original staircase and slightly shortened the fireplace. Both pantries made the

Libby and Caroline Slaymaker shortly after restoration of kitchen fireplace

room smaller. Although we plastered over the cellar entrance (there was an outside one) for the sake of authenticity, the pantries had to stay to provide modern kitchen facilities. The experts assured me that the earliest flooring was gone. The pine boards were probably laid during the Civil War restoration. Possibly, too, rafters were originally in evidence. But they had since been plastered over. An inordinate amount of time and money would have been required to uncover them.

Results were striking enough to win plaudits from the Museum Commission advisers and to evoke a feature piece in a local newspaper. I was pleased to better savor the idiom of the early Slaymakers while digging their story from heaps of their musty, yellowing papers.

4

AT LEAST A DECADE passed before Mathias Schleiermacher's family were integrated into the rapidly developing social life of the Pequea Valley. The early years had to be devoted entirely to sustaining themselves.

Around their cabin there was possibly enough open land for the seeding of vegetables. However, progressively more land was required for wheat, corn, and oats and that prerequisite of all settlers, according to the dictum of Penn's secretary, James Logan, an apple orchard to provide cider. So, as additional land was needed, it was "burned off."

Throughout autumn months hillsides echoed with reports from flintlock guns as Mathias and his oldest son, Lawrence, shot deer in surrounding woods. Hides were dressed, staked out, and dried before the women turned them into moccasins, breeches, and jackets. During summer evenings "outlines" were set in the Pequea for trout. Fish, venison, and pork were salted and cured in "smoke traps," those parts of the lower chimney just above the hearth which thoughtful James Logan included with building instructions. Children went on berry frolics and provided crab apples, which were hung over the hearth to dry for winter consumption.

The German Bible provided the family Schleiermacher with more than divine assurance of protection during cruel winter evenings. While work proceeded on crude furniture and garments, Bible readings provided a comforting diversion. Certainly there were few others during those first years. But if the family was at first typical of other German settlers of the period, a picture of increasing comfort soon began to emerge: an enlarged cabin, roofing done over more permanently with "shakers"—riven from blocks of pine and laid as shingles—the loft becoming a second floor, complete with a stairway. Pine torches were replaced by candles, now perhaps store-bought in Philadelphia. Trips there became more convenient after Mathias purchased a blue and yellow canvas-topped Conestoga wagon from a German wagonmaker. Later he would buy another.

In Philadelphia there was furniture to be bought with crop money; a corner cupboard, drop-leaf tables, slat-back Windsor chairs, tinderboxes, candlesticks and silver and pewter ware to grace the now improved log home. Catherine's colorful yarn rugs, her billowing goose-feather-filled pillows and coverlets, presented a picture of coziness at striking variance with the stark drabness of the wilderness cabin of ten years before.

Still, by the turn of that first decade, it was likely that a feeling of loneliness dogged the family. Religious toleration created unforeseen problems. After Madame Ferrée's death in 1716 they could not have had many close friends, since there were few Calvinist Germans in the valley. Their immediate area, known as Strasburg (after the European city from which they came), was settled mostly by Swiss Mennonites.

The ever-rising tide of immigrants, once predominantly Mennonite, now embraced other pietistic German sects such as Amish, Dunkers, Schwenckfelders, Moravians, and Baptist Brethren—white-robed male and female celibates who lived in cloisters to the north of the valley. A move was afoot to make German the province's official language. British Quakers, Anglicans, and Scots-Irish resented this and moved the Assembly in Philadelphia to require Germans to pledge allegiance to the Crown, although most had previously done so when staking their claims. Anglo-Saxon prejudice was also fueled by the sectarians' plain garb and otherworldly clannishness.

The High Church Schleiermachers had nothing in common with the German Pietists save their language. Even so, this probably did not sit well with those with whom they had more in common, the British groups. There was one simple way to allay discomfort. Mathias would speak English, Anglicize his name, and join a British church. This Rubicon was crossed in 1721. The name was written "Slamaker" at first. It became "Slaymaker" on the rolls of Pequea Presbyterian Church, where his growing brood would have the blessing of an English education in the Reverend Robert Smith's church-related classical school, known as the Pequea Latin School.

With the first glimmer of every Sabbath the Slaymakers donned their finest clothes and rode horseback over seven miles of winding rock-studded paths—paths that ruled out wagons—from Strasburg settlement to the church. Services lasted all day, so smoked meats, fruit, cider, and ale went along.

The church was made of stone and logs, plastered inside and out. Rough wooden benches served as pews on which the congregation sat uncomfortably while the Reverend Smith sermonized through the day, save for a meal break and occasional rounds of psalm singing. With the paucity of books, it was customary for the minister to "line out" songs for the worshipers, who followed him after he gave them the pitch from a mouth pipe.

In 1724 Mathias finally "arrived." He was elected an elder in the Pequea church, a happening as joyous to the family as news in 1729 of the building of the town of Lancaster, twelve miles to the west. That western appendage of Chester County known as Conestoga township was proclaimed by the Provincial Government to be Lancaster County. The county seat quickly grew into a charming Georgian town of red-brick, one-and-a-half-story dwellings with five hundred souls.

Here at last was a barrier against Indian incursions from the west. Notwithstanding Penn's reputed affection for them, Indians posed a perpetual threat as instruments of the hated French. When valley settlers gathered at area mills, news of faraway battles between the British and the French were discussed. Very probably Mathias received heavy doses of Francophobia from the Reverend Smith's sermons: full-throated warnings about the diabolical designs of French Papists in Canada and the threat posed by French trapper Peter Bezaillon, who sometimes appeared on the Great Conestoga Road on his way to and from the Susquehanna country, where he traded with Indians. Might he not be teaching them the occult mysteries of Romanism? Or assessing the region's manpower, as he sat in greasy deerskins over wine at Francis Jones's tavern? People liked "old Peter," but he could have been a spy for the French viceroy in Quebec. So by the 1730s the fast-growing Lancaster town was more than a nearby source of supplies. In a very palpable way it meant security for the Slaymakers over the coming years.

By 1740 Catherine had presented Mathias with four native-born sons: Mathias II, John, Henry, and Daniel. Throughout the 1740s the children sat in Pequea Latin School on wooden stools facing cold stone walls from which inclining boards were fastened as desks. Teacher-

Leacock Church

minister Smith, perched on a high stool at room center, unraveled the mysteries of geometry, drove home rules of syntax, and expounded on Scripture and catechism.

All the while Mathias developed as a community leader. He was active in road improvement projects and was a prime mover in the building of a new church, Leacock Presbyterian, the better to facilitate church-going, as it was only three miles from his home.

When he reached advanced age in 1754, Mathias could not have begrudged the Almighty's impending call, for his times of struggle had been capped with a serenity born of accomplishment. But the days of his remaining years were not destined to pass blissfully.

In 1755 the faraway French War erupted within sixty miles of the Slaymakers' hitherto secure homestead. Indians pillaged Scots-Irish settlements as far inland as the east bank of the Susquehanna. The nonviolent

Quaker Assembly in a safely distant Philadelphia refused to raise militia for the protection of the frontier. Terror-stricken refugees crowded Lancaster, now taut with fear as periodic tollings of church bells signaled continuing attacks along the river.

In the Court House burgesses prepared memorials to the Assembly for arms and a powder magazine for the dangerously exposed town. Throughout the county Scots-Irish and Anglican hatred of Quakers and their pacifist German brethren was never more pronounced. There was relief when General Braddock's British Army gathered at Wills Creek in preparation for a march west against the French stronghold of Fort Duquesne.

When Braddock's drive was delayed for lack of supply wagons and drivers, Mathias offered his two wagons, horses, and sons John and Daniel to drive them. Many pacifist Germans and Quakers refused to support the army. So Mr. Benjamin Franklin came out from Philadelphia to implore and badger, not very successfully. In quiet anger he posted handbills to the effect that if horse drivers and wagons "were not delivered in fourteen days time Sir John St. Clair, the hussar, with a body of soldiers will immediately enter the Province and take them"—signed "B. FRANKLIN."

The pacifists came across with horses and wagons.

In the middle of May, 1755, to the relief of even the pacifists, General Braddock's army departed for the west. After two months of anxious waiting for word of victory, dispatch riders clattered into Lancaster bearing news of Braddock's defeat. Refugee crowds from western townships increased. They engulfed the simple elegance that was Lancaster town and left stranded the swimming flotsam of brown-gray homespuns mixed with the floundering jetsam of the muddied, bloodied blues and reds of a discredited military.

Mathias's sons returned unharmed, minus their horses and wagons; John to a hero's welcome. It was reported that when early volleys killed two of his horses, he, with some British soldiers, hitched the two remaining to a cannon and tried to get it in action, but these horses also fell under a rain of bullets and arrows.

Lancaster's Court House bell tolled on October 20 and again on November 30 at midnight: more massacres by France's Indians. Horror tales were rife. One concerned a Moravian colony in Northampton County where "stakes were found driven into the private parts of the women and men's . . . cut off . . . a mother stretched on the bed with her newborn child horribly mangled and put under her head for a pillow. . . ."

Popular hatred of the pacifist Provincial Assembly peaked. Mangled bodies of massacre victims were carted in wagons through Lancaster to Philadelphia. The stinking cargo was dumped in a pile at the State House doors so the Quakers could see firsthand the fruits of nonresistance.

The pressure on the Assembly's Quaker hierarchy finally brought it down. Two deputy governors resigned. A third was able to negotiate a peace between the province and the Shawnees and Delawares.

Mathias received from Mr. Franklin a notice of reimbursement:

By wagon and team lost	£59
by 39 days	£39
by travel expenses	£37 lls.

In 1760, on mill days and at church, Mathias could at last joyously savor good news of victories; Forbes at Fort Duquesne, Amherst in Nova Scotia, and finally Wolfe at Quebec, whose death in victory signaled the end of the war in North America.

Mathias Slaymaker's will was drawn in 1762. The erstwhile Palatine refugee whose dawn had broken over a Europe in the throes of religio-political distemper was content to watch his sun set on rich valley land, now fashioned after his effort to provide sustenance for the brood he fathered on it. He willed his sons the land, equally divided. The two daughters received one hundred pounds each. Daniel was the executor.

Mathias died in 1763; coincidentally, at the time of the Peace of Paris, which officially closed the Seven Years' War. The funeral at Leacock Church was said to have been uncommonly large. This is certainly understandable, for the last of the valley's first settlers was now gone.

After the war, Lancaster, now the largest inland town in the colonies, was a study in red-brick serenity. Women and children in nut-colored garb padded barefooted down wide, graveled West King Street to a stream. There, amid pleasantries, they filled oaken buckets and plodded carefully uphill, stopping sometimes to observe bewigged burgesses wending their solemn way from the Grape Tavern off the square to its center and through the white doors of the stately Country Georgian Court House, whose two-faced Eberman clock clanged hours on a languid air.

Lancaster's burgesses spent most of their time enforcing a multiplicity of corporation ordinances: homemakers so careless as to permit chimney fires were fined thirty shillings, drunks twenty, craftsmen twenty when they plied their trade on the Sabbath. Ball-playing boys were a problem. They sometimes injured country visitors on horseback. No one could carry arms without the burgesses' permission, but there were often teenagers learning to stomach liquor who discharged guns "loaded with bullet and shot" in the town.

Larger problems such as those posed by the Stamp Act were handled by the burgesses with the same quiet, efficient aplomb. Their seaboard-wide correspondence with juntas similar to their own had brought the wrongheaded ministry in London to heel. Lancaster's burghers rarely questioned the actions of Jasper Yeates, Esq.; Edward Shippen, Sr.; William Augustus Atlee, Esq.; William Henry; and Dr. Edward Hand. For these were men of learning and means, well versed in the law and business. Living in the most imposing homes, like-minded on all issues, they were a happy phenomenon, abetted by intergroup marriages. Even before their anti-Stamp Act correspondence, Lancaster's rulers were on close terms with celebrities throughout the colonies. Grateful freeholders cherished the town's well-ordered existence. Thus the junta found it easy to perpetuate itself and extend its influence throughout the county.

Jasper Yeates and his confreres' link to the more populous, and hence most important, "east end" was a tall, portly young man with reddish hair, of pleasing mien and sentient eyes. He was Henry Slaymaker, a younger son of the pioneer, Mathias Slaymaker.

Henry, a landowner and storekeeper in the Pequea Valley, also practiced law. He was politically ambitious. His rate of advancement was in direct proportion to the value of his services to Lancaster's leaders in keeping the Pequea Valley posted on their views and carrying intelligence about what could be expected of whom back to headquarters in Lancaster's Grape Tavern. Henry was acceptable. He was well read in the classics, knew some law, and was married to Faithful Jones Richardson, the grandniece of one of the Pequea Valley's first settlers, the late tavernkeeper and justice of the peace, Francis Jones.

Bred in the relative luxury experienced by his family at the time of his birth in 1734, the youthful Henry Slaymaker escaped the hard labor borne by his pioneering elder brothers. Farm chores there must have been. But his father, perhaps noting his intelligence, might have spoiled this younger son, for while still in his teens the boy started a law library. Storekeeping and the management of his share of land possibly antedated his father's death. He practiced law well enough to be made a justice of the peace.

By the mid-1770s Henry was sufficiently well off to afford a red coach, a body servant named Peter, and a "mansion-plantation," Mt. Pleasant, on the Great Conestoga Road.

Even with plenty of indentured help, Faithful Slaymaker fulfilled the Biblical injunction to "look well to the ways of her household and eat not the bread of idleness." For besides bearing ten children over twenty-two years, she evidently participated in running the farm and store, not to mention "doctoring" her brood. She deftly plied her practice as laid down by William Penn's *Book of Phisick* and Benjamin Franklin's edition of John Tennant's *Every Man His Own Doctor* (for those who cannot afford to die at the hand of a doctor). Like her contemporaries, she had learned at her parents' knees something of the doctrine of "signatures," based on the belief that God made some herbs in the shape of human organs as an indication of their intended application to ailments. Since the trick of curing lay in having the right herb at the right time for the right organ, the better the wifely practitioners in the valley, the larger their herb gardens. Faithful's must have been satisfactory, for she lost only one child (at the age of a year). When cures failed, Faithful probably went to a midwife, the real professional.

By June, 1774, Faithful's responsibilities increased as Henry became progressively involved in political activities. It looked like the Stamp Act troubles all over again.

Early in June, 1774, Charles Thompson, Esq., clerk of the Philadelphia Committee of Correspondence, wrote Lancaster's chief burgess, William Augustus Atlee, about the town's sentiments concerning the latest "illegal act" of Parliament: namely, the dissolution of the Massachusetts Assembly and the dispatching of General Gage to Boston in May.

Now Burgess Atlee was not likely to have been deluded by the flattery. Philadelphia's leaders did not so much care about Lancastrians' opinions as they did about having a cooperative group of co-workers on the western frontier. This, it turned out, they had.

On June 15 Edward Shippen, Sr., acting as head of the town's Committee of Safety, resolved that Lancastrians unite with other colonists and use the most effectual means to procure repeal of the "unjust" Acts of Parliament against the town of Boston. "Firm allegiance" was professed to the King. This was logical. For Lancaster's leaders were not radicals. They were gentlemen of business and the professions who wanted to get back to the good old days of nonintervention in their affairs. And what was good enough for them was good enough for those many citizens who never bothered to come to the meeting in the Court House on that hot afternoon in June, 1774.

At the Grape Tavern and from his *Pennsylvania Gazette* Henry learned of Dr. Franklin's solicitations to the English court, to which that venerable sage had gone to protest Parliament's unrealistic approach to taxing policies. There was much news about the American boycott of English goods. It could only have set Henry to worrying. Taxes on his business were damaging enough, but the countering boycott could have threatened its existence. He might have guessed that American businessmen would rue the day they began it, but he had to go along. After all, Lancaster leaders had published a manifesto stating that any townsmen who handled English goods would be "abhorred as traitors to the interest of their country," and the rest of the populace "would never have any fellowship or correspondence with them, any of them!" The Lancaster chiefs further stated that they would "publish his or their names to the world to remain as a lasting monument of infamy."

With the inevitable collapse of the Penn family's proprietary government in early 1776, Henry Slaymaker received his greatest accolade from his sponsors, Jasper Yeates's Lancaster junta. It was arranged that he would be elected as a delegate to the State's Constitutional Convention called by Revolutionary leaders for the summer of 1776 in Philadelphia's State House. Proceedings were bound to reflect the immemorial conflict between "leather stocking" western Pennsylvania settlers and "silk stocking" eastern business and professional men, principally over extension of the franchise.

Henry sweltered through protracted and tempestuous meetings during which the state's emerging Constitution was written in the Supreme Court room. Another instrument was being debated across the hall: the Declaration of Independence.

While in Philadelphia Henry was moved to have his portrait painted by John Hesselius, a leading Colonial portraitist, whose famous father, Gustavus, had painted wife Faithful. Henry's canvas was sized to hers, and they were placed in matching frames.

After the new Constitution was completed in the autumn of 1776 Henry was rewarded again by being commissioned to administer oaths of allegiance to the state and nation and to "suppress neighborhood Tories." In all likelihood the latter task involved observing a few Church of England families on the Chester County line and reporting their activities to his superiors. Dossiers were kept on those who repeatedly refused the oath or outwardly aided the British. Later, these dossiers would be used as evidence to attaint them as traitors.

Henry's work continued to please Jasper Yeates. He was made a judge, an appointment which required more time in Lancaster. But his sons were now sufficiently grown up to assume full responsibility for home-front operations. Particularly his eldest son, Amos—twenty-one in 1776—showed great promise in storekeeping and evidenced interest in Henry's lawbooks.

That Amos was destined to be Henry and Faithful's most accomplished son became obvious shortly after hostilities with England began. Amos had two brothers, Henry, Jr. and Samuel, and seven sisters, Mary, Hannah, Faithful, Lydia, Sarah, and two Sophias, the first being the child that died. Amos, Henry, Jr., and a clutch of cousins enlisted in the Leacock V Battalion of Militia upon its formation in 1776. "Sammy" was too young to join his brothers. All the Slaymaker boys were private soldiers with the exception of Amos, who quickly achieved rank of ensign. They served in a company commanded by Judge Henry's brother, Captain John Slaymaker. His brother, Mathias II, was also a captain in command of a company. Their brother Daniel, his service in Braddock's campaign notwithstanding, remained a private throughout the war. Daniel's was a checkered military career. While serving in Virginia (according to his family history), he "became exasperated" with a Hessian prisoner and shot him dead. Daniel was court-martialed and cleared.

Lancaster County's Revolutionary effort was dominated by Presbyterians, the majority being Anglican-hating Scots-Irish. Militia battalions were usually formed by individual church groups. Invariably congregational leaders became officers. The V Battalion, commanded by Colonel James Crawford, was created under the aegis of Leacock Church's Reverend John Woodhull, a typical anti-English Calvinist.

The late Jay Warren Kaufman, historian of the Leacock Church, described the V Battalion's departure for Long Island on August 5, 1776:

Old Leacock's widest fame is in the story that John Woodhull took along with him . . . all the able-bodied men of his congregation. . . . Our imagination is thus free to picture these men meeting at the church early in the morning . . . accompanied by members of their families, to whom they said their farewells here: their assemblage in the church for an exhortation, a psalm and a prayer: their march eastward down the Old Road until they passed out of sight over the hill, led by James Crawford and James Mercer, to meet Robert Buyers and his company from Pequea [Church] on their way to New York and Long Island by way of Philadelphia and Princeton and Morristown.

The Leacock V was a ragtag force. Most of the soldiers wore large, loose homespun coats, dyed various shades of brown and maroon. Unkempt shirts were of gray-yellow flax. Trousers, mostly leather, were sloppily fastened just below the knee, tightly enough to hold up heavy woolen stockings. Few wore military boots. As if to compensate, huge buckles on cowhide shoes were highly buffed. A few officers had tricorns. The ranks wore large, round-top broad-brimmed hats. Most men were slung with crude knapsacks. There were no standard firearms. Many carried smooth-bore fowling guns, other long, graceful, and accurate rifled pieces—not long removed from the shops of Lancaster County's riflemakers—and perhaps some had Queen Anne blunderbusses.

Only a few of the men saw action in the Battle of Long Island, and the Slaymakers were not among them. The battalion was enlisted for only six weeks. Jay Warren Kaufman writes: "As early as September 5th of that year, just one month after the men marched away, John

Woodhull was writing to his wife that he did not need to write any further letters as he expected the men to soon be dismissed and sent home."

On their return Leacock Church's leaders dissolved the V Battalion and formed the VII, under command of Colonel John Boyd, an individual who would become the nemesis of the family Slaymaker in years to come.

For several months the war was easy on the Leacock VII. There were drills and reviews but, since fighting was far off, no campaigning. Militia troops were mainly charged with guarding their home grounds, a situation probably pleasing to practical Judge Henry. For young Amos and Henry, Jr. were able to attest to their patriotism while remaining useful at home. The war was costing Henry little and advancing his station—as long as fighting remained clear of southeastern Pennsylvania. The situation took an unexpected turn for the worse in August, 1777, when Henry's family's safety became threatened and he, as a Revolutionary oath administrator, faced possible execution.

On a Sabbath morning dispatch riders brought news of Sir William Howe's invasion of Pennsylvania. Fifteen thousand British troops had disembarked from transports at Head of Elk in Maryland. The objective was Philadelphia, about fifty miles to the northeast. Immediately, area militia were raised to assist Washington's regulars. They prepared to halt the British advance along the Brandywine Creek in Chester County, only thirty miles from Henry's home.

On a day in late August, 1777, Henry and Faithful bade farewell to Amos and Henry, Jr. as the battalion left Leacock's churchyard for the Brandywine encampment. The high resolve of Leacock warriors led to naught. General Washington's earlier experiences with such ill-trained, badly equipped, and unblooded part-time soldiers was not encouraging, so when battle lines were drawn along the placidly meandering Brandywine, he placed Pennsylvania's militia troops on the strategically less important southern flank. The main attack was expected a mile to the north at Chadds Ford on the main road to Philadelphia. There the principal American defense positions were manned by experienced Continentals. The blow fell here, in concert with a massive flanking movement to the north, of which Washington was unaware until it was too late. The American line collapsed in the envelopment.

Henry's boys to the south saw nothing, but they heard the battle upstream, became frightened and confused, and joined the rest of the militia in a pell-mell retreat east toward Chester, where the main body of Continentals retired in good order.

During the autumn weeks following the American defeat at Brandywine, both armies parried and feinted until Sir William Howe effected a successful crossing of the Schuylkill and entered Philadelphia to the cheers of thousands on September 26, 1777.

Some militia troops remained with Washington. Others faded into their countryside hamlets. Most likely the Leacock troops returned home, for they were only thirty miles away. Meanwhile, the British seemed content to consolidate their forces around Philadelphia.

The call to action came again in early October. Washington devised an eminently commonsensical plan for attacking British outposts at Germantown. Again, Pennsylvania's militia, including the Leacock VII, was placed where it could do little harm, on the far left flank of the main attacking forces. Because of an early morning fog and confused command decisions, the attack degenerated into ignominious retreat. The Leacock VII returned home again, and drills and reviews continued at comfortable intervals.

With the onset of the cruel winter of 1777–78 Ensign Amos Slaymaker and his brothers probably enjoyed festive Christmas holidays in the warmth of his father's home, Mt. Pleasant, on the Great Conestoga Road. All the while Uncle Daniel, who had since joined the Continentals, blue-skinned and shivering, barely existed in the white hell that was Valley Forge.

In the spring of 1778 the British realized that their occupation of Philadelphia had not dimmed American morale, and General Clinton led his army north to New York. Washington was determined to goad General Clinton into battle during his trek across the Jersey flats. Again the call for militia was aired, and again Leacock troops responded. In the vicinity of New Jersey's Monmouth Court House on June 28, 1778, the harassing Americans were turned on by the British with a vengeance. A toe-to-toe slugging match developed. For once the VII troops were caught in the action.

They beheld an awesome panorama. The green countryside was smeared with the reds and whites of British regulars whose arms sparkled in the sunshine of a 96-degree afternoon. From behind hedgerow defensive lines American troops heard the shrill of bagpipes followed by a swelling thunder of artillery which presaged human-wave attacks by the British. They came on gracefully in spread-eagle platoons toward the hedgerow. Like his compatriots, Amos probably fired, reloaded, and fired, while straining his smarting eyes at targets in the reddish wave that swam through a blur on the smoking landscape before the hedges. Perhaps Amos saw his minister in action. When a cannoneer fell wounded, the Reverend Woodhull served his gun.

The hedgerow positions held up under continued assaults.

During the night American soldiers slept on their guns. They expected attacks to continue in the morning. But with dawn the field was empty. The British had crept off to New York in the darkness. Leacock's troops had finally tasted bitter action and had distinguished themselves. The army was to repair to English Town, where word had it a celebration was to be held. But Ensign Amos Slaymaker was unable to be there.

In the heat of the action he lost contact with his battalion and found himself with a group of Chester County militia commanded by a Colonel James Fleming. Colonel Fleming had been wounded and was to be sent to a field hospital. He wrote a note to that effect to his family, who lived near the western end of Chester County, within a dozen miles of Mt. Pleasant. The note was entrusted to Ensign Slaymaker, who set off the morning following the battle.

After trudging and hitchhiking for almost a hundred miles, he arrived at the Fleming farmhouse, dirty and depleted. The family ministered to him for more days than were necessary for a lad who lived only a short distance to the west. He was attracted to Colonel Fleming's daughter, Isabella.

In very short order, Amos and "Sibby" were married in the Scots-Irish Flemings' Lower Octoraro Presbyterian Church.

Judge Henry felt constrained to provide for his soldier son and new daughter-in-law. He did so by buying for them the old Francis Jones tavern property. There was some sentiment attached to the place. His beloved Faithful's great-uncle had built it. She had known it as a child. Indeed, after she was orphaned by her parents' death, she might well have lived there with her Uncle Francis.

PART II

Federal

The mansion around 1820. Painting by Hannah Slaymaker Evans

It has often given me pleasure to observe that independent America was not composed of detached and distant territories, but that one connected, fertile, wide-spreading country was the portion of our western sons of liberty. Providence has in a particular manner blessed it with a variety of soils and productions, and watered it with innumerable streams, for the delight and accommodation of its inhabitants. A succession of navigable waters forms a kind of chain round its borders as if to bind it together; while the most noble rivers in the world, running at convenient distances, present them with highways for the easy communication of friendly aids, and the mutual transportation and exchange of their various commodities. . . .

JOHN JAY, *The Federalist Papers*

5

It was impossible to ascertain the life styles of the valley's first settlers, let alone their aspirations and apprehensions, from White Chimneys' earliest papers. Those covering Mathias's years were meager. Henry's era was better represented, but not so well as to preclude continuing background study. Amos's period was enlivened by a plethora of papers.

I studied them on long winter nights in 1957 by the very hearth where young Amos had totaled up his storekeeping accounts after he went into business in the onetime Francis Jones house. I was pleased with the prospect of getting to know Amos well—even intimately—through his voluminous correspondence.

Among his papers was an early likeness, a silhouette. He was wiry, with a craggy face, and remained so, as is attested by his portrait, painted years later when he served in Congress. Amos's personality suited his physiognomy. He was intently purposeful in pursuing ends, and hawkishly opportunistic in pouncing on their means. His correspondence revealed that he was not sidetracked by a sense of humor.

Amos Slaymaker was little inconvenienced by the remaining years of the War for Independence. He attended drill enough to remain on the muster rolls. Now and again his company was assigned to guard British prisoners in Lancaster.

The store opened for business on May 18, 1783, while peace was being negotiated in Paris. Amos probably started in an outbuilding on his new property. One Captain N. B. McCurdy made the first purchases: 142 pounds of iron, 44 pounds of "blister steel," and 5 pounds of "London Steel," totaling £14 10s. 4d.

Other sales followed briskly and in mounting volume, as well they should have, since the inventory had been carefully chosen to meet the needs of every man, woman, and child in the valley's east end.

Silhouette of
Amos Slaymaker, Esq.

Silhouette of his wife
Isabella Fleming Slaymaker

For the ladies Amos carried linens and side saddles; for the men, riding boots, cowskin whips, hats, and a variety of hardware items, while children were offered paper quills, primers, and spelling books.

Since money was tight, Judge Henry—living four miles to the west —did not stake his son to the store, for Amos was over twenty-one, married, now a father and a farmer in his own right. But Henry Slaymaker probably gave Amos advice as to the advantageous time to begin. The way seemed clear when the war began to peter out in Virginia.

At three o'clock in the morning of October 22, 1781, a dispatch rider arrived at the President of Pennsylvania's house in Philadelphia and announced to a sleepy-eyed chief executive that Lord Cornwallis had surrendered at Yorktown in Virginia. A watchman picked up the news and cried along quiet, cobblestone streets, "Past three o'clock and Cornwallis is taken."

News got to Lancaster before noon. There was wild celebrating in the streets by those who did that sort of thing. Sumptuous dinners were held by those who celebrated properly in the stately homes along Orange and King streets.

With peace in the offing, Amos began to buy inventory, but not in Philadelphia or Lancaster. Better deals could be made in outlying parts of the seaboard. The Southern states seemed the place to look. Judge Henry advised Amos to look south and purchase cheap.

The lad was put in touch with one Anthony MacCracken, who had money to lend to a son of a judge. Amos went into hock for probably not more than a couple of hundred pounds and was soon off for the South. He kept a meticulous ledger on the trip, noting every stop along the way through Virginia and North Carolina. His lodgings, the "corn and mush" breakfasts, and occasional "whisky" and "oats" and "corn for my horse" and "tools" were all carefully noted. There were no "sundry" entries.

By winter of 1783 he was back home. In the spring his wagon-loads of merchandise began to arrive in time to meet a continuing flow of returning soldiers. These men were about to settle down after months and years at war. Many of them had separation pay. The officers, of course, were better off. So above all others, Amos sought them out. "Major Harris" bought implements of iron; "Capt. Burns," rope; "Capt. Mullen," linen; "Capt. Watson," playing cards; and so on.

Possibly the judge counseled him not to extend credit, for he didn't do so. When he came up against a customer who for one reason or another he could not very well turn down, he took skins of panthers, wolves, beaver, bear, foxes, and raccoons.

Children were coming rapidly to Amos and Sibby. The first boy was named James Fleming, after Sibby's father. The second, most appropriately, was baptized Jasper Yeates Slaymaker at Leacock Church. Perhaps Mr. Yeates himself dropped in for this occasion. The third boy was named Henry (after Amos's father) Fleming. Over two decades Amos and Sibby had eleven children. James and two others, John and Jean, died in their teens, but the rest survived to marry and raise families.

Shopping traffic was heavy around the little house now filled with children and indentured help. Plainly, an addition was in order.

Amos was too busy to hew stone from the quarry. So building materials and labor were supplied by area contractors, and a southern wing was added to the house.

A portion of the southeastern wall was knocked out for a door opening onto the addition. As wide as the old house and extending 20 feet, the entire oblong house now measured 35 feet by 15. The new wing

1790
AMOS SLAYMAKER'S
FIRST ADDITION

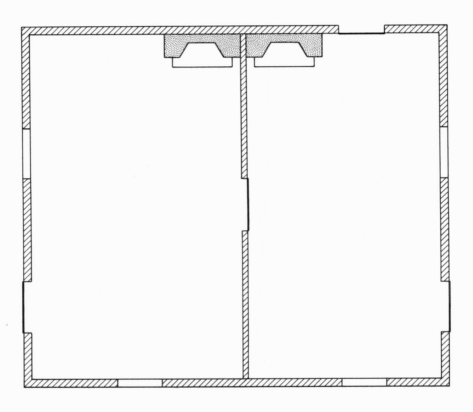

was split lengthwise by a first-floor wall. A door in the wall's center joined the two resulting rooms. One was a living room; the other was for dining. Both had windows in their southern extremities overlooking rolling fields, cut through straightaway by Francis Jones's north–south road. In the distance, along the base of the valley's blue-green southern barrier ridge, summertime dust clouds marked traffic on the Great Conestoga Road to the west.

Each new room had another window and a door: one set looking west, the other east. Since the east side bordered the Jones road, its door probably superseded the kitchen's as the main entrance. In the wall separating the new wing from the old, two fireplaces were built and bordered by Classic Revival wooden mantels. A new chimney was added. Now there were two.

The second floor of the wing comprised three large bedrooms. The new garret and cellar were extensions of the old.

Amos ordered oak shingles, so it is probable that all roofing was now shingled rather than thatched in straw.

It was unrealistic for me to plan restoration of Amos's first wing, for its interior had been altered greatly through Victorian renovating. Two classic pillars replaced the ground floor's center wall and lent support to the ceiling. The entire area had become a dining room. Amos's original Federal mantels were replaced by a mid-Victorian marble monstrosity. I found one original mantel in the garret and toyed with the idea of resetting it in the dining room. Since much work would be required, this plan was shelved—as it was to turn out later, much to my relief.

The dining room had last been papered in the 1930s. It was done gloomily with a heavy sepia-colored paper. Woodwork was painted a high-gloss white. Oak flooring had been dark-stained. I uncovered six distinct layers of wall paint. Like the kitchen's, the first layer comprised a sour milk–pigment mix, this time a light green. I matched it with a flat wall paint. If the area could not be reconstructed to Amos's original two rooms, it could certainly be made more cheerful and bright, as it probably was in his day. Our sanding of the floor to its original oaken luster entirely dispelled the previous state of gloominess.

Scraping, painting, and sanding in the dining room began in the late fall of 1956 as a fill-in job—for Lloyd continued working with tenants on weekdays, and I joined them on Saturdays. When embers fell away in the kitchen's hearth late at night, and I left Amos's papers, it was hard to resist an urge to scrape wallpaper in his first addition before turning in. It was slow work, but it came naturally, almost as if the intent and demanding Amos of the papers had ordered me to it.

It was imperative to keep dining room progress slow. Along with the tenant house program and ever-gathering incidentals around the farm, there was little with which to finance continued mansion renovating. Then in late autumn, 1956, Don hit upon an idea which provided an unexpected windfall. We went into the Christmas tree business.

In the early 1920s my grandfather turned two acres of the west lawn into a pine grove. He planned on periodically thinning trees by transplanting in his Lancaster real estate development. In the thirties his arrow-straight pines served as a striking backdrop for the large lawn parties which he threw for his two daughters. But he never transplanted many trees. Crowded and ridden by blight, they were dying by the mid-1950s.

If only, I thought, the grove could be cleared away and turned into pasture to compensate for land robbed by the new farm pond. Once this land was blended into the old pasture, lawn maintenance would be reduced and the area made productive. White case fencing could tie it all up, vastly improving the appearance and enabling me to vie with Chester County's horsy set just down the highway.

The government refused to help with stump removal. This would have contributed to farm surpluses. But Big Brother didn't shrink from tendering advice and financial help toward the seeding and fertilizing of the pasture once it was cleared.

I contracted with a pulp wood company for the cutting and sale of tree trunks. Work began late in November, 1956. The shambles of branches on the west lawn resembled pictures of Belleau Wood after its shelling. Through cold, gray days of early winter the lawn appeared sometimes a miniature Alpine range of snowy peaks and valleys. When limp with rain it seemed a sea-green tide, swelling before a storm. And on crisp, clear mornings, while making breakfast, I glanced on a fairy land, floored in frosty white satin, covered with glittering diamonds and sapphires. So what if the gems were illusionary; a sizable amount of gold would be mined from the mountainous ruins of evergreen.

Lloyd went halves with me in retailing Christmas greens and trees (cut from pine tops) along the highway. We also wholesaled into Philadelphia.

The staccato rattle of our chain saw rent icy air until March, when we had all the firewood we could scavenge. Then, with crankcase oil and used tires, we fired the thing, creating the largest controlled blaze ever seen around Gap. The fire company stood by.

We hired a bulldozer to bury the stumps. The ground was seeded to pasture in the spring. More than enough cash from the sale of Christmas greens was left over for the dining room's rehabilitation.

During a pre-World War I mansion renewal my grandfather had installed a coal furnace and radiators. Hot water was fed by gravity. Prodigious amounts of coal were required to heat the place. The heating plant was so constructed that wing and room cutoffs were impossible. Even if I could have afforded to heat the house properly, it would have been wasteful to do so for myself alone, since I was away during weekdays. The answer was to keep enough fire in the boiler to heat bathwater, to place an electric heater in my bedroom, and to live as close to the kitchen hearth as possible.

In that unkempt museum that was the front garret, I found an iron "ten-plate Franklin stove," vintage 1840. Its maker was one Henry Y. Slaymaker of York, Pennsylvania, a nephew of Amos's. One of his stoves was bought by President James Buchanan and is in his restored home, Wheatland, in Lancaster. Conceivably, my stove had been used in the kitchen room, because a pipe hole, leading into the chimney, had been cut in the wall to the upper right of the fireplace. It was plastered over. Lloyd and I opened this aperture, placed a stovepipe, and positioned the Franklin stove to the right of the hearth.

On winter mornings before I came down, Lloyd built wood fires in the stove, and I prepared and ate breakfast in a well-warmed room. Directly on arriving in the evening, I laid a fire in the kitchen hearth, dined, and went to work on Amos's papers.

Saturdays and holiday weekends were devoted to entertaining my young daughters, tenant house work, and two new farm projects.

In the 1930s my grandfather had experimented with a new kind of fencing, concrete posts strung with page wire. Posts were easily chipped by farm equipment. Successive frosts expanded breaks, rendering the fencing entirely unserviceable by the time I took over. Since the contour strips and revised pasture boundaries required new fencing, we decided to refence the entire farm. The white case panels were to frame the property in the front; wooden posts and page wire would enclose rear areas. The lumberers at work on the felled pine grove had assured me that they could pay in kind more handsomely than in cash. So our pine trunks were swapped for enough oak railings to enclose both east and west pastures along the highway.

On sparkling, cold Saturday mornings Lloyd and I drove twenty miles to the Mason-Dixon Line "barrens" where my father and his brother and sister own woodland. We took packed lunches, axes, and a chain saw and felled the largest cedars for fence posts. By spring we had almost enough posts to fence the front portion of the farm. The only cash outlay required was for nails and paint. Both were wangled at wholesale. A job that could have cost a couple of thousand dollars was budgeted for two hundred. It would take three summers to complete it.

When inclement weather rendered post cutting impossible, Don and I embarked on another project that would lead to lucrative results.

Don's half of our corn crop was fed to his milk cows; mine was sold to the Gap feed mill for cash. Were I to fatten steers with my share (and hit favorable fat cattle markets), a much better return could be realized. However, steer market vagaries can work cruel havoc on shoestring operators—not to mention that we had no quarters for steers. Nevertheless Don assured me that an unused portion of the rear barn, where horses were once kept, could be converted, and money was borrowed for "feeder" steers.

Steer stable plans from a farm magazine were adopted. We cleared the area and installed windows, a water trough, and wooden railing. Central to the new steer stable was a "self-feeder," the base of which we formed with ready-made concrete. The upper portion comprised a wooden funnel opening at the top in the barn's second floor. Above was a trap door through which chopped corn could be dumped to steers feeding in the concrete troughlike base below. Such feeders are studies in perpetual motion. The grain level is kept constant, and steers eat on.

The wooden funnel required a considerable amount of lumber, the going rate for which seemed steep. We found the answer in an old dance floor which had been stored in the main tobacco shed for more than thirty years. It had been built in the 1920s for my Aunt Jane's debutante party, held on White Chimneys' lawn and graced by the Lucky Strike

Orchestra. Of well-finished oak, it made for the most elegant steer-feeding apparatus in the Pequea Valley.

We began the steer-fattening operation with fourteen head of Black Angus "feeders" averaging seven hundred pounds each. After six months of feeding, they averaged twelve hundred pounds. We were fortunate in being able to buy "low," sell "high," and turn a handsome profit. An added bonus was the extra manure. It supplemented that of Don's cows and the government's prescribed chemical fertilizer, greatly enhancing the soil's growing capacity.

Over the next two years we handled more steers. By no means were all turnovers as auspicious as the first. A couple of times I was made bitterly aware of the truth of that old dictum of cattlemen to the effect that you never lose money fattening steers, but sometimes their manure "costs like hell!" Overall, the steers made money. Thanks to the steadily improving land, corn yields grew from 45 bushels to the acre to 90; wheat from 25 to 45; and tobacco from one-half to three-quarters of a ton per acre. All the while, higher rents reflected a steady improvement in the tenant houses.

After two and a half years the property's total income was more than doubled and operations were in the black. Any fear on behalf of the tenants that I might lose interest was dispelled. Despite business trips I was seldom absent for more than a working week and was rarely away over weekends—only in the spring for Pocono Mountain trout fishing. On autumn Saturdays I hunted White Chimneys' fields for pheasants that bolted over browning, brittle stands of corn. The throaty blast of my gun and the smell of cordite and dead leaves signaled the approach of winter's leaden skies.

To friends in Lancaster I was a social dropout; even worse, as I realized myself, a recluse whose self-centered aims were futilely unrealistic. For notwithstanding the success of the rehabilitation, it was obvious that the plantation was still a white elephant, destined to be destructive of my substance and freedom as long as I chose to stick with it.

The seeming hopelessness of my plight was humorously, but pointedly, brought home in a luncheon conversation with a well-heeled industrialist. He had bought a Lancaster County farm and was also farming "on the halves." When asked how White Chimneys was coming on, I replied that it was making a small profit.

Over a half-raised martini glass he stared at me incredulously and said, "A profit! Hell, you're not running the place right!"

And so I wasn't by his lights. But my tax bracket was too low to allow of a plaything farm with which to take tax-saving losses.

Ever so slightly my predisposition to revel in being a country squire weakened. It wasn't that I was fed up. The life was still enjoyable. But there was the unpleasantness of collecting from slow-pay tenants. Their incessant wrangling and prolonged bouts of nonspeaking became progressively tiresome. I worried about Don's future. He had to pay increasingly higher wages to field hands. Would I lose him? I was sure that it was only a question of time until he was forced to quit farming. Then whom would I get? In all likelihood a farmer who would steal me blind.

Still, there was a dogging desire to continue. It was inexplicable at first. But soon I realized that something in, about, or of the house was incipiently thwarting my power to give it up. I cringe at writing such lines. For the self-absorption they reflect should prompt a writer to unstuff his shirt. Let it be known that I was among the least spiritualistically oriented; so little so that I got in trouble with undergraduate friends in England when I was so rude as to question the existence of our college's ghost. Never mind the unattractive implications of my statement above, or even its credibility. A force *was* beginning to be exerted. There were no roving, misty materializations, no poltergeist, no ectoplasmic manifestations.

The force appears to have been aroused by my study of Amos Slaymaker's private papers, and I began feeling it, faintly at first, during that first winter of 1956–57.

The portraits were all in the unoccupied forward parts of the house. Earlier I had been trying to identify with Faithful and Henry. Examination revealed that her face had been dubbed onto a previously painted torso, a not uncommon practice of some mass-production-minded Colonial portraitists like Gustavus and John Hesselius. Faithful wears a pleasant smile that seems vacuous; but coupled with the creamlike glaze of her skin, it lends an aristocratic touch.

Henry appears a full-cheeked, ruddy, healthy-looking gentleman, bedecked in a cream-colored vest which sheathes an ample paunch. His posture is almost pompously erect. He seems a study in prosperous and solid Colonial respectability.

There was nothing about these earliest portraits to attract unduly, let alone mesmerize, probably because identification with their idiom had required studios effort. But the very personal nature of their son Amos's extensive correspondence facilitated intimacy, particularly because I was one of only three or four persons over almost a century and a half who were privy to his innermost thoughts and the machinations to which they gave rise. So the painting by his daughter Hannah fascinated me. It was obvious that her brush had uncovered the real Amos, not simply the accepted version of the revered elder statesman with a Revolutionary War background.

Amos sits leaning slightly forward, hunched over, in three-quarter profile. His left hand is raised to his jaw. In the right lower foreground lies an open book from which he has just glanced away, seemingly lost in thought about its contents.

There's the faintest trace of a smile on the thinnest of lips. The jaw is full, definitely protruding, and it appears large in contrast to the firm, small mouth. Light blue eyes glance obliquely at the viewer from under ever so slightly hooded lids—eyes that ponder some matter of long ago buried in the pages of the book: possibly a journal of the Congress, or the Bible, or Blackstone's *Commentaries*.

If the full jaw doesn't dominate the face, then the long, aquiline nose does. It is crowned by finely defined and not greatly arched eyebrows. However you look at him, with his ample forehead, topped by slightly unkempt wisps of white hair, you walk away with the pronounced impression of a perceptive man, a purposeful one, a thinker.

One snow-filled night while poring over his letters, I felt an urge to have the old man's visage present. Immediately, I brought the portrait back to his first wing, "the dining room," and hung it on the east wall. From my chair by the hearth I could glance through the kitchen door and, as I first thought, be at home with Amos. After a couple of evenings I became aware of a discomforting phenomenon.

Everyone has experienced "feeling" a stare. You're in, say, a library, absorbed in a book. You become uncomfortably aware of someone looking at you. You glance up, catch the other party's gaze, divert it, and go back to reading, free now of the previous sense of disquietude. Suppose, however, that you can't find the gazer. The feeling of being stared at, then, becomes unshakable. This is the phenomenon that began to dog me.

Amos Slaymaker, Esq. Painted by his daughter Hannah Slaymaker Evans

My first reaction was to blame the portrait. Since one can't force a painted likeness to avert its stare, I took the logical course of putting it back in the front house: out of sight, out of mind, I hoped. It didn't work out that way. The sensation of being stared at persisted *as long as I remained with the papers.* On leaving them it diminished, slowly though; not instantaneously, as it would have had the onlooker's gaze been observed and redirected.

Plainly, any effect that Amos's portrait exercised was secondary to that of his papers. Could some otherworldly coercion be manifested through them? Given my impatience with things occult, such a possibility seemed as absurd as it was distasteful. But, imperceptibly, a fascination with the phenomenon began to militate against rationalizations of it. Then, paradoxically, fascination replaced determination as the driving force behind my investigation of White Chimneys' bizarre beginnings.

6

WHEN JUDGE HENRY SLAYMAKER bought the Francis Jones tavern, he had more in mind than acquiring for his son, Amos, property once owned by his wife's great-uncle. It was an investment that promised to pay handsome dividends when the war ended.

A decade before the war the Pennsylvania Assembly recognized the need for a more serviceable route between Philadelphia and Lancaster. The old east-west King's Highway was often rendered impassable by rain and snow. In 1767 the Assembly ordered that a new and proper east-west road be surveyed. It was to pass through the Gap in the Hills and bisect the Francis Jones land. But hostilities began before work commenced.

Jasper Yeates, Esq., was to prove himself the most farseeing of Lancaster's leaders. While the others were undoubtedly preoccupied with the war, Jasper pondered speculative possibilities which the road would present when peace came, and the price of land in its path would soar. The time to buy was during the war, and quietly.

It was clear that Jasper Yeates discussed the future with his faithful aide in the east end, Judge Henry, for Jasper was a silent partner with Henry in the Jones property.

In 1779 it was owned by one Josiah Irwin and a silver merchant, John Ewing. With Jasper staying in the background, Henry dickered with the owners, arrived at the price of £6,500, and bought the property of two hundred acres in his own name on June 2, 1779. An agreement was drawn up on July 4, with Jasper noting that he reimbursed Henry half the purchase price, £3,260, and that they would hold the property in "undivided halves" until such time as they decided to split it; assuredly, after the road was a fact.

In order to facilitate their future split, young Amos was not given the house and farm outright. Jasper and Henry stipulated that on April 1, 1780, they would lease to Amos the two hundred acres, house, and outbuildings. Amos agreed to return to them yearly one-half the crop income from "hay, flax, cider, apples, peach brandy, barley, Indian corn, wheat, potatoes."

On September 25, 1785, two years after the Peace of Paris, Judge Henry Slaymaker died unexpectedly at the age of fifty-one. The keen sense of loss felt by his family and friends was epitomized by his unmarried daughter Lydia, who penned a rather morbid poem. More touching were the lines graven on his tombstone in Leacock churchyard, probably Lydia's also:

> A Patriot most firm
> A Saint without disguise
> Has took his unknown flight
> Above the areal skies
> O Slaymaker the wise, the good
> Thou art gone
> To sit together with the Savior on his throne

Henry willed Mt. Pleasant to his widow, Faithful, but directed that young Henry, Jr. be the master of the estate. Faithful's rights on the place were carefully described by Judge Henry:

The sum of 20 £ per annum out of my mansion plantation during her natural life and her bed and bedstead and furniture and case of drawers, my table that I used in my office and the one half of my kitchen furniture, 6 of my best chairs, and the one half of my table linnen as also the following privileges and maintenance to be continued to her out of my mansion plantation only during her widowhood to wit the privilege of the room she now lodges in or in lieu thereof the storehouse if she pleases and also her necessary share of the kitchen, and cellar and garden and orchard and spring house and firewood cut sufficiently short laid to the door for her and liberty to milk for her use any one cow that is kept on my mansion plantation aforesaid that she shall chuse so that she may at all times of her life have milk not exceeding the milk of one cow at any time. And one hundred weight of pork well fattened and one hundred weight of Beef yearly and one quarter acres of flax ground put in good order for her and her choice of any of the hackneys kept on said plantation at any time she pleases to ride abroad. . . .

The older daughters each were slated for between £100 and £140 and assorted furniture, bedsteads, saddles, and silver. Each also was to receive a spinning wheel. And the five unmarried girls were to "live with my son Henry in my mansion house until they severally arrive at age 18." Henry must "school" little Sophia until "she can read the holy scriptures of the Old and New Testament and write a legible hand and be learned in the five common rules in arithmetick. . . ."

Little Samuel was to be schooled too and "put to some useful trade or occupation to get his living by honest industry."

On the date of his father's death Amos could have free title to the old Francis Jones homestead and "my new suit of apparel, and my large still . . . and all my law books." The Yeates-Slaymaker holdings, however, still remained unsplit. Presumably Amos continued to farm the two hundred acres on the halves for Jasper Yeates.

Amos passed the seven years between the death of his father and the start of the turnpike in 1792 siring children, completing the new wing, and running his store and farm.

He could not have been too busy to continue the study of his father's lawbooks. The store and active membership in Leacock Church (he was elected an elder after his father's death) kept him in continual contact with area folk of all walks. So there was no reason why Amos could not aspire to revive Henry's legal practice.

During Christmas week in Lancaster town in the late 1780s victual-laden Conestoga wagons from the country rumbled through town in early morning. Into the spacious market area just off the northwest corner of the square, they skidded on ice patches, rattled, and squeaked while whips cracked smartly.

Strung along the clean blue and yellow wagons, and before them on rugged stretcher tables, were heaping rolls of rich brown sausage, smoked joints of every meat imaginable, interspersed with wheat-colored piles of fresh plucked poultry. Amid those groaning tables stood crudely hewn barrels of cider, applejack, elderberry wine, and whiskey. And stuffed between these stood wheel on wheel of off-white cheeses, clustered about with bright green and white squashes and golden pumpkins and dark brown potatoes.

Spotted throughout the marketplace, too, were piles of greens—cedar and pine trees—awaiting purchase by the German burghers, who would dress them gaily in candles on Christmas Eve while their kinder watched—some quaking from fear of the Belsnickel Man, who was prone to seize and carry off in the dead of that very night all wee transgressors of the year just past.

Over a loud chorus made by hundreds of huckstering voices was heard the melancholy wailing of French horns and a squeaking of violins. The famous Moravian Church band tuned up in a practicing session in the small stone church a block behind the market square.

To Jasper Yeates, Esq., Lancaster's Christmas weeks were no different from those of the early seventies. Nor had the town changed much. About the only sign of structural progress that the roly-poly lawyer could note as he puffed his purposeful way about the wintry square was the building of a new courthouse. The old one had burned in 1784. Its replacement was to be more commodious. But the bar had seen to it that it would be Georgian and dignified. Pending its completion, Lancaster was run from the Grape Tavern and White Swan—a fact affording Jasper further comforting proof that nothing had really changed.

It was customary for gentlemen of affairs like Jasper to be "at home" over Christmas holidays and there to greet friends and relatives. One of his closest friends was General Washington's late adjutant general, Edward Hand, Lancaster's eminent prewar doctor. General Hand had married Jasper's niece. While the returned General could always go back to medicine, Jasper had a situation in mind that would be very rewarding for one in General Hand's exalted station. It's likely that the barrister discussed the General's future with the newly conceived turnpike company over a Christmastide during the late 1780s.

For Jasper the new highway would bring damages from the land

Henry Slaymaker had secretly bought for him back in 1779. Furthermore, he could build a summer mansion in the lovely valley of gentle hills and lush farmland. Since Henry Slaymaker's son Amos would be helpful in supervising construction, Jasper and Edward Hand would take the young man in on developing the turnpike, whose plans were still unannounced. They might give him one of the road-supervising jobs.

General Edward Hand could become a company manager. He could profit, too, from an early purchase of turnpike stock. It was sure to appreciate fast.

It was pleasing to both men to note the course that Pennsylvania's affairs were taking. As conservatives who opposed the rabble-written Constitution of 1776, both had come to admit nine years later that the maligned instrument had worked out pretty well. Untutored legislators in the unwieldy single-house Assembly had not been able to dominate the Executive, after all. But this was only because the state had been blessed with strong presidents (i.e., governors) of the Supreme Executive Council. Even those who represented the radical Whig Constitutionalists had become conservative enough after gaining office. The only real legislative innovations had been the Divesting Act of 1779, which relieved the Penns of their lands (but rightly enough remunerated the family), and the Act for the Gradual Abolition of Slavery, passed in 1789. Since the latter was drawn to be very gradual, most everyone couldn't have cared less. It was simply a sop to the German sects and the Quakers, who had been for abolition since William Penn's days. Like everyone else, the Pietists knew that slavery was uneconomic in Pennsylvania's balanced crop farming. Otherwise, thought many gentlemen like Jasper and the General, they would have found a way to justify it.

At the time Dr. Benjamin Franklin was President of Pennsylvania. Jasper Yeates and Edward Hand could not ask for more, especially since Dr. Franklin was known to be in favor of improvements to the old state Constitution.

So their big concern was no longer the state. It was the nation; more properly the lack of one—one which could legislate as a political entity under uniform law; one through which currency might be backed so that "Internal Improvements" could be fostered to the betterment of industry and commerce.

Their friends in Philadelphia—Messrs. Hamilton, Jay, Madison, and

Washington himself—were confident at the prospect for a strong federal government. Once the Constitution was a fact and business confidence was restored, the first Internal Improvement would be a reality, making rich men of them both.

This Internal Improvement was to be a turnpike linking Philadelphia to Lancaster. Word was that it would be 21 feet wide, peaked in the middle for proper drainage, and hard-surfaced all the way from Philadelphia to Lancaster. A Scot named Macadam had developed a new means of surfacing; crushed stones would bed the thing, and smaller ones—the size of pullet eggs—were to cover these. Finally, the top was to be of gravel.

News of the project spread up the rocky coasts of New England and down the broad reaches of the Chesapeake, through Virginia's Capes and onto the sleepy, plantation-studded plains of the Carolinas and Georgia. Here was the first palpable proof for a jaded world that America— through her divinely ordered institutions—was on the move!

On April 9, 1792, the General Assembly of Pennsylvania voted "to enable the Governor of this Commonwealth to incorporate a Company for making an artificial road from the City of Philadelphia to the borough of Lancaster." The total capitalization of the company was to be $300,000. One thousand shares of stock were to be issued—six hundred for Philadelphia and four hundred for Lancaster. The total cost, however, was $465,000.

Tollgates were to be placed at ten-mile intervals. A well-defined set of rules was laid down for every kind of conveyance. Freight rates were limited to seven tons per wagon in spring, eight tons during the rest of the year. No more than eight horses were allowed to a wagon, and those with wide-rimmed wheels weren't charged as much as those with narrow ones. Milestones were ordered for every mile, as were signs at intersections, beginning "from the west side of the Schuylkill River . . . so as to pass near to or over the bridge on Brandywine Creek near Downingtown and from there to Witmer Bridge on Conestoga Creek, and from there to the east end of King Street where the building ceases in the borough of Lancaster."

The turnpike was to be built in five sections. There was a district supervisor over each. General Hand was named to the board of directors, and at Yeates's behest, the General made Amos an assistant supervisor in charge of the upper district to the west of the Gap where the road would run about one hundred feet in front of the Slaymaker home.

Amos was charged with hiring laborers, directing and paying them from funds allotted to him by the company. He was also responsible for purchasing stone and seeing that it was delivered promptly on horse-drawn sledges. Laborers were principally occupied in the heavy, onerous work of sledge-hammering stone into sizes requisite for macadam construction. Large gangs slaved from sunup to sundown. Even after the road was completed, Amos had men continually at work keeping the road in repair. He paid one James Williams "for braking 1645 perches of stone at 20¢ per perche and for 83 days work at ⅔ of a dollar per day [$]384.33."

Tavern sites were in immediate demand. As expected by those in the know, land bordering the turnpike appreciated rapidly. But Amos had determined not to sell off any land when came the time for his division with Mr. Yeates. He would need every bit of it.

The foundation of his plan was a tollgate. Jasper Yeates, who had become a justice of the Supreme Court of Pennsylvania in 1791, seemed certain to get him one—especially since Amos promised to be of help in the building of the judge's grand new country seat, Belmont, a quarter of a mile behind Amos's home. Set on the crest of a gentle slope, the site commanded a striking view of the entire Pequea Valley. Belmont was begun with the turnpike in 1792; it was completed along with the road in 1794–95.

From the beginning, Amos practically took over the building operations for the judge, who was seldom available. There were his court sittings and his trip to western Pennsylvania, where President Washington sent him as a commissioner to help settle the Whiskey Rebellion. Amos was invaluable to the judge, meticulously keeping tabs on the disposition of building materials and faithfully reporting on the mansion's progress.

All the while, Amos was building four houses of his own for rental properties. Of half timber and stone, plaster covered, they were placed conveniently near his own house, on both sides of the turnpike. To help foot this bill, Amos borrowed from mother Faithful £200 in "gold and silver, lawful money of Pennsylvania."

All along his eye was on that tollgate. He saw it as an ideal spot to build an inn—a perfect stopping place for the mail stage.

The mail-stage idea was particularly intriguing. It also occurred to Amos to begin a stage line of his own. The location was splendid, midway between Lancaster and the Brandywine stop. He counted on Judge Yeates to expedite his license before too many others got the same idea.

On July 2, 1795, Judge Yeates, having accomplished the purpose of his 1779 land-buying agreement with Judge Henry Slaymaker, namely, to buy land through which a turnpike would run, dissolved (with Amos) said agreement "to hold in undivided halves." Amos Slaymaker was on his way.

Three weeks later, on July 24, 1795, Jasper Yeates wrote Amos from Lancaster regarding details attendant on the completion of Belmont and the judge's moving in. He asked that "Mrs. Slaymaker" permit his tenant's wife, who was already there making the place ready, the use of her oven until theirs was built. There were a few remarks about building lumber which the judge had bought "at the river" for some remaining construction. Then came the good news!

Tho I was much fatigued and very worn on my return from the farm, I did not fail to write Genel. Hand by the stage on the subject of the gate near your house. There seems to me considerable weight in your observations, which I will not fail to communicate to the General when he returns home this evening or tomorrow. I shall then know what he thinks of the plan we have adopted, and if it is not inconsistent with the general system of the turnpike company I am persuaded it will be received. At any rate, you may depend on my using my utmost endeavor on the subject both in my atten. to the Board as well as otherwise.

Our best respects to Mrs. Slaymaker.

I am dr. Sir.

Your friend and hul. servt.

J. YEATES

Amos Slaymaker Esq.

In the wake of Amos's appointments as turnpike supervisor and toll-house keeper came those welcome ordinations as justice of the peace and postmaster of Salisbury—the name given his recently built village of four houses. Thanks to increasing turnpike traffic the store's business grew so handsomely that by 1797 he was out of debt. He even felt flush enough to take on a full-time business manager, one Davis Ostler.

Ostler was ensconced, rent-free, in a tenant house. He looked after the farm, the store, and road-supervising duties. Now Amos had time for magisterial duties and their remunerative offshoot, the practice of law, and time to ponder his final and deepest plunge. By April, 1797, the squire of Salisbury felt ready to start the stage line and build his inn.

Since Lancaster was about to become the new state capital and explode with more population and commerce, it seemed worthwhile to plan for an inn there as well. Two inns, coaches, horses, and help would cost Amos dearly. However, with his reputation and Jasper's Philadelphia banking connections, he foresaw little difficulty in raising the necessary funds.

On April 24, 1797, he borrowed from a George Aston, a merchant of Philadelphia, £1,356 in gold and silver currency of Pennsylvania. For this loan Amos mortgaged all his land (now a hundred acres), his tenant houses, store, and home.

The Salisbury inn was begun with spring plowing and finished by harvest, 1797. He located it two hundred yards west of his home on the same side of the road and designed it himself. The actual building operations were left under the direction of Davis Ostler.

Ostler was meticulous in his dealings with the various tradespeople with whom he contracted—William Bird furnished shingles and spent thirteen days in laying them to the tune of £4. William Linville did carpentry, and from his bill certain "goods" purchased from Amos's store were deducted from the workmen:

Brandy sling, gill gin, mug cider 2s.8d
Pint Wine 1s.10½d
Gill Whiskey 5½d

When Ostler felt that materials could be had cheaper than the contractors offered them, he bought direct and turned them over to the builders. Such was the case with pine boards, cedar rails, planks, pine scantling, and later "two tons of plaster and twenty-one pounds of nails."

All through the bedlam of building, the sweating homespun-clad foreman Ostler kept the turnpike in repair; Moses and Robert Eliot sup-

The Sign of John Adams Inn, as it stands today

plied him with "one-hundred-eighty load of flintstone for the turnpike road." And on turnpike letterhead: "Resolved that Amos Slaymaker, Sup of the upper district of the road be authorized to have the Bridge built by Mr. Henry Witmer repaired as soon as the season will permit. . . ."

Dutiful Davis Ostler saw that Arthur Linville did the job and paid him £11 8s. 6d. At the same time Davis kept after the farm's indentured help and the few slaves that Amos had begun to take on. He saw to it that fences were mended, washes filled, and reported all to Amos in horribly misspelled little chits: "I foiling the bad gulley in the large north field at its opening in the road."

Amos was not so wrapped up in justice of the peace duties, church chores, storekeeping, and postmastering, though, that he failed to keep close tabs on Ostler's activities. So well pleased was he that he felt a special bonus was in order. The only public office that had somehow escaped the squire's grasp was that of tax collector for Salisbury township.

Time-consuming though the job was, there were advantages in having it under his own roof. Even though the cut wasn't large, it would be appreciated by Ostler. So he got the job for him.

The inn, Ostler's most special handiwork, was grand to behold. Snuggled against the foot of Salisbury Hill, it was the most commodious and graceful hostelry on the new highway. Unlike others—now rapidly springing up—Amos's was not placed flush to the road. It sat back a full fifty feet behind lawns that were always well tended. Built entirely of stone, covered by softly rippled white plaster, its porticoed front faced the road with a dignified unpretentiousness that served to de-emphasize its large rear quarters; these constituted the supporting or base leg of the T. Amos named the inn the Sign of John Adams—a Federalist appellation sure to please Jasper Yeates.

It looked to be exactly what Amos had envisioned, an inn for gentlemen travelers. Cattle drovers, wagon drivers, and the like could stop at Robert Kennedy's tavern, the Sign of the Rising Sun, down the pike near Gap. Not until the Lancaster–Chester County line was there another gentlemen's stopping place, the Sign of Mt. Vernon. To the west, there were no gentlemen's inns for five miles until the Sign of the Indian King, and this was getting pretty close to Lancaster.

Amos's proposed hostelry in Lancaster was also bound to succeed. With the growing population of state job holders and legislators he was assured of boarders, no matter how the passenger trade was running. He knew just the right building in Lancaster and had word that it could be bought for much less than an entire new construction. Built as a home by a bricklayer of substance, the building was as comely a structure as Lancaster could boast. Four stories high (the top floor was marked by three handsome dormers), it had twin brick chimneys at both extremities of the roof. The doorway was porticoed with two white pillars; second-story front-facing rooms had neat little circular balconies set before tall windows.

The inn had distinction, but as important to Amos was its size. The location was right—the State Capitol Building was only half a block away. The Pennsylvania Arms, he called it, after engineering the purchase for £1,034 on September 18, 1801.

Taken with the cost of building the Salisbury inn and purchasing stage equipment, not to mention increasing payrolls, this figure contributed to a large total outlay. Money, however, was no longer a worry; business was good with no sign of a letup.

The wellspring of Amos's future success lay in his justice of the peace duties. At first they seemed nothing but boring drudgery. There were constant neighborhood quarrels to settle—devilishly picayune little affairs. On January 29, 1796, he examined a "James Walker, a peddler . . . who saith that on Tuesday night before Christmas he lodged at Peter Elmaker's and gave his pack to a girl living with said Elmaker named Eleanor Murphy and in the course of the night his pack was cut open and fourteen dollars was taken out of his pack and two silk handkerchiefs . . . with fringe all 'round."

Such affairs were legion. But Amos dutifully heard them out in his J.P. office in the Sign of John Adams Inn, amid the comings and goings of stages, the loading and unloading of passengers who had to be fed and boarded.

There was one delinquency case which Amos took particular pleasure in pressing home. In milking each of his contrived facilities to capacity, Amos was willing to be downright mean. The area's population center was Gap, not Salisbury. Dwellers in Gap resented the post office's being placed a mile distant by virtue of nothing more than Amos's political bulldozing. To add insult to their injury he required them to pay at the tollgate before entering the post office in the inn.

Five angry burghers petitioned the Court of Common Pleas in Lancaster to the effect that they: "divers inhabitants of the township of Salisbury . . . sheweth that Philadelphia and Lancaster Turnpike Company have lately erected a tollgate, adjoining land of Amos Slaymaker Esq. . . . which subjects your petitioners to considerable inconvenience, as an obstruction to the only convenient way to the post office through which we obtain our letters and newspapers and other places which our business necessarily calls us. . . ." Amos's tollgate was an "obstacle to the diffusion of that knowledge which is the support of our free institution. . . ."

They went on to ask for the appointment of an overseer who would lay out a road so that they might have free access to the post office.

Amos was given a copy of the petition, which carried the name of a Mr. Rambo. The road was never built, but provisions for the good people were obviously made, for the matter was dropped. The petition led to an act of the legislature prohibiting Amos's kind of gate management.

Mr. Rambo, however, had the tables reversed on him August 13, 1799, when Squire Amos vengefully had him hauled "before me to answer William Thompson on a plea of debt under forty shillings."

Between 1795 and 1799 there were as many as five and six such cases in one day. While delinquency settlements afforded a percentage for Amos, the total amount was small. But he fast became the lord high arbiter of the "east end." There were wills to write, promissory notes to draw up, agreements to witness, and estates to settle. The larger the estate, the more his fee.

His first big estate broke in 1798 with the death of an old Leacock VII Battalion crony, George Leech. Both of George's Gap hostelries were sold, along with his "plantation of 70 or 80 acres in Salisbury township." As administrator, Amos arranged for sale of the inns to Thomas Henderson, thus cementing relations with that well-fixed clan. When some of them packed off in Conestoga wagons, along with Sibby's brother, Daniel Fleming, for "the western country" (Westmoreland County, Pennsylvania), it was Amos who looked after their affairs back home. He kept in touch with the western Hendersons through consistent correspondence with his brother-in-law—always keeping the Salisbury Hendersons posted.

Plainly, Amos's estate business was in the cross-pollinating stage, considering the mounting flood of wills, agreements, and the like. The harvest would be coming; all Amos needed was longevity, the better to reap it.

So at forty-five—at the century's turn—the squire of Salisbury was tirelessly occupied twelve to fourteen hours a day with his multiplicity of responsibilities, all the while making the rounds of farm and inn with a swift, determined gait.

By way of using a nagging family problem to cut operating costs, Amos put his brother Henry, Jr. in charge of the Pennsylvania Arms hotel in Lancaster. Henry, Jr. had been left in charge of Mt. Pleasant by Henry, Sr. After Faithful's death in 1792, Henry, Jr. lost interest in the

Silhouette of Amos's brother, Henry Slaymaker, Jr.

place and began dabbling in Lancaster politics as a part-time building contractor. Sammy was incapable of coping with Mt. Pleasant. All of Amos's sisters, save Lydia, had married and left. Mt. Pleasant deteriorated around the sole survivor, poor Lydia. She passed lonely hours penning dreary letters to sister-in-law Sibby. Lydia was a hypochondriac—understandable, since she suffered from an incipient cancer or a tumor. She wrote on January 7, 1793:

... how I shall spend this winter is best known to Him who knows all things. The very thought of it makes me shudder—oh, had I but one sister that I could speak to I should not be so miserable but even that is denied me. Or had I but my dear parents . . . not one left in the house of our nativity but myself. Every room that I go in seems as if it wanted something but when I go in the room that my dead mother occupied it is more than I can bear, to express my feelings. . . .

There was no convenient way that Mt. Pleasant could be incorporated into Amos's operations. It was four miles distant. Eventually, it might be sold and the proceeds split among his brothers and sisters. If Lydia still lived, she could be farmed out. In the meantime, Amos

68

benefited from the estate by putting its manager, whom his father had willed to perpetuate it, to more constructive use.

In less mundane ways Amos's in-laws also proved useful. The marriage of his sister Hannah to Samuel Cochran of Cochranville, a member of the Governor's cabinet, enhanced Amos's social worth. It was not lessened when sister Faithful married landed George Duffield II, comptroller general of the Commonwealth, whose home, Duffield Manor, was contiguous to Amos's village, Salisbury. So by the century's turn the Slaymaker fortunes were on the upswing.

Highly developed as were Amos's imaginative powers, they did not bless him with a sense of history. He left no record of "opening day" at the inns and the departure of the first stage. But the turnpike could not have been open long before his two handsome red coaches clattered briskly along the pike, scattering drovers' cattle herds and forcing Conestoga and farm wagons to the shoulders.

The "Slaymaker Line of Stages" was a moneymaker from the start. Sales volume grew steadily at the store. Since the Sign of John Adams catered to genteel travelers, Amos commanded top rates. Income from his other projects was rising steadily. Presumably by now he had paid off his large debts and had surplus cash to lend. So it was logical for Amos Slaymaker to become a banker. He could not very easily have ducked the honor, even if he had tried.

Moneylending had been as much a part of the storekeeping game as bartering back when he had first set up shop after the war. He learned the ropes, got to know the good prospects from the bad, and developed a reputation as the valley's "man to see" for ready cash.

It was a perfect time to move into the field. Lancaster had its first bank in 1803 when the Bank of Pennsylvania set up a branch there. And in Philadelphia a rival to the State Bank appeared, the Philadelphia National, with the result that even in country areas west of "the City," people were beginning to lose their inhibitions—give up hoarding and bartering and invest instead. Valley farmers might find it vexing to journey to Philadelphia and Lancaster to bank. Amos would make the trips unnecessary.

From around the valley farmers and tradesmen flocked to the Sign of John Adams, where Amos sat hunched at his desk, intently and neatly recording interest and principal payments of his many debtors. Most interest charges were collectable once a year. There were scores between 1800 and 1807, mostly in the range of ten to twenty-five dollars each.

With the turn of the century came new emoluments. Amos was named assistant assessor of thirteen townships. Then he became a county commissioner. And on April 21, 1806, for his "zeal, patriotism and fidelity," Amos was named "Brigade Inspector of the Fourth Division, composed of the militia of Lancaster County." With the job went the rank of major. The parchment commission, when unrolled, was a full 17 inches across, 16 high, beautifully engraved and heavily sealed by Thomas McKean, Governor of the Commonwealth. Amos had come a long way from the cold, bare schoolroom at Pequea Church, from that confusing and frightening night on the Chester Road after Brandywine.

Manifest Destiny was lending a hand which grew more powerful by the day. Every falling of the sun saw Lancaster town filling up with westbound transients. Then when dawn's first glimmer sneaked up behind chimney and spire, the chock-full wagons took their monotonously screeching course west on King Street. On they rumbled, along the now extended turnpike to Wrights Ferry on the Susquehanna. Wagons and livestock were rafted across, and the trek commenced again toward Chambersburg, beyond which the turnpike was being lengthened across the blue-green mass of the Alleghenies to the frontier hamlet of Pittsburgh.

To the Slaymaker brothers there seemed no end in sight to the pike and immigrants alike, so little time was lost in pushing their line on to Chambersburg. More drivers and horses were employed—only the most dependable of both. There was that unbeaten record to hold: Philadelphia to Chambersburg in forty-eight hours for only two dollars!

State officials, merchants, traders, gentlemen of the professions, land speculators—all such who were impatient of delay swore by the Slaymaker Stage. "Intend to travel 14 miles to Mr. Slaymaker's on Tuesday afternoon," wrote Governor McKean to his son in 1805, "and there to breakfast and embark in the stage. . . ."

7

In 1806 Judge Yeates and his Lancaster power structure tapped Amos for the State Senate. This latest accolade bespoke need for a more impressive home. A mansion commanding the turnpike seemed in order. Amos entered the Senate for the term beginning December, 1806. Ground for the new addition was broken in the spring of 1807—after the term's end—so that he could supervise the work.

The advent of the turnpike left the old Francis Jones house (and Amos's wing) awkwardly positioned. The south end of the home faced a lovely expanse of meadow overlooking America's most impressive highway. The front door did not face the turnpike because, of course, previously there had been no turnpike to face.

Symmetry dictated that the new wing should front on the turnpike. What better opportunity could present itself for construction of a Classic Revival front! There was the sweep of the road, grandly climbing Salisbury Hill to the west. Set back fifty yards on the north side, in meadowland that sloped down to the turnpike and the tiny hamlet that was Salisbury, would stand the new mansion, all-commanding.

There was one major architectural problem to overcome. Were the new wing's first floor to be built on a plane with the old, the house would appear too squat to command the turnpike with dignity. So the addition's floor would be raised. How to join the houses? Amos hit on a characteristically practical solution.

He decided on chipping the bottom out of both turnpike-facing windows so that their bases would be even with the new mansion's floor. A set of steps under each window would turn them into doors leading from his first wing into his second. The window-turned-door on the east side would lead into a drawing room, itself opening wide and undoored into a front living room. Before the west portal would be a

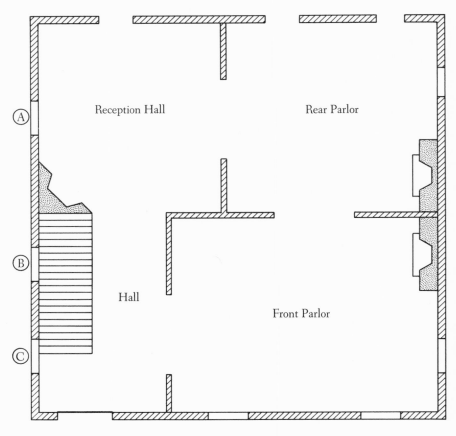

(A) Became Passageway in 1923
(B) Became Portrait Niche in 1923
(C) Window Removed — Opening Retained in 1923

reception area, from which would run a long hallway to the mansion's front door.

Amos envisioned a wide balustrade staircase facing the front entrance, hard against the west wall. It would go straight to the second floor, where he planned three large bedchambers and a small front sitting room, and on up to a third-floor garret and servants' quarters.

There was no sense in keeping the ceilings at a low seven feet to conform with those in the old house. For more breathing space Amos thought they ought to go to twelve feet. And since the new rooms were going to be large, the ceilings would be supported by columns, in the classic motif. Each new room's fireplace would have a classically carved mantel to match the columns. He chose flooring of fine oak, cut more narrow than the wide boarding in the farmhouse behind. Whether he realized it or not, Amos's empirical plan was going to lend a feeling of tasteful, rambling unity to old and new wings alike, signifying a restful sense of permanence.

When he entered the Pennsylvania Senate, plans were well firmed. Davis Ostler had signed on contractors and laid in supplies. Beams, joists, and girders were lumbered from Amos's woodlands and set aside to age throughout the winter. As had been the case with the Salisbury inn, Amos determined to supply as many materials as possible. Contractors would furnish the labor.

The cellar came first. Ostler's team of hired diggers heaved picks, axes, and shovels from dawn to dusk, stopping only every couple of hours for a whiskey break. Amos probably watched in snatches. He had to check on the inn, talk with travelers and the help, and then return to Ostler and the toiling gang in the cellar. He might have chinned occasionally with an old comrade-in-arms of the Leacock VII, Adam Cowan.

Adam supplied the stone; it was carried on a large ox-drawn sledge from a nearby quarry. At job's end his bill read: "The number of lodes I haled to you on the turnpike is seventy-six lodes of stone as witness my hand. To Amos Slaymaker, Esq. Adam Cowan."

Levi Bailey and his team of masons took over in April. Quickly the cellar cavity's walls were lined with lime and flintstones, deftly fashioned by chipping until quite smooth.

Then Bailey tackled the walls. In keeping with those of the old house, Amos wanted them 21 inches thick. This had to be the longest and most laborious job of all. Through blazing summer Levi Bailey drove his men relentlessly on. In stifling heat, in flash thunderstorms, they lifted, sledged, chipped. Hard on their heels came the plasterer, Nathaniel Williams, and his gang. Outside and in, walls were sloshed over and smoothed, all in a matter of days.

Amos told them that the first frost had to be beaten. And it must have been. For he paid the mason promptly on November 11, the receipt reading: "From Amos Slaymaker the sum of one-hundred-and-fifty dollars for the mason work on the house. Levi Bailey." The plasterer got his $19.50 soon after.

Days shortened ominously. The buffeting wind began to make its bite felt to Amos's marrow. Surely it seemed that the last stage would take forever. There were so many pine shingles to be laid. Jasper Thornbrough's bill for nails, brads, and ceiling lath covered paper sixteen inches long and came to $43.

The fireplaces in the mansion's two new rooms and reception area fed three new chimneys.

Happily, with winter's first snowy gusts, the completed mansion stood serenely ready. The excited family could have viewed the two lofty attic dormers, that solid-looking stone porch, and its four graceful pillars supporting the overhanging roof with a thrill that they had never before experienced. It must have seemed very large and empty. Possibly they wandered about the place almost aimlessly, like a ship's passengers testing their sea legs on a first cruise. The mansion's interior probably seemed cold and dreary. It was heavily limed, a gleaming, monotonous white; floors were garnished to a pale yellow by sweepings of sand. There was probably no carpeting, only a few rag throw rugs which Sibby placed. Made from strips of castoff clothing, they could have livened the whited-sepulcherlike appearance of the place. The only other color shone in the gleaming likenesses of Amos's parents probably hanging over the mantel in the front drawing room. So he painted all rooms, upstairs and down, a lemon yellow.

It must have been great fun for Amos to play hooky in Philadelphia and Baltimore, where he browsed at cabinetmakers, dickered, and bought. From one he picked up a mahogany secretary for $27.50. At $4.50 he got a portable desk, perfect for commuting use. From another, one John Dorsay, came a lovely Empire sideboard with two taper holders, a set of prints (for those bare walls), a box of dueling pistols (just for the fun of it), and a traveling trunk, all coming to $9.20. There were Chippendale and Hitchcock chairs, a rocking chair for himself, and that "organizer" piano that he couldn't resist, even at $150, since little Hannah had taken so well to music.

An especially prized possession for the new wing was Amos's "Washington-Yeates" Chippendale sofa. He enjoyed relating its circuitous route to his mansion. It was said that General Washington had a matching pair and presented one to Jasper Yeates. He, in turn, gave it to Judge Henry Slaymaker, possibly for political services well rendered.

More practical than aesthetic was Amos's washing machine. The thing was patented to a Simon Willard, Jr. of Massachusetts, and Amos was given in the agreement of sale "the full power and authority to use the said patented washing machine in his family and not elsewhere. . . ." He was admonished to see that the operator "put in ever so few clothes, not so many as to choke the machine, and not use too much water, if you mean to have the machine work easy. If you have very dirty collars and wrist bands of shirts, rub the soap on such places previous to putting them into the water."

Shortly the mansion was superbly outfitted. Windows were trimmed with spotless silk hangings. Perpetually tremulous in drafts, they shimmered in sunlight and cast soft shadows across the amber gloss of Sheraton and Hepplewhite furniture, delicately rendered in cherrywood, sandalwood, and maple.

Chests and a grandfather clock of heavier, darker mahogany lent an elegant balance. Bright Oriental carpeting supplemented the throw rugs and provided warmth. In the large space between the living room's two front windows, he had a large gilt-trimmed mirror built into the wall. Perhaps the children enjoyed standing in the rear mansion room and looking through it into the front living room's mirror. They could see their reflection a full twenty-five feet away!

It seemed proper that the farm buildings should be in keeping with the new mansion. So Ostler was put to building a large new barn "half of stone at the ends, of wood in the middle, with a shingle roof." A new smokehouse was put up in the east lawn, and a washhouse at the well by the kitchen door of the old Francis Jones house.

Off the west lawn, by the little stream separating mansion and inn,

Ostler built a tilt mill, a metalworking shop to serve both the plantation and the village.

The leisurely gentleman's avocation that was "scientific farming" was becoming great fun. Amos eagerly absorbed the latest word from Philadelphia on cattle breeding, orchard care, the wonders wrought by red clover in haymaking. He pondered with Judge Yeates the bright future of Merino sheep and grape culture. Both of these latest fads seemed promising.

Amos hired a young man named Robert Smith to run the inn, bank, store, and post office. He was assisted by three hired hands. The squire could now devote himself fully to Senate duties, estate settling, magistrate chores, and farm overseeing.

Adolph Ulrich Wertmüller was "First Painter" to the King of Sweden during the 1780s. He migrated to Versailles, where he painted Queen Marie Antoinette. With the onset of the French Revolution's Reign of Terror, Wertmüller shipped to Philadelphia. There he was befriended by the Swedish American artist John Hesselius, who painted Judge Henry Slaymaker. Through the Hesselius family, Adolph met a niece of Amos Slaymaker's, Betsey Henderson. They were married in 1802.

Adolph painted President Washington, French Ambassador Citizen Genêt, and a classical tableau, *Danaë and the Golden Rain*. The latter subject was a nude. This precluded Sunday viewings in Philadelphia.

Wertmüller suffered a malady which to an artist can be worse than death: incipient blindness. He bought land in Naaemen's Creek, Delaware, and with childless Betsey took up farming. His diary, reflecting pathos spiked with comedy, reveals a bumbling and unsuccessful farmer whose travails were cut short by death at sixty in 1811. He willed his land, personal effects, and some paintings to Betsey. The paintings were unsold because they were of his immediate family: parents, sisters, an unidentified woman, and several self-portraits, the most revealing of which was done in Versailles in 1795. These paintings were supposedly bestowed by the artist, as a grateful suppliant, on his "sponsor," Squire Amos. At least this was the handed-down story. Actually, they probably never met.

Within a few months of Adolph's death, Betsey expired, still child-less and intestate. Uncle Amos Slaymaker was made executor of the estate. Henderson heirs were scattered to Pennsylvania's northwestern extremity. None was about to return to Naaemen's Creek and claim shares in the farm. Amos computed the heirs' shares, wrote each—under-scoring the inutility (to them) of their distant and minuscule portions—and offered to buy their claims to the farm. After a couple of years of dickering (of which more later) the heirs came across and Amos took over the farm, placed a tenant farmer, and awaited a propitious time to sell it. There was no one about to claim the portraits, so they were auc-tioned. Some paintings were needed to cover the empty walls of Amos's new mansion wing. As an alert executor there were ways for him to pick some up at little or no cost. Maybe he considered his eight Wertmüllers part of his cut for settling the estate.

On July 12, 1811, John Boyd, Amos's friend, neighbor, and onetime battalion commander, died unmarried with no issue, and intestate. The absence of a will represented no oversight on John's part. He had planned it that way.

For the 466 acres of rich east Pequea Valley farmland that he left behind didn't really belong to him. So John's favorite next of kin stood to gain nothing from a stuffy old will. It was better that his brother James be given sufficient latitude to shift for himself, just as John had been doing so successfully for forty-nine years.

Ever since his father died without a will back in 1762, John had been using the Boyd plantation pretty much as he saw fit. After all, he was the oldest of eight children, some of whom could not read or write. Someone had to look after their affairs, and he was that logical someone.

Of course, John would pay them all for their share in their father's estate—someday. So all the legal gobbledegook from the courts about dividing the land in parcels among widow and children could wait until he was good and ready.

Anyway, who was there to press claims? His brothers and sisters would never be so ungrateful. He had always taken care of them, and they had all seemed to be happy enough for twenty-eight years. Even when his widowed mother died without a will, no one complained, since

John continued to handle her share of the estate just as if she were still around.

Then in 1790 John Boyd's sister Margaret, egged into becoming difficult by her husband, James Hamilton, demanded her share in her parents' estate and took John to court. Margaret and James Hamilton got an award of £184 14s. 2d., including back interest.

John dragged his feet on the settlement for two years, during which time he was cited twice by the Hamiltons to pay up. He sought, successfully, to convince them that he would, as soon as he could split up the property and effect a sale. In order to put this date as far as possible into the future, John strove to cultivate his other brothers and sisters.

Two spinster sisters, Isabella and Mary, were ensconced with him in the old Boyd mansion. He convinced them that he was their protector against the covetous Hamiltons who wanted to break up the old family seat. John made it worth the while of his brothers James and George to share "management" responsibilities with him. Meanwhile, lest anyone else become difficult, he persuaded them and the two old maids to renounce their rights to accept the real estate and request the courts to confirm it to him.

Only two brothers remained as potential troublemakers. Happily, they moved south.

As for the Hamiltons, he played them by ear as before—stalling on the sale, promising, then stalling some more and talking his sisters into pleading that the homestead be kept intact. John Boyd lived happily ever after. When brother George died, his share continued under John's suzerainty. As money poured in from lands and rentals, John reinvested in still more land, and the administration account of his late father waxed richer.

On John's death, the second-in-command took over. Reared in the estate-managing traditions of his brother, James Boyd's methods were John's, with one difference. John had always played everything close to his vest. But when facing the cruel and often unsympathetic world alone, James felt the need of a consultant.

The perfect man would be easy to get. James had known and trusted him from school days and through wartime campaigning. This gentleman had more estate-settling experience than anyone in the valley. Though possessed of substantial wealth, he was never unwilling to look for more.

As one of Lancaster County's leading politicians with connections at the top, he was universally respected. The old-maid sisters would trust him implicitly. The courts would be solicitous of his wishes.

If the settlement could be dragged out and the sale put off interminably, there would be handsome administration fees to be paid on a long-term basis. The large corpus would ensure plenty for James and his new administrator and old friend, Squire Amos Slaymaker. Unlike John, James Boyd wasn't hoggish.

On July 13, 1811, James Boyd and Amos Slaymaker, Esq., filed John's inventory as administrators. Amos would rue the move until his dying day.

In earlier years Amos probably would have kept clear of James Boyd's affairs. Boyd's designs were so transparently dishonest that eventual detection and legal retribution were foregone conclusions. But by 1811 Amos must have felt confident enough to make right any situation and to profit from it as well.

Contributing to Amos's "era of good feelings" was the realization that his children were getting a first-rate education. They were under the tutelage of a learned scholar, corpulent Reverend Nathaniel Walshard Sample, an alumnus of Pequea Latin and Princeton College. Of religion there was plenty in the Reverend's Strasburg School. But knowing well the imbalance in curriculum in other church schools, he included bookkeeping, surveying, and navigation for boys; sewing and needlework for girls. In 1803 he merged the little school with that of Robert Elliot, M.A., into the fine, large Strasburg Classical Academy—a boarding school housing children from some of the finest families of Delaware, Maryland, and Pennsylvania.

There was Latin, Greek, history, mathematics, geography, and "the English language taught grammatically," as the advertisement read. This modern curriculum was made more so with the addition of dancing, fencing, drawing, and painting. For "one hundred dollars per annum for board and tuition" the older children were boarded. The latest copybooks were bound with blue paper covers and printed in Philadelphia. "Writing," it said on the cover, "is not only an useful, but an elegant accomplishment."

Amos had high hopes for the two eldest boys, Jasper and Henry.

Silhouette of Amos's son,
Henry Fleming Slaymaker

Silhouette of Amos's son,
Jasper Yeates Slaymaker

Both were slight of build. With hair neatly cued, they seemed at first blush a lot alike. But one could detect that Jasper Yeates Slaymaker in his late teens had a breath of restless energy about him. His full jaw suggested a trace of confident pugnacity, absent from the thin, more ascetic features of his younger brother, Henry F.

Jasper was of a cut to follow his namesake, old Judge Yeates, at law. The Reverend Sample had recommended Dickinson, in Carlisle, a new Presbyterian College. Franklin College in Lancaster was nearer, of course. But it was mostly made up of Germans of the Reformed faith. In 1804, when Jasper entered Dickinson, it became clear that Salisbury would not long hold him. His letters showed him to be a good mixer, one with an excellent future at law.

As a member of the Belles Lettres Society Jasper developed into a lively, convincing, and articulate debater. As eloquent in the rival society, the Union Philosophical, was one James Buchanan. Mutual respect began to warm into a friendship destined to be lasting.

Amos's second son seemed more fitted to Salisbury's sedentary quietude than the first. Always respectful to his father, kind to his mother and the younger children, diligent—if plodding and a trifle unimaginative—

Henry F. was fast becoming his father's favorite, and closest confidant.

Like Jasper he joined the Belles Lettres Society at Dickinson and became a tolerable orator. On February 18, 1809, "Mr. Slaymaker then delivered an elegant oration on the Contemplation of Future Happiness." On March 18 he was one of those sustaining the position in debating that matrimony, rather than celibacy, is "most conducive to the happiness of man." He won. In April, he stood for the affirmative on the issue: "Are a good name and the esteem of our acquaintances preferable to a large estate?" He won again.

But to shy and withdrawn Henry college life held little appeal. He constantly longed for the familiar security of the tight little world of Salisbury's humdrum ways. "Dear Brother," he wrote from Dickinson to Jasper on November 13, 1808:

> your letter I rec'd and also the plates, and you cannot imagine the pleasures I derived from hearing how you all are and that business is still going on with its usual perseverance. But while I thus contemplate the pleasures derived from the business of the old walks, I am here spending days and hours in this solitary room without any person to converse with to pass the many long and lonesome hours of the days and nights. How much more happy would I be if I had a companion like you. But I find there is none here, they appear all to be given up too much to the imperfection of our nature. . . .

He went on about his studies in "mensuration," some parts of which he found "a little difficult," but which he would "get over" with some tutoring. He complained that college regulations were enforced more strictly than when Jasper was there. After describing the current state of the Belles Lettres Society, he asked for newspapers as often as they could be sent "as they will be my only amusement in the evenings. . . ."

Amos tried to build Henry up by asking Samuel Cochran to stop at Carlisle on his frequent jaunts to "the western lands." On one occasion the comptroller general accompanied the surveyor general. But neither Uncle George Duffield nor Uncle Samuel Cochran could assuage the melancholy student's discontent. He wanted to come home.

Finally, Amos relented. Henry left Dickinson for the last time in June, 1809. His failure to graduate with the class of 1810, though, didn't upset Amos unduly. Jasper, with his far-reaching interests, would soon be lost to Amos. Were young Henry kept in Salisbury, he, at least, might stick and some day take over.

When he left college, almost everything about the inn was dumped on Henry F. Slaymaker's frail shoulders. Thomas Smith, the previous manager, assisted him.

Henry took complete charge of the tollgate. Arrangements were made with the powers that were for his postmastership to become official, the honor being bestowed on November 6 in a most impressively printed letter—a masterpiece of stilted redundancies—from the General Post Office, Washington City. Jasper would have laughed to think of his younger brother "applying" to their father after having helped to do the job on and off for all those years. But Henry took it seriously, as he did everything.

He spelled Amos as turnpike supervisor, meticulously listing amounts paid out for road-mending labors. The long lists were sent off to the turnpike office in Lancaster, but only after duplicates had been carefully drawn for his father's files.

Even so delicate a matter as quality control of the inn's victuals was left to his willing hands. "The tea must have the right quantity of dandelion," he penned for the bound help; "ripe peaches to be washed clean and put into a stone pot with a large handful of peach kernels"—these two recipes coming under the headings of "Tea making" and "Peach Cordial."

By itself, running the Sign of John Adams was a full-time job involving long bills to check and pay and the help to jog in the broiling kitchen so that guests were served quickly during twenty-minute coach layovers.

8

ALWAYS WANTING THE BEST for his children, Amos was increasingly able to give it during these glorious years. As he mellowed and enjoyed them as never before, he became more solicitous of their every wish. Particularly, he doted over the youngest, bright little Hannah. He must have taken pride in her obviously artistic bent, encouraged her dabbling in paints, and generally set about spoiling her, as indeed he did to a lesser degree the two youngest boys, John and William Daniel.

There was little farm work for them. As potential gentlemen, they were being drilled hard at Strasburg Classical. Then would come college —followed, if Amos had his way, by the law, medicine, or the ministry. These two boys were his last hopes for the professions, since their brother Amos Henderson Slaymaker wanted to go into business on his own after Dickinson.

The squire was a slave to every whim of the older girls. They had no heavy housework and no need to make their own clothing. From Philadelphia Amos ordered the finest of silk and damask dresses, hats, gloves, ribbons, and shoes. Each was bought a side saddle and a horse. He wanted them well equipped for the young people's outings al fresco at Duffield Manor and Cochranville.

Amos had ensured this leisurely life for his girls with plenty of household help. Three Negro slaves, two women and a twelve-year-old boy, were shuttled back and forth between mansion and inn.

Amos was devoted to one of the women, Diana Scott, known to the family as Black Dinah, and she to him. Her son Abraham was born just before Amos bought her in 1795. Apparently he had rescued her from an unhappy and unsettled life. While the law required that the son be given his freedom at the age of twenty-eight, from all appearances Abraham, as well as his mother, were fixtures at the mansion for life.

For gardening and milking, there was a never-flagging stream of indentured girls. When one finished her stretch, another was taken on. Such was also the case with boys charged with mastering the "mystery of farming" at the feet of Davis Ostler. Some stuck. Some didn't. But all got a fair shake; they had clean, warm quarters in the mansion's garret, took their meals at the common board, and Amos saw that they were schooled. Not at Strasburg Classical; Amos would certainly have considered that an extravagance. But he did make it his business to locate itinerant private adventurer-teachers such as Edward Henry, whom he paid $7.75 for "three months tuition of Elizabeth Thompson," or Samuel Higgins, who charged $2.50 for "one quarter tuition of Mary Ann."

Yet, notwithstanding the invidious state in which the bound help found themselves in relation to the squire's children, long-termers like Charles Frederick Eadmen, a German boy, John Armstrong, and a son of a Dianna Brown became accepted and integral parts of the ongoing good life of the white mansion.

For Amos's part Salisbury life probably seemed anything but ongoing in these lazy years. Save for the turnpike's perpetual bustle, the hamlet slept. In the summer of 1811 the squire's lot was a serene one.

A gathering cloud soon obscured Amos Slaymaker's sunny vistas. On June 19, 1812, President Madison declared war on England. Like staunch Federalists throughout the country, Amos saw this conflict as the work of Western "War Hawk" Congressmen who had long plotted to expand U.S. borders into Canada at the expense of a distraught Great Britain.

Pro- and antiwar factions in Lancaster town went at each other's throats through their respective newspapers, the anti-Federalist *Intelligencer* and the Federalist *Journal*. Animosities eventuated in brawling and fistfights. A typical *Journal* attack was waged on Federalist politician Timothy Matlack, who was rumored to have been pro-British in the Revolution.

I am told [wrote the editor] that when you read my paper of Saturday last, you flew into a tremendous passion . . . that you ran bare-headed like a maniac through the greater part of Orange St. . . . that you fumed, grinnd, stamped, and raved in alternate seconds . . . that on returning to your house about noon you cursed the wife, and the cook, upset the dinner table, plates, dishes, kicked a poor lap dog and thrw a cat out of the window.

Next he worked over Tench Cox, another ex-Tory:

Good news . . . Great news . . . Glorious news . . . Let the harsh trumpet sound . . . sing the loud clarion and the pealing bells. Let the children squall, dogs bark, cats mew, cocks crow, horses neigh, cows bellow, frogs croak, hogs grunt, pigs squeak, and turkeys gobble. Let every bird and beast and creeping thing extend its lungs and roar jocundily. Let the people of this once happy borough rest from their labors and join in rejoicing for the happy event. TENCH COX IS TO LEAVE LANCASTER . . . in a few days . . . we hope never to return. This extraordinary character has been found worthy of fresh honors and emoluments . . . and goes a step higher on the ladder of democracy. . . .

Eventually leading citizens of both factions papered over their differences and embarked on a unity campaign.

Federalist Jasper Yeates Slaymaker, Esq., was one of the prime movers, along with his lawyer confreres James Buchanan, James Hopkins, and other of their peers, such as James Humes and John F. Steinman, Jr., son of an anti-Federalist hardware merchant. They formed an outfit of their own, the "Lancaster Phalanx," designed fancy uniforms, and elected James Humes their captain.

Amos was probably grateful that he was no longer inspector of the II Brigade, that the Reverend Sample's son, Nathaniel, Jr. of Strasburg, now had the hapless job. Just how impossible was the state of the militia, Amos knew only too well from a report by his old friend, the former Governor's son, Thomas McKean, Jr., who was struggling to head up the Commonwealth's entire militia effort. This report to the Governor stated openly:

The Brigade Inspectors generally represent the want of a disposition on the part of the Captain in complying with their official duty in consequence of which they incur considerable difficulty and great delay in making returns to me. They also represent the arms with few exceptions, as being out of order occasioned by the deficiency of the funds appropriated by law for repairing them, and also by the neglect on the part of individuals who possess them. . . .

Amos's cousin John Slaymaker, Jr. from Strasburg formed a rifle company. This was announced in the *Democrat Intelligencer*: "With pleasure we state that the Pequea Rangers, a volunteer rifle corps, commanded by Captain John Slaymaker, Jr., of this county and composed of gentlemen of different politics, on Wednesday last, unanimously resolved to tender their services to the governor for the defense of their country, as a part of the quota of Pennsylvania." Young Henry joined this company as a private.

On May 9, 1813, Lancaster County was struck by a shock wave of high emotion. Up from the greening moors of the Eastern Shore it came, leaving in its wake badly stunned populations. Some British ships had been sighted in the Chesapeake. Only a few were reported but enough to start the wellsprings of rumor boiling. When the news flooded the valley, these few had become squadrons. The invasion, it was shouted, had already begun.

Jasper left at once with Captain Humes's Phalanx for Elkton, Maryland. After fervent praying by the Reverend Sample, Captain John Slaymaker's Pequea Rangers left Strasburg. The colorfully uniformed troops marched smartly, their band blaring a stirring quick-step, burnished arms glistening menacingly in May's sunshine. Henry F. Slaymaker was among them, trim in light blue trousers and a dark blue tunic, tight at the waist with crossed white belting, topped off by his handsome, beplumed stovepipe hat, minus a brim. Elkton was to be the rendezvous point for all Pennsylvania militia.

Mention of Elkton probably struck a familiar chord in the far reaches of the squire's memory. It was there that Sir William Howe had landed thirty-six years before. At twenty-two Amos had been younger than Henry was now.

The crisis was short-lived. The British did not invade, and the boys were soon home again, drilling and parading. The real blow fell in August of 1814.

A large British fleet had entered the Chesapeake—transports and men-of-war, carrying the pick of British troops now free with the defeat of Bonaparte to humble the United States. It all seemed preposterous to Amos. The faraway war, the unreal war, the needless war, was now at their very doorsteps.

On August 20 word reached Lancaster County that General Winder, commanding the Tenth Military District—which covered the soon-to-be-attacked areas—had called on Pennsylvania Governor Snyder for five thousand Pennsylvania militia.

Henry's Pequea Rangers and Jasper's Phalanx were ordered to bivouac outside of Lancaster. In a matter of days both units were expected to be thrown into the defense of Philadelphia.

Any lingering hopes that this emergency would pass like that at Elkton the year before were dispelled on August 26. The British had landed near Washington. Militia opposing them broke and ran. "Washington City" was in flames.

Shortly after news of the arson was received in Lancaster, notice from the Governor in Harrisburg was published to the effect that he expected all militia of the eastern counties to respond to a forthcoming call to arms with alacrity—"superior to local feelings and evasives that might possibly be drawn from an imperfect military system."

This total of five thousand men were to rendezvous at York, Pennsylvania, on September 5 so as to be ready for the march to the Washington-Baltimore area. Concurrent with the news of the burning of Washington, a general town meeting was called in Lancaster. A list of resolutions was drawn up containing many "whereases" and "resolveds," the tenor of their entity being that all privately raised companies should heed the Governor's call and head for the York rendezvous to prepare for the march on the Baltimore area. Rumors were flying thick and fast about an engagement between British General Ross's troops and defending militia near Baltimore.

Word of what the *Intelligencer* was to headline "The Glorious News" got to Lancaster at 5 P.M. on September 15, 1814. In a battle before Baltimore on September 12, General Ross had been killed. The British had retreated back to their ships, harassed by American militia. The next day British ships bombarded Fort McHenry unsuccessfully. The emergency was over.

The remainder of the war seemed an anticlimax to Amos. When the immediate region was safe, the young men were no longer needed to run hither and yon with the militia. Jasper's Phalanx had to stay in Baltimore—where it had finally gone too late for the battle—for an extra three months. Since it was fairly well established that the British would not be back, Amos probably thought this foolish in the extreme. But at least Henry returned to banking, storekeeping, and the running of the inn. Amos especially needed young Henry now, since the elder Slaymaker was soon to become a Congressman, completing the term of resigning Representative James Whitehill.

Patriotic revelry—Lancaster's principal contribution to the war effort—evidently did not interest Amos; it passed unnoted in his correspondence. He might well have been grateful, however, for the parades, days of mourning, and meetings (at which Jasper Slaymaker, Esq., was a prime orator). Since these celebrations often involved the Pennsylvania Arms, Amos's brothers Henry, Jr. and Sammy Slaymaker gained new business to compensate for the loss of customers occasioned by the state capital's removal to Harrisburg in 1812. Also, the inn's reputation as the town's premiere hostelry was advanced by those martial galas hosted by the brothers Slaymaker.

The Arms was very much in the limelight when Sammy Slaymaker invited a distinguished artist, one Thomas Birch, to exhibit what the *Intelligencer* called his "superb picture"—an oil painting of Perry's Lake Erie victory—in the Arms. Afterward there was a large parade, at which, according to the warmongering *Intelligencer*, "The joyful citizens, with martial music and lighted candles paraded the streets 'til near midnight and a number of houses were illuminated. At four the next morning the cheerful bells awoke the happy citizens. About ten the volunteer companies of Captain Humes and Shippen, with an excellent band of music, enlivened our streets by firing repeated volleys in honor of the splendid victory, and in the evening there was a general and splendid illumination."

On December 18, 1812, there was a particularly impressive celebration of Decatur's Azores victory over the British frigate *Macedonian*. Both Jasper's and Henry's companies paraded amid the largest display of flags ever placed, all illuminated by torchlight, to the tune of massed bands whose renditions were punctuated by rifle salutes and loud huzzas. Church bells rang. The former State House—now the Court House again—was illuminated as never before; its cupola was festooned with flags.

The Pennsylvania Arms was the scene of memorial meetings to honor fallen servicemen. Such affairs ended with resolutions to the effect that gentlemen of the town wear crepe on their left arms for thirty days.

More celebrating on Tuesday, December 6, 1814, was the order of the day when Jasper's Phalanx returned amid loud cheers, gun salutes, bonfires, and band music.

The last "big parade" took place on February 20, 1815, when the confirmation of peace arrived. The anti-Federalist *Intelligencer* described the jubilee on Tuesday morning as being

ushered in by the ringing of bells and the beat of Reveille. All business appeared to be suspended, except that of providing transparencies and decorations for the evening's illumination, which was general, and was superior in brilliancy to any we have ever witnessed.

The jubilee was continued on Wednesday in honor of Washington's Birthday. The different volunteer companies paraded and performed many evolutions and firings in a truly soldier-like manner. They were accompanied by a band of musicians, composed of gentlemen amateurs. The ringing of bells, the repeated volley of rifles, musketing and pistols, the variety of music and the shouts of the populace, were calculated to fill the mind with extraordinary emotions. An appropriate and excellent oration was delivered in the Court House to the Washington Association pursuant to their request by Jasper Slaymaker, Esq., after which about eight members of the Association sat down to an elegant dinner at the house of Colonel Slough.

In the evening, a splendid ball was given at Mr. Cooper's [Red Lion Tavern] which was attended by a large and brilliant assemblage of ladies and gentlemen.

It gives us pleasure to add, that in the rejoicing of two or three days no accident of importance has occurred and the utmost harmony has prevailed.

Amos, like most businessmen, was greatly relieved to be done with a war he had never wanted. Now he and his sons were free to expand their enterprises to meet the needs of the nation's in its unimpeded march westward. The family's feelings were reflected in March, 1815, by Amos's sister Hannah Cochran in a letter to her boys in boarding school:

Dear Boys, How pleasing it is to see spring once more unfolding her charms and the face of nature resume its long wished for appearance. And likewise with peace onto our land again. I hope and pray that the sound of war may no more be heard in our land and that everyone may turn their hearts to the Bountiful Giver of all our blessings with thanksgiving and praise. There surely never was a time that the land throughout had more reason to rejoice and give thanks than the present when we have peace and the prospects of a plentiful year of the Bounties of Providence . . . adieu from your ever affectionate Mother, Hannah Cochran.

Amos had little time for thanksgiving. He had taken his place as a Congressman two months before at the seat of the nation's government, dank, cold, foggy, and burned-out Washington, D.C.

The House of Representatives' chamber had been burned by the British only four months earlier. So the House convened on December 13, 1814, in a crowded Post Office Building. Living conditions were miserable in Washington. And Amos was not used to being away from Salisbury for so long a time. There was much supervising to do back home. Most probably the work of the Congress seemed as tedious as it certainly was foreign to him. Deciding upon completing his term, that that was enough, Amos left in the spring of 1815 and never again sought public office.

On his return from Washington Amos had reason to be more confidently content than ever. For everyone sensed a swelling national conviction that the Manifest Destiny of an ever-expanding U.S.A. was certain. Amos was sure that his business would prosper concurrently. A pleasing harbinger was his winding up the estate of the late Betsey Henderson Wertmüller, the artist's widow.

Amos was able to buy from Betsey's heirs in western Pennsylvania their claims to the Wertmüller farm in Delaware. He used his brother-in-law in Westmoreland County, Daniel Fleming, to collect from the heirs on a commission basis. Amos did so well at $50 per head that he could afford to offer as much as $250 each to a few holdouts.

Storekeeper Daniel Fleming, nervous about handling such large sums, was afraid that he might do something "unlawful." Amos replied, impatiently, urging Daniel to get on with the job. He, Amos, knew what was legal and what wasn't. Daniel asked for Jasper to come out to advise him. Amos was annoyed. He did not want to be second-guessed by his learned son. Jasper did not approve of his father's ad hoc estate-settling practices. He had written his brother Henry saying, "It is regretable that father ever had anything to do with the Boyds. I knew that they would bring nothing but trouble. . . ." Relations between Jasper and his father cooled. So Amos sent young Henry over the mountains to corral remaining Henderson-Wertmüller heirs, and the boy did so with dispatch.

The inns, stage line, bank, store, and miscellaneous operations were doing well, as was the Boyd business. Money continued to flow into the Boyd kitty, and "expenses" came out. The two old-maid sisters, Isabella and Mary, had given Amos a carte blanche for running "their" place and seemed pleased that he was making the operation pay off.

The latest judgment against his colleague, James Boyd, had been large, totaling $4,810.33, but Amos had been able to get James's suing brother-in-law, James Hamilton, to accept back interest and sit still for the principal until the time was ripe to sell the property. Evidently, James Boyd's brother-in-law trusted Amos more than James, which is exactly what James had counted on when he sought Amos's counsel.

Amos was also immensely satisfied with the budding love affair between his niece Rebecca Slaymaker Cochran and his son Henry. Lovely young Rebecca was in a girls' finishing school in Newport, Delaware, from which she made repeated sallies to visit with friends in Philadelphia and New York.

On February 29, 1816, Rebecca married her first cousin, Henry Fleming Slaymaker, at the old stone Faggs Manor Presbyterian Church near Cochranville. The minister sent "Becky" off with a letter to Leacock Church stating that "the bearer, all along supported a good moral character," that "her walk and conversation were becoming the gospel," and that "she is free from scandal and every ground of church censure."

The couple settled in the Sign of John Adams and fast became the most culture-conscious of the valley's young marrieds. They formed something called the Friends of Literature, which met periodically at the mansion. On November 20, 1817, a special meeting was called to discuss the founding of a Sunday school at Gap.

When Henry and Becky's first child, Hannah Cecelia, was born in 1817, the old squire surely believed that his home's future was as promising as the new nation's.

On the afternoon before Christmas, 1814, James Buchanan, John Reynolds, and Jasper Yeates Slaymaker set out by sleigh from Lancaster for a cross-country holiday pub crawl. Heading west on the turnpike, they reached Columbia late in the day, well buttressed against the season's nip by bounteous measures of liquor. Up Front Street they charged, roisterously singing, mufflers flying on the chill wind, and their top hats doffed to a knot of well-bundled humanity crowding the now defunct old ferry property, hard by the new Columbia Bridge.

The Lancaster sleighing party was not so high at this point not to know what was going on; the old ferry house was being auctioned off.

For the fun of it Jasper Slaymaker stood up and, with a deep bow in the direction of the auctioneer, called out, "Six thousand seven hundred" as the sleigh slid past the shocked group of Columbia burghers.

On the Christmas morning after the night before, Jasper awoke to the unsettling news that he had bought a Christmas present for which his aching brain could have found no earthly reason. The figure was much too high. James Buchanan wanted no part of the deal. Fortunately

John Reynolds, editor of the Lancaster Federalist *Journal*, felt constrained to go along on a fifty-fifty basis (perhaps he put Jasper up to it). Both came across with the money on July 13, 1815.

Jasper wasn't too concerned about buying what might have seemed on the surface a white elephant. Along with his Uncle Henry, the builder, Jasper was a stockholder in the Bridge Company and involved in its affairs. As its attorney and judge of stockholder elections he wrote its regulations and ordinances, typical of which was one outlawing "pipes and lighted seegars on the bridge." Dividends had been good and promised to get better. The bridge was becoming so great a success that shareholders decided on founding their own bank.

The strikingly picturesque landscape along Susquehanna's meandering sweep near Columbia held a great attraction to travelers; so much so that the spot was considered as a site for the capital city of the United States. Hence, the name Columbia. Later it was mentioned as a good location for the state's capital.

Situated on a major route of western migration, Columbia's boom seemed assured. Jasper knew well that river-front properties there would appreciate. But Columbia had a far greater future than that of a stopover point for western migrants.

The "American System" of Clay and Calhoun had taken on the aspects of a crusade. "Internal Improvements," such as the new highway from Cumberland, Maryland, to Wheeling on the Ohio, were confidently expected to conquer the hinterlands in the name of Manifest Destiny. In 1817 the first steamboat went upstream from New Orleans to Cincinnati. Steam navigation and the planned-for Erie Canal connecting the Hudson with the Great Lakes and their outlet rivers assured the Eastern seaboard access to America's heartland. New York was due to pick up the lion's share of Western commerce. Philadelphia would be the loser.

Plainly, Philadelphia (and all Pennsylvania) had the answer in the Susquehanna River.

For a decade communities on the upper Susquehanna and its tributary, the Juniata, floated their produce downstream on rafts and river arks. Shallow of draft, like immense floating barns, the arks dotted the river from the New York State line in the north to Columbia in the south. They were heavily stocked with lumber, grain, tars, salt meat, and fish. Soon steamboats would make it possible for upriver traffic in finished goods.

The Susquehanna's occasional rapids and shallows made for some difficult navigation. But whatever waters shallow-draft steamers couldn't traverse, riverside canals could. When a proposed canal linked the Susquehanna-fed Chesapeake Bay to Philadelphia, Philadelphia could more than compete with Maryland's Baltimore and New York City.

Even before the canals were completed, anyone with a trading establishment on the river could have been in an excellent position to serve the needs of wilderness settlers on the one hand and Baltimore and Philadelphia merchants on the other. Columbia, it seemed to Jasper Slaymaker, was the perfect spot for a wholesale house.

And the times were right, too. In Washington the Federalist Party was a memory. For a dozen years the country had grown accustomed to quiet but purposeful leadership at the hands of the Virginia dynasty— now under Monroe and unsullied by any taints of political radicalism.

State politics, at the fount of which Jasper now sat as a member of the legislature, mirrored the nation's. The Federalist Party had all but ceased to exist. Everyone was a Democrat. The question was only one of degrees. As in Washington, this was measured by a man's temperature on the Bank of the United States; most were either hot or cold, few lukewarm. All, though, were infected by the virus of Internal Improvement. It was only a question of who knew best how to realize progress.

Harrisburg's era of good feeling was vividly described in Surveyor General Samuel Cochran's voluminous correspondence with his wife, Amos's sister Hannah. There were legislative sleighing parties on the frozen river, the Governor's receptions, and holiday balls; July Fourth's was always the *pièce de résistance*.

With a political eye on this encouraging picture in Harrisburg, Jasper felt the time propitious for his Columbia plunge. He would need his father's help. Possibly feelings between them were still strained because of Boyd affairs, for Jasper decided on working through brother Henry.

Young Henry was to have overall charge of the Columbia business. He would move with Becky from Salisbury into the house adjoining the ferry property, and brother Amos H. would live in the old ferry house, itself now converted to the warehouse. In Salisbury young brother William was charged with the inn and the postmastership.

Since money was needed, it was incumbent on Henry and Amos H. to sell father Amos on the idea. The old man went for the scheme enthusiastically. As a longtime expert in the field of transportation, he was intrigued with getting in early on the dawning age of steam and canals. He gave the boys $5,000. Amos wasn't worried. The venture seemed promising, and were he to need extra cash, the Boyd administration account was available for borrowing. He could always make good on it if he had to.

By the winter of 1819 plans were well along. Squire Amos went happily about building a starting inventory. He bought heavily of hardware from his old friend, ironmaster Daniel Buckley. And with that new, up-and-coming entrepreneur in iron, Charles Lukens, on the Brandywine, he arranged a running account for bar iron to be delivered in Columbia as needed. He bought dry goods, notions, and small wares in Philadelphia and inspected and dickered as in the old days.

Nothing could hold the squire down—not even a serious coach accident which interrupted one of his buying trips to the city.

Becky wrote to mother Hannah in Cochranville that Amos "had started in the morning stage for Philadelphia. They had not got but a mile or two when the horses ran off. The stage either upset or the passengers were thrown out. However, they were all hurt, but none so bad as Henry's father. His head was very much cut. The skullband and his shoulder was very badly hurt. He was brought back home."

Soon, though, the squire was up and about his purchasing, no worse off for his accident.

On March 11 Henry and Becky's clothing, furniture, and china were shipped ahead to Columbia. A few days later the couple, with their babies, Hannah Cecelia and Isabella Angelica, bundled tightly into the Dearborn carriage (borrowed from the Cochrans), set out for a new life of their own.

Henry's sister Isabella Green helped them to settle into the small and cozy brick house along the river and introduced them to the Columbia Presbyterian Church, to which they had been formally transferred from Leacock.

Notwithstanding the bustle of moving in wet and windy weather, which gave both babies colds, Becky loved Columbia. Excitedly, she wrote back to mother Hannah of the beautiful view they had of the river: "The ice is going out—the big arks will soon be sailing in. . . ."

Henry and young Amos opened for business on April 1 with $20 in the till. Sales boomed throughout spring and summer. By December 21 they had $9,844 in cash. A year later in 1821 their balance stood at $21,015; in 1822, $37,112.

Theirs was an import-export operation. From middlemen upriver in Mexico, Lewistown, Thompsontown, Middleburg, the brothers took in grain, whiskey, butter, cheese, lumber, tar, and increasingly large quantities of coal, the use of which was being expanded from factory forges to front parlors. Together with delectable Susquehanna River shad, these staples were shipped down to agents in Philadelphia.

From "the City" they took in groceries, dry goods, and hardware, each neatly drawn bill of lading indicating the transactions being separate and distinct as to routing instructions and special requests of haulers; one noted "30 lbs of herring, wine, assorted groceries, and 8 doz. sickles to be shipped through the Del. canal and Sus. River to near the mouth of Conestoga and by wagon to Columbia. The boatman will be careful of rain and heat."

By 1821 Columbia's leaders recognized Henry as enough of a comer to be made chief burgess of the town—no mean recognition for a young man who had arrived only two years before. In 1821 Henry and Becky's happy little family was expanded by a third daughter, Beckie Ann. Henry's sister Isabella Green was the first Slaymaker in Columbia. Now with the marriage of Amos's youngest daughter, the artist Hannah, to A. L. Evans of Columbia, and Jasper's marrying Mr. Evans's sister, Jane, the family was fast developing a colony of their own in the bustling river metropolis.

Becky kept up a consistent correspondence with mother Hannah Cochran, reporting in minute detail every illness of the little girls, of Henry and relatives and friends. And her mother answered in kind about those in the Cochranville-Gap area, mentioning also the bitter running fight at Faggs Manor Church between adherents of old and new theology, and her heavy duties in the Cochran store and farm.

Back in Salisbury, Amos had never been happier. The boys' first year in Columbia had been promising; many better ones lay ahead. He wrote them two and three times a week. The letters were short, newsy, and warm. The only sad notes struck concerned their mother. Some days Sibby was "up" or "about," others "in bed." Always, though, she remained "unwell."

But Amos's outlook was generally comfortable and optimistic. For him there could not be many years left. He would relish them, puttering around the farm and working with stage and inn accounts. Justice of the peace duties and estate work were chores to be carried through at a more leisurely pace.

9

WHILE AMOS COULD NOT have seen it as such, his fall from the coach was a harbinger of things to come, but the next blow was more comic than grim.

Gossip about the valley had it that Amos had bought two white horses for a new four-wheel phaeton. It was said that he dearly loved white horses and always had them for his stages. Shortly after being delivered, they were stolen. Anxious to drive in the new phaeton, he quickly bought two more and made do with black when white horses weren't available. On his first ride he was caught in a thundershower. In shocked disbelief Amos watched the trotting steeds turn white under the lashing of relentless raindrops.

The horses were his white ones, painted black and fenced back to him. Amos immediately became a member of the Lancaster County Horse Thief Detection Association, the organization that eventually laid low the thief. He was tracked down and shot to death in the Welsh Mountains.

Then came a string of more serious misfortunes. Amos's brother-in-law Samuel Cochran had become overextended in his "western land" speculations. Creditors took all but the Cochran home, farm, and store. There was no ready cash, so Samuel and Hannah sponged farm supplies from Amos.

His brother Henry Slaymaker, Jr., owner of the Pennsylvania Arms, went bankrupt. Since ownership of the Lancaster hotel had been turned over to Henry, Jr. by Amos, there was the possibility of its going on the auction block and out of the family.

The summer of 1821 brought the worst drought in memory, and with it came an extremely virulent typhoid epidemic. Leacock's grave-diggers worked around the clock. Amos's immediate family was among the few to escape. Young Henry's in Columbia was sorely hit. Becky's morbid letters made her children's death appear imminent. Fortunately they all survived. But in Harrisburg Samuel Cochran and his son Stephen were infected and Stephen died.

Cold weather had barely put out the plague when Amos experienced a blow, the magnitude of which was in no way lessened by its long imminence. On January 27, 1822, Sibby died.

Amos now became terribly depressed, quite mixed up, and very difficult with those around home. Son William's running of the inn did not please him. He complained of the bound boys continually—"They are so mischievous when both are home there is no doing with them." He wrote of "Black Dinah's" son: "I have been obliged to turn Abraham out of his business. He had become so wicked I could not bear him any longer." Of a man involved in the Boyd business with whom he couldn't see eye to eye: "I have to be in Lancaster on Saturday next to attend a reference in a case of John Wilson against John Boyd estate. I wish I was done with him. He is such a vile creature it's disagreeable to have anything to do with him."

Perhaps these difficulties led to his stroke.

"My complaint," he wrote the boys in Columbia, ". . . was entirely in my head and brought on tremors in my whole frame so that I could scarcely write or walk without staggering and it seemed to affect my memory very much."

In this debilitated condition Amos faced up to Boyd litigation, which was now taking an ominous turn.

James Boyd had died in 1820 and willed what he believed to be his share in his brother John's estate to his two maiden sisters, Isabella and Mary. They could live on the farm until the last one died. Then it was to be sold and divided among the descendants of brothers in the South. He left only fifty dollars to Sister Margaret Hamilton.

Margaret thought James had no right to make such a will. For, like his brother John, he never really owned the lands. So she contested the will. But Amos knew that it wasn't really Margaret making the trouble; all along it was her son, George Hamilton. Amos probably saw him as a formally educated gentleman who thought he knew more than longtime squires—typical of so many college types, now more in evidence than in the old days. Surely, Amos guessed, when the state got "free schools" there would be even more of them, meddling into the affairs of their elders, who had always known better about what was right in their own bailiwicks.

It was vital that Amos get James Boyd's will approved, for failure to do so would bring public discredit on his head, as he had been James's adviser. More important, if the will was disallowed, a complete rehash of the entire tangled mess from its beginnings would be certain. Then Amos's accounts would be held up to public scrutiny.

Far be it for the squire to think that anyone might believe him dishonest. Ready money had been needed for the Columbia venture, and he did borrow from accounts entrusted to him. After all, he was a banker and a respected one. He had known for many years how to cover himself. After his stroke, however, he did admit to being forgetful. So, should the account get pawed over by enough people, embarrassing errors just might crop up.

Amos had banked on Jasper's being able to get the will approved. He gave him permission to hire the best backup talent available. In the absence of James Buchanan in Washington, this would be James Hopkins, Lancaster's highest-priced lawyer.

Well aware that Jasper had been opposed to his handling of Boyd affairs from the beginning, Amos wanted to make sure that his temperamental son would go along. So he got the two old maids to agree to pay Jasper and Hopkins $1,000 each if they got the will approved; $400 each if they didn't.

The high-powered legal talent did its duty. The will was approved.

But Armageddon was only postponed. Sooner or later the old maids would die. Then Margaret Hamilton and her heirs would be back. The accounts would be viewed again. He had to build up more cash with which to cover himself in the meantime.

Boyd affairs were now far and away too much for Amos to handle alone. With the sale of those Boyd lands not in the hands of the old maids, distribution of funds had to be made to that swelling multitude of heirs who were forever turning up all over Virginia, the Carolinas, and Georgia. In establishing contact with them, James Buchanan had been helpful through his Southern contacts in the U.S. House of Representatives. But it soon became evident that an on-the-spot lawyer would be needed to cope with Southern claims. One Andrew Hoyle, Esq., in North Carolina was retained. Still, the necessity of figuring portions of the estate down as low as "$\frac{1}{2}$ of $\frac{1}{10}$ of $\frac{1}{24}$ equaling $\frac{1}{480}$" (or in decimals .0020833) was too much for Amos. His dutiful son Henry in 1828 relieved Amos of Boyd affairs.

Plainly, the time had come for sons Jasper and Henry to take over completely from their father. They began with a plan to save the Pennsylvania Arms for the family. A gentlemen's agreement resulted. The boys' Uncle Henry Slaymaker, Jr. was permitted to continue as proprietor of the hotel. His brother Sammy assisted him. Jasper bought the place from the assignees for $6,200, $4,000 of which was borrowed from James Buchanan. Jasper planned on sprucing it up and arranged for the hotel to be named headquarters for the Lafayette festivities; the General's visit was expected in a few months. Of all hostelries in town, there was no question about whose was the premiere stopping place.

Young Henry felt that his father's deteriorating health necessitated his leaving the Columbia store in charge of help and moving back to Salisbury with the least possible delay.

In the winter of 1823 the roads were bad and Becky, pregnant again, wasn't happy about so fast a move. She wrote her mother on February 9 that "Henry expects his father's wagon up tomorrow for a load. He wishes very much to send me and the children down, but I can't get everything done so soon. I would rather see more of our goods sent away first."

But Henry pushed the moving anyway. With the help of his

father's wagon and phaeton, along with the Cochran Dearborn carriage, the move was carried off in ten days' time.

A new, more decisive, and forceful Henry F. Slaymaker was beginning to come out of his shell. Within days he took over the postmastership, was sworn in as justice of the peace in his aging father's stead, and became involved in the formation of a new Presbyterian church, built around the recently established Sunday school, Bellevue, at Gap.

On March 17 Becky's fourth child—a boy, at last—was born at the mansion; he was joyfully christened Amos Fleming at Leacock by the Reverend Joseph Barr.

Wednesday, July 27, 1825, dawned bright, and by 10:30 A.M. waxed uncomfortably hot. A swelling host of farm folk crowded the Mt. Vernon Tavern at the top of Gap Hill, along the turnpike road, near the Chester County line. All wore their Sunday finest; many dutifully sported spears of wheat in their hats as emblems of plenty. The committees on arrangements in Lancaster had asked this of them.

At eleven, picked cavalry units of Lancaster County's militia rode up to the tavern green, their banners, sashes, and cockades flashing a pulsating blur of colors. Gleaming sabers and side arms rattled smartly. The awe-struck farmers hung back respectfully, then craned anxiously to catch a view of the carriages.

Three elegant barouches followed the troops, each drawn by four fine horses. One had dapple grays, one bays, and the other whites. Slowly they moved up to the Chester County line. But not over it. The great event, a year in coming, was only minutes away.

General Porter dismounted. He nervously fingered a written address of welcome. Would the most famous guest ever to land on America's shores reply in understandable English? General Porter fervently hoped so. He wanted no hitches in this opening ceremony over which he had been placed in charge.

Around noon the Chester County cavalry troop approached at an easy clip-clop before flanking, and behind a fine four-horse carriage in which rode a splendidly dressed, kingly-looking figure. It was that most distinguished visitor himself. On the Lancaster County side there came the rattle of drums, a crackling rifle salute, and loud, unrestrained, unorganized cheering.

The Marquis de Lafayette, corpulent and beaming, was helped down within the Chester County boundary. Cheering subsided as he was ushered into Lancaster County to hear General Porter's welcome. General Lafayette answered off the cuff, eloquently, in quite comprehensible English.

To renewed cheering he mounted one of the three barouches, and in company with the other two—filled with Lancaster County's welcoming committee—the cavalry-led procession set off on the turnpike for Lancaster.

The General had been on the road from West Chester since early morning. For his comfort it was agreed that there would be a brief stopover in Salisbury at Squire Slaymaker's mansion. A luncheon for the General, his party, the welcoming committee, and the horse troop was to be provided al fresco.

About twelve-thirty the procession reached Salisbury. Inn help, farm hands, and tenants clustered along the roadway. In the shade of the mansion's veranda stood white-thatched Amos Slaymaker, Esq., in a dark suit. Flanked by exquisitely dressed sons, daughters, and grandchildren, the bent old man moved slowly down the steps and across the lawn to the front gate. It swung wide. Deferentially, and with great humility, the squire bowed greetings to the man whom the President of the United States would soon entertain.

Lafayette was particularly fond of meeting representatives of that fast-dwindling body of old Revolutionary soldiers. It was entirely appropriate that Amos was his host for that brief reception at Salisbury.

Amos could not go into Lancaster. He very rarely traveled anywhere since his stroke. Before leaving, the General presented Amos with a walking stick, capped with a carved likeness of himself. Heartfelt adieus were exchanged, and the procession began again. Sun-flecked dust settled with the quiet on Salisbury.

The procession arrived at Grove's field, two miles east of Lancaster, at 3:40 P.M. Amid a vast concourse of citizens the town's infantry battalion and the crack Strasburg Blues were drawn up for review. After inspection by the General, a large parade formed. By 5:30 P.M. Lancaster was plunged into the most gargantuan celebration of its history.

In each of the four streets leading to the square huge triumphal arches were constructed. Hung in floral greens and bunting, they were bedecked with large pictures of Washington, Wayne, Hand, Montgomery, and Franklin. As Lafayette's carriage cleared East King Street's arch—emblazoned "Hail, Friend of Liberty," and "Brandywine, 1777, Yorktown, 1781"—pandemonium broke loose and thousands of spectators sent up a mighty and sustained roar. Streets were jam-packed. Windows along King Street were hung with gaping humanity, as well as bunting.

When the carriage reached King and Duke streets, massed bands sounded "Hail, Columbia" while fifty Revolutionary veterans saluted the General from a specially constructed platform facing the Farmers' Bank. As the music died out, Lafayette stood in the coach. With tear-stained cheeks, he broke into an impromptu oration and the cheering died down. Those closest by heard him call out in a breaking voice, "These are the wrecks of that gallant band that in the vigor of youth and full strength of manhood, stood by me side by side in the hour of their country's peril. That country—that grateful country—will smooth the pillow of their declining years."

Through the square and out to Franklin College the parade moved, then back again through the square to the Pennsylvania Arms. As the General was being met at the door by Henry Slaymaker, his brother Sammy, and their nephew Jasper, the town was being illuminated.

The spectacle was breathtaking. On every windowsill stood a lighted candle. The largest buildings were fronted with immense transparencies. The street arches were brilliantly lighted.

After an address of welcome by the mayor, the General, his party, and the town's elite assembled beneath the soft glittering lights of the hotel's dining room candelabra. Tables were laden with immense quantities of geese, ducks, chicken, ham, beer, fish, and vegetables. Among the wines were Lisbon port and champagne, vintage 1800.

At the table's head sat Lafayette, flanked by the mayor, the hosts, and General Porter. Nearby was the top echelon of the town's legal hierarchy—Jasper Slaymaker, James Hopkins, John R. Montgomery, William Jenkins; only James Buchanan was missing. His excuse was probably business in Washington.

Many toasts were drunk, at first rather stiffly, to the memory of Washington, Hand, and other Revolutionary generals; but later on, more boisterously, to just about anyone who was anyone. While some tableware was broken, it was agreed by all that the evening was completely "harmonious."

In the morning a delegation of the clergy called at the hotel to pay its respects. At eleven the General was met by 320 schoolchildren, the boys with blue sashes. Each held a bundle of laurel. Girls were in white with pink sashes, carrying bouquets of flowers.

On Thursday evening another dinner by subscription at five dollars per head was held on the upper floor of the Court House, after which a ball was thrown by the ladies of the town in the Masonic Rooms.

On Friday the town was astir at daybreak for the General's departure.

At six, the three barouches drove up to the crowded hotel. At the door Lafayette exchanged bows with his hosts. The heads of the city's military then marched up and saluted him. He got into his coach and was escorted to the Maryland line by the same cavalry troop that had brought him in.

Lancastrians could now get about their business, content that they had done as well by General Lafayette as any town in America. Jasper Slaymaker was happy for another reason. Now that the landmark value of his Lancaster hotel was assured, its business would boom and its value appreciate. Good times surely lay ahead for all of the family.

PART III

Victorian

Colonel Samuel Cochran Slaymaker   Jane Cameron Redsecker Slaymaker
Painting by Baron Leo Von Oskb   Painting by Baron Leo Von Osko

The rights and interests of the laboring man will be protected and cared for, not by the labor agitators, but by the Christian men to whom God in His infinite wisdom has given the control of the property interests of the country. Pray earnestly that the right may triumph, always remembering that the Lord God Omnipotent still reigns and that His reign is one of law and order, and not of violence and crime.

> MR. GEORGE BAER, president of the Philadelphia and Reading Railroad Company, in the *New York Times,* August 21, 1902

10

THE SLAYMAKERS' PRE-EMINENT ROLE in the Lafayette festivities provided Amos with his only salubrious moments in a grim and drear decade. If the old squire was at all buoyed up at the prospect of his sons' expanding business ventures, he did not reveal the fact in his memoranda. Rather, he seemed completely preoccupied with mourning.

Amos's hopes for an afterlife predestined to be rewarding were reflected in a letter in May, 1829, written to Salisbury from Philadelphia, where he was attending the annual General Assembly of the Presbyterian Church, U.S.A.:

> If my health shall continue, I shall stay to the end as it is possible it will be the last time I shall attend the General Assembly in this life, and if I can get a seat in the next, then will my happiness be complete . . . may God be with you all and bless you, I am Amos Slaymaker.

His father's generation was long gone. March 14, 1817, had been a particularly sad day. His great benefactor and friend, Judge Jasper Yeates, died in Lancaster and was buried there in St. James Episcopal churchyard. Now brothers, sisters, and cousins were dying off. In 1825 Davis Ostler died. A year later brother Henry Slaymaker, Jr., late master of Mt. Pleasant, onetime innkeeper, builder, and politician, expired a bankrupt. On July 4, 1827, the papers noted the tragic death of the state's former comptroller general; brother-in-law George Duffield was killed by a horse's kick.

On August 3, 1827, Lancastrians were saddened and the family stunned by the sudden death of Jasper Yeates Slaymaker, Esq. At forty, he had been cut down by dysentery, and two days later all branches of the family moved into town for the large, impressive funeral at the First

Presbyterian Church. Members of the bar appeared at the church en masse and afterward retired to the Court House. There a select committee prepared a memorial. James Buchanan was chosen to present it to members of the family. He appeared before them late in the afternoon at Jasper's home on Duke Street and read the stirring instrument. Later it was run off on silk and distributed about the town.

It was for Jasper's administrators, John Reynolds and James Buchanan, to make good his unliquid estate and to set up guardians for his six children. Since one of them was named James Buchanan Slaymaker—not to mention that Buchanan himself was a principal creditor—Amos and young Henry could be certain that Jasper's estate would be expeditiously handled. Jasper's Pennsylvania Arms was a valuable property. But now it would go out of the family. Dreams of another successful hotel venture in Lancaster faded with the passing of Lancaster's most brilliant and attractive lawyer-businessman.

When his Uncle Samuel Cochran died intestate and insolvent in 1829, Henry F. grabbed the reins from the strong hands of his Aunt Hannah. As administrator he told her that the old Cochran farm at Cochranville in Chester County must go. He would try to run the Cochranville store through the youngest Cochran boy, John Beaton. If it was too much for him, he would sell the store, too. Aunt Hannah was put up in the Salisbury mansion, where her presence served to cheer up her brother Amos.

Each death, perhaps, seemed to Amos a harbinger of his own, for which he was well prepared. The subdued old squire sat brooding in the mansion, annoyed by grandchildren who made "the house so very crowded." Summer's heat became harder to bear: "The weather is so warm that I cannot go much about except morning and evening. I have been obliged to sit as near the door as possible, so that I can go out and take fresh air," he wrote relatives in Columbia.

He was furious with a broker who sold the Wertmüller farm for "only $7,830 . . . $2,000 less than expected."

By the early 1830s the two old maids, Isabella and Mary Boyd, and their sister Margaret Hamilton had died. It was natural that the now thoroughly fed-up Boyd heirs would demand an accounting of Amos's stewardship. They did so through the Orphans' Court in Lancaster.

After writing one of his lawyers, John R. Montgomery, to the effect that he would be "satisfied" if a certain friendly judge heard the case, Henry dragooned a stellar band of character witnesses—mostly Harrisburg legislators—to testify to the ancient defendant's sterling qualities. Amos's administration account was speedily approved by the court.

If Boyd heirs felt bitterly disposed toward the Orphans' Court because of its decision, they must have become infuriated with Amos when one George Boyd accused him of having someone filch records, ostensibly from their lawyer's Lancaster office. On November 6, 1833, George Boyd (probably a Southern heir who came north for his claim) wrote Amos:

SIR:

I have rote to you so often to come to Lancaster to see me. I am undur determination not to leave the place until you produce the records that some-one took out of the offfice and I have no doubt but you have them or no where they are as no other living being has any use for them but you and H. F. Slaymaker. Now sir a man that would be gilty of so degrading an art for viliness purposes is two degrading for any man to be continanced in any civil-ized country. I am determined to advirtise you in the Publick papers. For your son it will be very rough. I am sorry to have to do so, but your treatment is such that you can't expect less from me. I am of opinion that any one that wuld slip records out of the office is more base than the basest counterfiters in Lancaster jail. And my opinion is there is not a man in Lancaster but what thinks you have or no where the records is and this is my opinion myself. I have no doubt but your lawyer has them. I am of opinion that your whole aim is to employ lawyers to cheat and defraud the legatees of James Boyd deceased and pay them out of our money which is degrading to human nature. I am sorry sir to tell you, you ought to reflect and consider the letters you have rote now in my hands and you would be ashamed of your conduct and I will say your old friend, William Hopkins, had seen the papers and he is truly sorry for your conduct and so is every high-minded gentlemen in Lan-caster. I will hope you will come up and let us have an interview.

I am in more information than you are aware of.

I am your humble servant,
GEORGE BOYD

The Boyd heirs now retained one of the most respected attorneys in the state, tall, angular-faced, and bespectacled Amos Ellmaker, Esq., who would later run for Vice President of the United States. Ellmaker appealed the case to the Superior Court, which was to sit in Lancaster in September, 1834.

The measure of Amos's excellent reputation in Lancaster—George Boyd's comments notwithstanding—was manifest in the townspeople's description of the forthcoming legal melodrama: "The great trial of the Boyds," they called it. But, of course, the Boyds weren't being tried. Amos was. And for him and his family the affair was a tragedy in three acts.

The first trial in the Boyd case, billed "Attorney of Isabella Boyd, deceased vs. Amos Slaymaker," was crucial. The next two—"Mary Boyd deceased" and "Margaret Hamilton deceased"—were routine; their decisions rested entirely on that of the first. For if it was found that Amos Slaymaker had withheld Boyd income from one heir, he had withheld it from all, in the still unsplit estate of the two deceased spinsters, Isabella and Mary Boyd.

Amos's counsel had to be well prepared for the 1834 trial. The Superior Court expected more than character witnesses, who had meant so much to Lancaster's judiciary in 1830. So Amos's attorneys obliged with a lengthy and learned defense, charging that the Boyd heirs' claims constituted "stale demands."

The Slaymaker counsel was impressive, by far the best that money could buy. Courtly William Jenkins, polished John R. Montgomery, and dignified Evan R. Evans were surely worthy successors to the old squire's previous helping hands, his late son Jasper and the recently deceased James Hopkins. Everyone knew that James Buchanan would have been on hand, too, were he not tied down by duties in the U.S. Senate.

The crowd around and inside the courtroom was said to have been large. Its center of attraction was the seventy-nine-year-old, white-thatched, and wizened defendant, constantly attended by his son and daughter-in-law, Henry and Becky. A friend of Amos's, Attorney Ellmaker, treated him deferentially enough, probably with an eye to the feelings of the town. Nevertheless, Ellmaker proved to the court's satisfaction that circumstances peculiar to this case rendered Boyd heir claims anything but stale; the court ruled that Amos Slaymaker must make good on funds for which there had been improper accounting.

The decision, no doubt, stunned the audience. Here was a tragic comedown for a grand old man, a onetime Revolutionary soldier and Congressman. Perhaps some present thought of the sentiments about old soldiers of the Revolution expressed on the streets of Lancaster by Lafayette almost a decade earlier. Here, truly, was one of those "wrecks of that gallant band. . . ."

Even before the Boyd trial Henry F. Slaymaker was emerging as the new squire. Around the Pequea Valley he played his part perfectly. In nattily laced shirts, frock-coated, and with a beaver top hat, he smartly drove his phaeton between Salisbury, Gap, Cochranville, and Lancaster. During his first years as master of the plantation, he rebuilt the barn and had the brick chimneys plastered over. These small, but very visible improvements—not to mention the many portraits—made the mansion more of an area showplace.

A name seemed in order. Perhaps it was his artistic sister Hannah—or his cultured Aunt Hannah—who suggested "White Chimneys." But so it became known to all in the valley.

By way of increasing his income to a level commensurate with his station, Henry hit on an idea which seemed promising.

By the mid-1830s popular enthusiasm for railroads was fusing with the canal craze. Lancaster with its port of Columbia was bound to become increasingly important as a trading hub between Philadelphia and the West, as well as between Baltimore and the North.

Clearly, steam locomotion would be the coming mode of transportation on land as on water. Henry F. Slaymaker knew that every politician in Harrisburg was committed to spend massive sums on further "Internal Improvements"—specifically, an east–west chain of railroads and canals that would link Pittsburgh, and its river highways to the heartland, directly to Philadelphia. If navigational improvements on the Susquehanna had not been enough to outflank the growing metropolis of New York, then the Erie Canal would be met head on. Pennsylvania would recapture its old place as the east–west trading backbone of America!

From Philadelphia to the West a railroad was to parallel the turnpike. Eventually, it would knock it out. The old Sign of John Adams Inn was sure to go with it.

Henry saw a new hotel-store located along the railroad at Gap as a perfect answer to the financial bind in which he was placed by the Boyd case decision. Here would be a repeat performance of his father's old game! But now the vehicle for moneymaking would be the Columbia and Philadelphia Railroad.

It seemed senseless to continue with the stage line. Accordingly, Henry urged Amos to sell out to another, the Good Intent. But by way of keeping his hand in the old horsepower age, Amos took stock in this company as a partial payment.

Henry guessed that the Salisbury inn might continue for a while. As a well-known landmark it still had considerable traffic. Brother William and paid hands could run it, overseen by Henry.

Henry's main concern was to be his new Railroad Hotel and store, which he would be in charge of building and running, while his younger brother, Amos H., operated the Columbia wholesale house. To build the new Gap establishment, $1,000 was taken from the Columbia operation, and Amos, Sr. borrowed $12,000 from rich Lancaster moneylender John N. Lane. Inventory from the old store in the Sign of John Adams Inn was transferred to the new Gap store.

The Gap railroad establishment was an immediate success. Its gross was less than half of Columbia's in its prime (Henry averaged $10,000 per year in Gap), but profit margins were more substantial, for at Gap he dealt as an over-the-counter retailer in stable sundries, not as a wholesaler in commodities whose prices along the river could fluctuate with the weather's whims.

The new building was a large and handsome brick structure in Georgian style, an ideal overnight stop for gentlemen with business in the valley's east end. For all travelers on the Columbia and Philadelphia Railroad, ladies included, the hostelry was a most delightful comfort station where tea was taken and hearty meals served in the spacious front room overlooking the iron-topped wooden rails. These were a great boon to business. Frequently, the strips came loose, causing protracted stopovers at the hotel. Heavy weather helped, too. Then the horse-powered stagecoachlike cars (steam engines were still experimental) had to halt for the comfort of drivers, who sometimes sat in an open box atop the first car.

Such delays gave Henry opportunities to cater to bored lady travelers. He got an importer's license from the state permitting him to deal in foreign finery such as jewelry, French perfume, and clothing. For gentlemen there were the finest of liqueurs and shaving brushes, cigars and tobaccos. Staples for Gap burghers he carried also—hardware items, cedarware, candles, and stationery.

While tobacco and much of the hardware were bought in Lancaster, the major share of Henry's merchandise came from Philadelphia. To facilitate shipping from "the City" and to cut costs, he bought three freight cars of his own. Not very impressive, they looked like rough-boarded little outbuildings on wheels. But they were the talk of the valley.

Henry F. Slaymaker was off to a good start. While the Railroad Hotel and store was to be his main stock in trade, he clung like a leech to those other Salisbury moneymaking machines set up by his father years before: the tollgate, the postmastership, the justice of the peace office, and the Sign of John Adams Inn. His paucity of ready cash, of course, dictated an end to the banking operations. Henry dominated brother William completely. Not even a wage slave, the young man was bedded and boarded and worked while Henry played the up-and-coming squire.

11

IT WAS ALMOST as if the mansion's new name, White Chimneys, afforded it a new identity. It was more than ever Henry's place. He became obsessed with clinging to it and the proper mode of living it bespoke.

But deep down the emerging squire was a troubled and driven man. Toughening to the point of heartlessness, he embarked on a series of self-serving extralegal maneuvers destined to ruin his younger brothers, Amos Henderson and William Daniel Slaymaker. Henry's plotting began in 1831, before the Superior Court trials.

Henry's difficulties lay not so much in demands which would be made by the Boyd heirs. Were the court to do its worst by his father, two to three thousand dollars would be needed to square the Boyd account. Even though his father and he had no ready pool of cash, Boyd heirs could very easily be taken care of. There was the Gap Railroad Hotel, the Columbia store, shares in the Good Intent Stage Line, some turnpike stock, and insurance. And, of course, the old Sign of John Adams.

The big danger lay in his father's loan from John N. Lane for $12,000. What might happen if Mr. Lane called the loan? He probably wouldn't while he lived. But what if he died? The situation looked the grimmer since the Columbia store, under young Amos H., wasn't doing well. For three years Henry had been trying to sell the inventory, but he couldn't find a buyer. And he had no equity in the building, now partly in Jasper's estate and in John Reynolds's hands.

The idea settled on to protect the White Chimneys' mansion, farm, village, and the Sign of John Adams Inn was probably entirely Henry's. Had he had legal advice, it's reasonable to suppose that the instruments which he drew up would have been filed in the Court House. They never were. Evidently either Henry believed them power enough in themselves to divest his father of his real property, or, more likely, he decided to hold paper for filing at a later, more urgent date.

He prepared an agreement for his father's and his own signature to the effect that mansion, farm, and village had been "sold" by Amos to him for $6,500. He wrote a second agreement between his father and brother William stating that the Salisbury inn had been sold to William by their father for $5,000. In both cases, no money passed.

Henry believed that no one could now claim these properties from his father. The old man owned neither anymore. And Boyd claims could be made only against Amos. For any trials coming up would be concerned only with Amos's handling of the account, *before Henry became administrator in 1828.* The Lane loan, too, was strictly the old man's.

These guardhouse lawyer tactics gave Henry little peace of mind. If he could manage to save the Salisbury holdings, what of his father, now with no real property? While there were moves afoot in New England to abolish imprisonment for debt, five-sixths of Pennsylvania's jail sentences were for just that. The thought was too awful to contemplate.

114

Anxiously, Henry cast about for means to build up ready cash. He was able to browbeat his father into selling more Good Intent Stage Line stock—"⅓ of all my interest west of Lancaster for $3,300.35." The remainder Amos wouldn't part with. The same went for his insurance holdings and his shares in the Gap-Newport Turnpike.

With desperate intent Henry squeezed every holding to the last drop of profit. The food garden was partially let out, as was barn space, to neighboring farmers. When possible, permanent boarders were installed in the Gap and Salisbury taverns. The tilt mill was rented. Occupancy of a tenant house was doubled.

Untiringly, he experimented with different farming arrangements. One year it was a farmer on the halves; the next another on a fee basis. Then still another on the halves, with modifications always slanted toward extreme penny-pinching. Nastily worded things his farm agreements were, harping as they always did on picayune detail. It was small wonder that farmers could take no more than a year on the place.

His work load was very heavy. There was the Cochran estate to settle, the Cochranville store to oversee, his own store and Railroad Hotel at Gap, the running of which was turned over to his sister Faithful's boy, Jervis Mott. Relations with brother William continued to worsen as the Salisbury inn, with declining traffic, became a growing headache. Brother Amos H. in Columbia had to be checked on constantly. All the while, there was the farm to run, the post office to oversee, and justice of the peace duties to attend to. The latter load he sought to lessen by having as many forms as possible printed and by making use of that new innovation in stationery, the envelope, so as to be done with the tedium of sealing wax.

When it came, after the Superior Court's decision, the final Boyd judgment against his father probably seemed to Henry an anticlimax. Only $2,379.40 had to be made good. And, happily, Attorney Ellmaker gave him a grace period; payment could wait until all Boyd lands were sold and Henry would take his cut as the late James Boyd's administrator. It was also amicably agreed by both parties that proceeds of the sale would be put in safe, blue-chip Bank of Pennsylvania stock.

Old Amos's health was declining rapidly. Dr. John L. Atlee's trips from Lancaster to Salisbury were becoming frequent. But there was little to prescribe for just plain deterioration. Dr. Atlee was simply checking.

His father's worsening condition caused Henry to reassess his situation.

The John N. Lane loan to Amos was still outstanding. Henry would have to make good on it when his father died. It had never seemed possible that the seemingly indestructible old man would go under. Otherwise, Henry would never have made that divesting agreement back in 1831. For it was good only as long as his father lived. Another way to save White Chimneys would have to be found, and fast.

Henry pondered and came up with a new compact. Like his first agreement, the second (of May 5, 1836) was probably drawn without benefit of counsel. In it Henry stated that his father was "bound" to him in the amount of $10,000, but that since Amos had put roughly $5,000 of his own into the property that Henry would inherit, the old man would be in debt to him by only $5,000. Henry believed that this simple statement would give him a claim against his father's estate which would precede claims by anyone else.

On the same day, he prepared a will for his father, designed to supplement their agreement: Amos left the White Chimneys property to Henry, with the stipulation that Henry must pay two-thirds of Amos's debts first. Henry was also charged with small sums to his father's other children and grandchildren.

Now claimants could not hit Amos while he lived, as he was "bound" first to Henry; no one could go after the estate after his father died because it would still be owing to Henry, who, in turn, could not claim it until he satisfied the requirements of the will.

The old Sign of John Adams property was willed to brother William. But William would have to pay the remaining one-third of his father's debts before claiming it.

In order to give himself more latitude for maneuver, three weeks later Henry added a codicil to his father's will noting that Henry could sell White Chimneys and its land if he deemed it necessary.

The agreement, the will, and the codicil, then, gave Henry what he believed to be free rein for protecting himself. Of course, he desperately wanted to keep the codicil from coming into force—from having to sell White Chimneys.

So he took a radical step to cover himself against the Lane loan. He sold his pride and joy, the Gap Railroad Hotel and store with railroad freight cars, to merchant Hawthorne Freeland for $6,950. With scant regard for a possible future rise in commodity value, he unloaded all inventory from the Columbia store. Brother Amos H. and his family were told to leave. Henry promised to help his brother get a storekeeping situation in Philadelphia.

Still desperate for more cash, he decided on selling that famous landmark where his father began his meteoric rise, the old Sign of John Adams, still dear to the hearts of all the family.

The agreement of 1831 with brother William—in which William was said to have "bought" the inn—had, of course, been superseded by the 1836 agreement and will. On February 14, 1837, Henry unilaterally voided these. He told William to get himself, wife, children, and baggage out. The place was sold for $3,824 to a James Buyers, who later sold it to one Clinton Himes Martin.

William's pathetic wailings were probably too shrill for Henry's comfort around the valley, in general, and Bellevue Church, in particular. So he promised to buy William a small farm somewhere in Chester County.

Slightly more than the $12,000 needed for the Lane loan had been raised through the sale of the two inns, Columbia inventory, and the earlier sale of stagecoach stock. Henry put the remainder, with the Boyd funds, in safe and sound Bank of Pennsylvania stock.

For the first time in many years Henry could have felt in the soft spring air the warming balm of security. It had cost him dearly. For now all he had was White Chimneys, its farm, and the village. But through them, he might live that proper life for which he had always longed. Later, perhaps, when he could accrue some cash, he might go back to trade. He had promised Freeland to stay out of business for six years. Six years might be just about right.

But the first fragrant winds of early April carried a malignant fear fever. For Henry F. Slaymaker, Esq., like every gentleman of business the country over, the spring of 1837 was a nightmare. "Internal Improvements"—those glistening handmaidens of an incipient Manifest Destiny that had spelled the millennium, appeared now furies, intent on dragging the nation to oblivion. An awful truth dawned on the business fraternity: the much-heralded age of steam and canals had not, after all, provided income sufficient to support a jerry-built investment structure in state and nation. Banks fell like tree limbs in a storm, which when past presents a cleanup almost too futile to contemplate.

The Panic of 1837 laid prostrate the business of the land. White Chimneys, like surrounding homes and institutions, seemed certain to go under, only to surface again in strange hands. A natural supposition this was, on Henry's part. For the Bank of Pennsylvania had gone, carrying with it Boyd funds and his own. Then, too, he had never been born to succeed. He lacked a flair for which even the harshest forms of self-sacrifice—not to mention the wanton sacrifice of others—could not compensate. Still, he had striven to be ethical. For the sake of appearances he had carried a terrible burden in the name of the family. And he had vouched for the welfare of brothers Amos H. and William D. even though he considered the latter next to worthless.

Henry could steel himself against depletion no longer. He became ill. Becky worried greatly—she wrote her sisters-in-law that he seemed "so sad" and "so delicate." He longed to start over again, far from these scenes of failure. At forty-eight, there might still be time enough to go west, once he was free of his responsibilities.

He debated with himself, finally confiding to his lawyer, John R. Montgomery, by letter: "I have been speaking of visiting Illinois, but with no intention of remaining there until I see the country, and not then, if we ever go, until I see the whole of my father's business settled."

He mentioned, too, that there was still the Cochran estate to wind up. Unmentioned, of course, was the fact he would have to await his father's death. Even if old Amos had been well enough to be moved, the very fact of doing so was too tragic to imagine. Amos still knew where he was and was determined to remain until the end.

On June 22, 1837, the household awoke to sounds of a typical early summer morning. Perhaps a cock crowed. It was time for farm hands to harness teams and for the first wagons to crunch their squeaking ways on the pike. The post office flag would soon be raised. Since youngsters are always up and about early in summer, it's probable that one of his grandchildren found Amos Slaymaker in his large, canopied four-poster bed in the south front bedroom. He had died the night before.

One of Amos Slaymaker's grandsons, Squire Samuel Evans of Columbia—the artist Hannah Slaymaker Evans's son—attended the funeral as a small boy. He described it later, in the 1890s, as one of the largest in the memory of Lancaster Countians. According to Squire Evans most, if not all, of Amos and Sibby's six remaining children (five had died previously) attended with their wives, husbands, and children. Business associates from Philadelphia and politicians from Harrisburg debarked from the railroad train at Slaymaker's Hotel in Gap, where they passed the night preceding the funeral. It was held at Leacock Church. While Henry, Becky, and their children were members of Gap's Bellevue Church, it was evidently felt that Amos's remains should be placed by the church with which he had been associated since his baptism eighty-two years before.

The crowd was too large for the little church. So the Reverend Joseph Barr conducted the service in the yard, under trees heavy with verdant foliage. The area was jam-packed with dark-clad mourners and circled about, Squire Evans reported, by massed carriages.

After hymns, prayers, and a soul-moving oration by the Reverend Barr, Amos Slaymaker, Esq., went to his last rest next to Sibby in Leacock churchyard's "Slaymaker Row."

12

AMOS SLAYMAKER, ESQ.'s, second and mansion addition to the Francis Jones house stands today very much as he built it. Close examination of its two rooms and hall afforded me only one exciting "find."

Between the two turnpike-facing windows in the front room there was hung years before a massive, life-size portrait of my grandmother, flanked by my father and one of his sisters, circa 1910. Since it was too large for the room, and I wanted to replace it with paintings of Amos's period, Lloyd and Don lent a hand in removing it to the 1923 wing. Beneath was that oblong, gilt-edged mirror, 6 by 3 feet 4 inches, which Amos had placed. Evidently, a sheet of glass of sufficient size was not available to him. So two sheets were spliced. No effort was made to disguise the resulting horizontal seam in the mirror's upper extremity.

Imperfect gilding, the crude affixing job, and that ubiquitous seam epitomized Amos's bent for practicality, and I liked it. It was kept uncovered.

The interior of Amos's 1807 mansion addition had last been done over in the late 1920s. Rooms on both floors were badly lighted by nondescript frosted-glass chandeliers and standing lamps. The downstairs rooms and hallway were exactly as I knew them in boyhood. Furniture was heavy, dark-stained, and late Victorian, chairs and settees being upholstered in horsehair.

Much of the eighteenth-century and Federal period furniture was in the rear of the house and the garrets. There were several tilt-top tables, two "piecrust" tops, Amos's four Hitchcock chairs and a highboy and lowboy, both Chippendale. An Empire dining table and sideboard, together with Chippendale chairs, were still in the dining room. Amos's grandfather clock stood in the hall.

Wallpaper in both rooms and the hall was heavy and oatmeal-colored. As in the adjoining dining room to the rear, floors had been darkly stained. I found the first layer of the mansion's wall paint to be a lemon yellow. While Amos probably left walls in the rear house unpainted for some years—as was often the custom in country houses—his mansion's walls were very possibly done with the yellow sour-milk wash when his family first moved in. It was pleasing to know that these rooms could be restored to something very like their original condition.

Scraping began in the fall of 1958, with the inevitable oyster and beer parties. Three were required for removal of all paper and high-gloss woodwork paint. Again, I rented a sander and the dark floor finish was removed. After "gym-seal" finishing, the fine oak flooring was revealed in those rich, light, amber tints that the home's first family would have recognized after Sibby's help had completed a sand sweeping.

By early winter, walls had been painted in matching lemon yellow, period furniture was set, and portraits hung; the Wertmüllers and Amos's were grouped in the front room. Sibby was never painted. Perhaps she was too self-conscious to sit. Her silhouette shows her to have been very plump.

Work on the "front house," as we called it, progressed rapidly because our tenant house program was completed. All dwellings were painted, the frame ones light gray, the double brick, red. But Slaymakertown, as Amos's village eventually came to be known, little resembles the Salisbury of his days. His tenant houses were of stone and half-timbered. Only two originals still stand: the larger "farmer's house," Don's, and Lloyd's to its east, directly across the "turnpike" (Route 30) from the mansion where the tollgate had stood. To the east of Lloyd's house Amos built another. Since it was in bad repair when my grandfather took over in 1894, he razed it and built the double brick house. He also demolished two of the original dwellings to the east of the mansion on its north side of the road. Small frame houses replaced them.

The Sign of John Adams stage inn, just to the west of the mansion, looks much as it did in its heyday. But now it's a private dwelling; about which more later.

In the 1930s my grandmother faced the entire front lawn with arborvitae trees. If it could not much diminish the traffic's roar, the sixteen-foot-high hedge could at least obscure it. By the time of my take-over it was full of bagworm, and I planned on replacing it with privet hedge. But the press of other projects left this one on a back burner.

Then on a winter night in 1957 there came a heaven-sent engine of destruction—a tipsy driver who skidded from the road and mowed down a good 75 feet of arborvitae. The young man had no insurance. I appeared in court and sued for damages. A couple of weeks later, in midnight sleet, another car hit the hedge, miraculously, at the point where the other had stopped; 115 feet of arborvitae were now wiped out! The second driver was a fit and sober gentleman who had insurance. Settlement was amicably made. While a good 210 feet of hedge remained, income from the accidents was sufficient for the purchase of privet hedge for the entire front lawn. Don removed what remained with his tractor.

In retrospect, the lawsuit business seems as wrongheadedly cruel as it was needless. For the amount involved was "peanuts," as I heard one of my business associates tell another when they thought I was out of earshot.

"Sam's changed," the other replied. "He's so wrapped up in making that damn farm go that he's beginning to act like a self-made man!"

A few months earlier an overheard deprecatory remark from a colleague would have stung; this one in particular. It reflected the dictum that in the nature of things "silver spoon" heirs are incapable of "amounting" to more than that. But now I stood stock-still in the office hallway, reflected momentarily, and felt a flush of pride as I moved on.

For I was changing: from a bubbling extrovert to a driven introvert, who felt for the first time that sense of economic insecurity that dogs the self-made on the way up. My colleagues were more right than they knew, I thought. In time they realized it. As the vicissitudes of business raised my station, I drove myself as hard at the office as on the farm. And when results proved economically beneficial, I found it easier to make self-serving decisions.

While the impetus of my drive was the need for funds to hold White Chimneys, I found, paradoxically, that the role of country squire was no longer fun—when I was on the property, that is. Elsewhere, when being introduced as its owner—or better, as its restorer—I still felt pangs of pride. The tenant houses were the sources of my troubles.

Improvements and higher rents brought tenants of better means. Still, some were a pretty rough lot. While the houses had conveniences, only Don's and Lloyd's had central heating. Space heaters precluded renting in the highest brackets. I was increasingly annoyed with the tenants' perpetual complaining, their fighting and my rent collection difficulties, and I let them know it. There were no more repair parties. Lloyd's help was permitted when we had to react to emergencies. Being always there, he took the brunt of their hostility. Bred in Slaymakertown's tradition of combativeness, Lloyd relished the ceaseless set-tos between the tenants as much as he did theirs with us. My father told me that before radio and television, fighting was a favored pastime in Slaymakertown. My studies revealed that such was the case from its beginnings.

I was able to turn some of the flare-ups to good advantage. Inflation and rising property taxes provided reasons enough for rent escalation. Since it was always easier to "up" rents when new tenants moved in, there were occasions when—if I thought the traffic could bear it—I helped fights along by way of hastening turnovers and hikes.

Too preoccupied to dwell long on introspection, I attributed my changed outlook to a process of maturing. Smugly, I took comfort in becoming pragmatic. It never occurred to me that my turnabout owed more to things spiritual then psychological. Then came an event that forced me to consider the possibility.

I was still bemused by that feeling of being watched while perusing Amos's papers. So it's likely that I sought subconsciously to destroy it, by moving them to his mansion's front room. This now seems a peculiar act. For any ghostly influence of Amos's would surely be more effective in his new wing, now appointed after his own taste. Perhaps the move was really prompted by an intuitive desire to test Amos's ability to haunt, as, say, a child tests a parent's will to punish. The question was not whether he could be stopped; inwardly, I think now, I wanted to egg him on.

I remember clearly a spine-tingling sense of dread fascination on laying the first fire in his refurbished front room. Now and again the water pump in the basement hummed as cows drinking in the barn triggered it for trough refills. Occasional tractor-trailers rattled front windows. Otherwise, there was an oppressive silence. In the soft glow of a table lamp, Amos's likeness above the mantel seemed almost benign. If ever a setting was conducive to the feeling of stares, this one was. But there were none. Nor did they intrude the following evening.

I had been reading letters to Amos from his sister Hannah Cochran, written from Cochranville in 1817. They were pleasantly newsy and concerned landscaping the new Cochran mansion grounds, minor illnesses of her children, and political gossip from her husband, Surveyor General Samuel Cochran in Harrisburg.

On the third evening, I unraveled the first of several large packets which my grandfather had labeled "The Boyd Case" when he packed the papers in their tin boxes in the early 1920s.

I could not remember my grandfather's ever talking about the Boyd affair, although my Aunt Helen once told me that he had mentioned it briefly to her years before. He had said that the Boyd principals were "difficult and dishonest" and that they had caused the family "a great deal of trouble." When I spoke to my grandmother about researching the family papers, she laughed and said, "Your Great-aunt Rebecca wouldn't have wanted you to get into the Boyd papers." Her old-maid sister-in-law was an especial guardian of the family's good name. In these particular papers, then, I expected to find the skeletons.

On first looking over the Boyd papers I felt no discernible stare. Then my eyes fell on the letter from Jasper to Henry in which Jasper regretted their father's ever getting involved with the Boyds.

I felt the stare strongly. Oddly, it caused no bedeviling unease. Rather, I felt an excited urge to open all seven packets, to go through their contents and search out information on the case from beginning to end.

There were enough neatly folded papers on the Boyd case to paper the front room and some of the adjoining ones to boot. So it was possible in this one sitting to extract only a very small segment. Small as it was, it was enough to reveal a side of Amos which wouldn't have inspired any of my earlier prideful feelings. Now, strangely, I had become so understanding of his ends and tolerant of his means that I exulted in both.

It was almost as if Amos had directed me to his dirty linen, content that I could finally appreciate his side of the Boyd affair. After all, I was now prepared. My personality had begun to blend with his, perhaps because of his ghostly influence during preceding months.

I left for my bedroom that night feeling more aggressively determined to hang on to the place then ever before.

Over a bright autumn noon hour in 1958 (after having researched the Boyd case) I stopped in Lancaster's center square, glanced at the Civil War monument, blinked it away, and developed a mind picture of the area when the Country Georgian Court House had stood there.

It's the first day of court in the fall of 1834. The red-brick building is surrounded by gentlemen in broadcloth coats and beaver toppers; ladies hoopskirted and bonneted by the primmest standards of *Godey's Ladies' Book*. There is a sprinkling of rough-dressed country types. Their hobnailed boots are heard clomping over the excited buzz around the Court House. To the northwest of the square, in the market area, Amish and Mennonite farmers await news about the legal melodrama. Their religion precludes attendance at affairs of law. Gossip is all they hear.

A hush settles over the crowds as a phaeton approaches the Court House. In it are Henry, Becky, their older children, and aged Amos. They alight and push their way through knots of well-wishers.

Amos's friends in the audience see nothing unusual about his trying to explain away shortages in the account as being covered by sundry expenses, the details of which he "couldn't remember," as they were "so long ago." They sympathize with the old man sitting bent in the dock, his white-topped head cocked as if to afford improved earshot, for he presents a touching picture.

I couldn't help but glory in the old man's being as tough as a leather boot. I sought to justify what had once seemed to me questionable dealing. So he had used political influence for self-aggrandizement. His brother-in-law, Samuel Cochran, was surveyor general as much for what the office yielded in terms of land speculation possibilities as in the emoluments of what today is called "public service." And history books are replete with records of more exalted nation builders with *modi operandi* similar to Amos's.

Did he really misappropriate Boyd funds? Or was he simply an unwary victim of the vicissitudes of estate-settling practices of the times? Evidence points toward his having "borrowed" Boyd monies for his sons' ventures. But to a great degree a contributing factor had to be the business milieu. And, I reminded myself, the magnitude of his sufferings surely exceeded that of his misdeeds.

The curbstone reverie was rent by the smell of diesel fumes and a screech of brakes. I boarded the bus and rode back to the real world of my office.

My total absorption in Amos's tribulations inspired renewed interest in those artifacts of his still remaining at White Chimneys. Many had left when his heirs and descendants married. His grandfather clock still keeps excellent time. The Lafayette cane was found in the garret, along with a couple of other walking sticks with ivory heads. Lloyd built a cane rack so that they could be displayed in the front hall.

There was the aforementioned "Washington-Yeates" Chippendale sofa, two gilt-edged hanging mirrors, a couple of spinning wheels, and the previously mentioned furniture. Many pieces are probably souvenirs of Amos's Philadelphia shopping trips. In the garret I found a "mourning picture," of the sort embroidered on silk by the women during periods of a family's bereavement. Possibly the girls did this one on the passing of Sibby.

After Samuel Cochran and his sons died, local Cochran holdings were sold to satisfy creditors. Hannah Cochran continued to live at

Samuel Cochran,	His wife,
Amos's brother-in-law	Hannah Slaymaker Cochran
Miniature on wood	Miniature on wood
by Jacob Eichholtz	by Jacob Eichholtz

White Chimneys until her death at eighty-three in 1847. She brought the large Cochran library, containing many valuable works; some had been printed in England in the sixteenth and seventeenth centuries—mostly theology. With a large manuscript collection was a letter written during the Revolution by General Washington to Samuel Cochran's uncle, General John Cochran, asking him to replace "an old and favorite penknife" which he had lost. She also brought two miniatures on wood of Samuel and herself and a portrait of Samuel. They were painted by the well-known Lancaster County artist Jacob Eichholtz, who studied in England under Gilbert Stuart and, ironically, as a beginning sign painter rendered the sign for the Sign of John Adams years before.

Paintings of Amos's era also included works by his youngest daughter, Hannah. One of her early efforts was a landscape of the mansion and turnpike. Her perspective was off, but it is a charming primitive showing the home's red-brick chimneys before they were painted white by her brother Henry.

Correspondence reveals Hannah Slaymaker to have been a temperamental and imperious woman, probably the result of being spoiled by her father. She married well into the Evans family of Columbia and divorced her husband. I could find no details. Divorces then had to pass the state legislature. Any records of this one were probably removed from the files by the family. I could only discover that brother Henry handled the divorce and that his expenses were $25.

Later she married again, this time to an older and evidently more tolerant man who referred to her in a letter as "Queen Victoria." She died in 1860.

Other early paintings by Hannah were of brother Henry and his wife, Becky. These were on the primitive side. Her best work, that of Amos, was painted later and marked her as the fairly accomplished artist that some contemporary critics declare her to have been.

It was normal for me to develop a heightened interest in Amos's antiques and furnishings. Actually, I became almost pathologically possessive—obsessed with the fear of fire, theft, or breakage.

One day I called in an appraiser to review values. As we talked it dawned that any assessment upward would be unrealistic, since these things could never be replaced. As the man left, I became aware of the fact that had been escaping me—or that I tried, subconsciously, to escape all along. Possessed by my possession, I was a captive of my mansion.

Realization should have come in a more dramatic setting, say, late at night while lightning riddled the sky and thunder rattled windows, and I could feel that inexplicable stare. But for months the stare syndrome had been receding to nonexistence. So it was more natural, if not so fitting, that I finally faced up to having been haunted while talking with an appraiser on a fall Saturday afternoon in 1958.

Acceptance of what I had sensed for so long brought embarrassment (I didn't dare talk about it) and surprise. For almost immediately my rigors relented. I no longer felt driven. My fear for the paintings and antiques subsided. So did frustration born of exceeded budgets and complaining tenants. The blow I'd been expecting since taking over— the departure of Don—was taken resignedly when it came. While the

Henry Fleming Slaymaker   Rebecca Cochran Slaymaker
Painting by Hannah Slaymaker Evans   Painting by Hannah Slaymaker Evans

next farmer would be hard put to match him, a way would be found to carry on.

Given Don's lack of built-in family help, he had little future in farming. The price of field help was too high. So he decided to join his wife in schoolteaching. He planned on "selling out" farm equipment to finance a course in teachers college. Nineteen fifty-nine was to be Don's last year at White Chimneys.

Relaxation brought at last introspection.

The unpleasing metamorphosis which Amos's haunting had worked on my personality should never have been laid to maturing. For this process is usually dependent on contact with others. Monkish aesthetes might grow in wisdom by living in a vacuum with musty piles of manuscript, but not, I ruminated, sales executive types. Further proof that those sourceless stares could not have been self-conjured was manifest when they were no longer felt. On my accepting captivity in "our" mansion, Amos left me alone. His job was done. There seemed no other way to explain the now total absence of a feel of his presence while I finished working on his papers.

His son and heir, Henry Fleming Slaymaker, was my next subject. His sister Hannah's portrait was not so primitive as to miss an almost anemic-looking face with a slightly receding chin. On first glance the painting suggests a languid and weak type, a dilettante. But there are those intent blue eyes burning nervously in a thin face. I had never before been aware of this quality of tension which his sister Hannah, it seemed to me, read in him. Bemusedly, I guessed that he was as driven as had been his great-great-grandson. Progressively my research bore this out. And there would be other parallels in a relationship more intimate than the one with Amos, and nonetheless eerie.

My grandfather had once confided to me that Henry was "a weak sort of person." He had some reason to think his grandfather a dilettante. While he never knew him, he had heard from his parents of Henry's culture-conscious life style. The portrait probably suggested as much, as long as the eyes evaded him. Also, my grandfather was relatively close in years to the Boyd scandal. Since Henry was responsible for family affairs in its aftermath, it was natural for him to blame Henry for mismanagement, by way of protecting the image of the illustrious Amos.

My research, of course, revealed Henry to be anything but weak. I was intrigued to discover how, as his father's grasp on affairs faltered, Henry's grew more firm. It became clear that if Amos had been devious in erecting his empire, his son was ruthless in salvaging its remains. The wellsprings of their strength were in Presbyterianism: Amos's in the classic sense, Henry's in relative latitudinarianism. Father and son perfectly reflected the changing theological patterns of their respective eras.

13

By the 1840s the village was becoming known as Slaymakertown. With the post office moved to Gap (where it should have been from the beginning) and the Sign of John Adams in other hands—and, because of declining stage traffic, no longer an inn—the place began to reflect the characteristics, if not the appearance, of its present state: a moribund hamlet that had lost its reason for being. But it served as an adequate backdrop for the new squire.

Henry's family appeared archetypical of others in the upper rungs of Pennsylvania's squirearchy. It seemed not to lack wherewithal for amenities, let alone necessities. His children attended local private schools. In their early teens all passed muster before the session of Gap's Bellevue Presbyterian Church and were placed on the roll. The rigors of scholarship and religion were spiked with the pleasures of good clean fun and games.

There were the annual Fourth of July celebrations at Slaymaker-town with the firing of rifles, beating of drums, and orations by Henry and/or his brother ex-officers of the War of 1812. Local militia marched to brassy renditions of "Hail, Columbia, Happy Land," courtesy of the Salisbury band. Punch and ice cream were served on the White Chimneys lawn. With evening came fireworks: Roman candles, illuminated pinwheels, firecrackers, and hand-held sparklers.

The family attended country fairs featuring crop and livestock contests and balloon ascensions. Circuses were always well attended. They usually consisted of a clown, an equestrienne, fiddlers, trumpeters, a drummer, and an acrobat. According to the rural Pennsylvania chronicles of Henry B. Plumb, some shows after 1812 had wild animals: "An elephant, a monkey, and a learned pig drew great crowds," he reported. Sometimes there were traveling waxwork shows. Henry's girls held quilting parties, attended church suppers and poetry readings, and took singing lessons from itinerant music masters.

After a hiatus caused in the 1820s by clerical opposition, cotillions and assemblies were coming back. Henry's second son, young Samuel Cochran Slaymaker, attended many and became a manager of a Chester County assembly. He also played a horn in the Salisbury band.

Samuel—his father's favorite, and the future squire—was born at White Chimneys on April 22, 1828. He began his education at Harmony School, a log building a mile from home, run by his Bellevue Church minister, the Reverend Philip J. Timlow. The fee was $18 per term. Within a few years the Duffield family opened a school in Duffield

Manor. Since George Duffield, late comptroller general of the Commonwealth, had married Henry F. Slaymaker's Aunt Faithful (old Amos's sister), Henry transferred his boys, Samuel Cochran and Amos Fleming, to the Duffield school.

On reaching their early teens the boys commuted by horseback to Moscow Academy several miles east on the turnpike. Here they studied under the Reverend Francis Alison Latta, a well-known and learned Presbyterian divine. They completed their formal educations as boarding students at one of the most respected schools in southeastern Pennsylvania, Parksburg Academy in Chester County.

Samuel was an excellent penman. His school copybooks show him to have been a promising draftsman. Unlike many of the mechanically oriented, Samuel had an affinity for good literature that was equaled only by a love of the out-of-doors. As a gifted and compulsive diarist, he evidenced the proclivities of a devoted naturalist.

His diarykeeping began in 1851 when he was twenty-three and ended the day before he died in Lancaster at sixty-six in 1894. The first beautifully scrivened notebook was titled "Memorandum of Weather and Work, Samuel C. Slaymaker 1851–52." It began with an entry for May 1, 1851: "Rather pleasant, too wet to plant corn. Hauled a load of hay to Samuel Neal. Hauling rails bought of AFS and SCS [his brother and himself]."

He had an eye for beauteous effects of weather on nature. February 9, 1852: "On Thursday and Friday there was one of the most sublime scenes ever witnessed by the inhabitants of the county caused by the sun shining on the trees which were encrusted with ice."

But all was not play for the boys, Samuel Cochran and Amos Fleming Slaymaker. They put in many hard hours on the farm. It wasn't that Henry wanted them to. He strove to avoid making farm laborers of his sons. He had never been one and was not about to start. But after experimenting with a long line of tenant farmers, Henry realized that there was not enough cash in "farming on the halves." Were the boys to take over, more farm income would accrue to him. So upon completion of their secondary educations they became full-time farmers.

Samuel, however, planned for another career. He studied surveying and wanted to become a civil engineer. Here was a field promising substantial income, enough perhaps to ensure the family's possession of White Chimneys. But Henry's penchant for hanging on to his genteel ways won out. For the time being, Samuel would have to farm.

Much less onerous was the boys' work than that of their grandfather Amos in the days after the Revolution. Small grains were no longer broadcast by hand. Horse-drawn seed drills made for speedier sowing and heavier yields. Arm-wearing scythes were replaced by horse-propelled mowing machines and hay rakes. Iron plows turned more even furrows less laboriously than those of wood, and horse-powered cultivators precluded back-breaking hoeing.

The grain-harvesting machinery that revolutionized American agriculture was now in the experimental stage. But grain was more swiftly cut and stacked by the cradle, a combination scythe and grain-gathering implement. No longer was grain threshed by foot stomping and flailing on the barn floor. Horse-powered threshing machines did the entire job.

Still, there was dawn-to-dusk activity: milking, butchering, fence repairing, and almost continual field work.

Little cash was available for new machinery. But Henry had inherited a well-equipped farm, and young Samuel's scientific bent was a help. He experimented with such soil-building additives to manure as gypsum, lime, and red clover. He was a constant reader of agricultural publications, a favorite being journals of the Philadelphia Society for the Promotion of Agriculture. An inveterate competitor in farm produce contests, Samuel won a large silver coin engraved: "The Pennsylvania State Agricultural Society, A.D. 1851, Awarded to Sam'l C. Slaymaker, Salisbury, Lancaster County, for Best Collection of Apples. Exhibition of 1855."

It could not have been lost on the more perceptive valleyites that Henry F. Slaymaker's genteel station was maintained entirely by subsistence farming. Few, though, could have realized how cash-poor he really was because of continuing Boyd payments and his children's education. And they most probably never found out. For the sight of the squire puttering about the farm as its manager, tending to his J.P. duties, advising locals in legal matters, and functioning as a learned elder in the Bellevue Church was a deceiving one.

Much of Henry's time was spent in trying to liquidate the Cochrans' western lands. These promised a windfall. While his Aunt Hannah would receive any proceeds left after creditors took their shares, he, Henry, would be the real beneficiary, since she lived with him.

While Henry had already satisfied his father's debt to John N. Lane through property dissolutions, Boyd affairs constituted a continuing worry. He corresponded with heirs and paid what claims he could from his own pocket. No one started legal action which could have led to foreclosure. Apparently, all accepted the loss of Boyd funds during the Panic of 1837 philosophically and did not hold Henry responsible. But he must have feared the worst. He continued to toy with the idea of selling out and moving to Illinois. There, perhaps, he might buy a farm for the boys to work while he went into storekeeping.

In the mid-1840s Henry went to western Pennsylvania to liquidate the Cochran lands. He decided to continue to Illinois and look over prospects there.

Certainly Henry was impressed by civilization's rapid advance westward. Almost forty years before, when he rode on horseback toward Westmoreland County to buy off Wertmüller heirs, highwaymen prowled the mountain fastnesses. Uncle Daniel Fleming had cautioned him to be well armed. By the 1840s railroads and canals made for relatively safe and leisurely travel.

He traversed what was considered a wonder of the world, the Allegheny Portage Railroad. It ran thirty-six miles from Hollidaysburg to Johnstown. Ten straight incline planes were constructed to meet a rise of almost fourteen hundred feet. Canal boats were placed on cars which were pulled up and let down the planes by steam power supplied by standing engines connected to wire cables. The railroad was tunneled through the Alleghenies for nine miles. This was America's first railroad tunnel.

After the Cochran land sale, Henry boarded a river steamer at Pittsburgh and sailed down the Ohio to Illinois.

It's likely that a polyglot group of passengers—gamblers, servicemen, drummers, ladies of the evening—discomforted the retiring aesthete from Slaymakertown's sheltered haunts. The seemingly endless stretches of shimmering river and broad green-ocher expanses of prairie might have inspired longing for the well-manicured hills of home. He was in his mid-fifties. It was late to start over again. In Slaymakertown there was a semblance of security.

While homesickness could have been influential in bringing Henry to a final decision, more important was his determination to have all Boyd claims met and his father's name cleared before considering removal to the West. Back in Slaymakertown on June 22, 1847, he wrote Andrew Hoyle, Esq., his lawyer in North Carolina: "Everything now paid will be out of my individual funds, as my father's estate, from heavy losses a short time before his death, is wholly insolvent and I am already a loser in the matter. . . ."

So perhaps, down deep, Henry knew that he could never go west. The proposed move might well have been pure whimsy. Even had there been no Boyd commitments it's unlikely that Henry would have left White Chimneys. He had always been a slave to his father's desires. Parting with the mansion had been unthinkable to Amos. Now that the old man was laid away in Leacock churchyard, deference was due his memory. Henry's religious convictions were not sufficiently latitudinarian to permit disregard of possible spiritualistic wrath on the part of his late father. No, the mansion would have to be taken from Henry. If not, he would only leave feet first.

The Cochran land sale meant that Henry's property would remain decently maintained. During the 1840s and 1850s Lancaster County farmers' rough-hewn "worm" fences were being replaced by boards and perpendicular posts, whitewashed. In all probability Henry emulated them and kept the fences whitewashed as well as the mansion and outbuildings.

Henry made no consequential structural changes in the mansion's interior. But it was certainly less pristine than during Amos's prime. Hooked throw rugs were giving way to carpets, heavily flowered in bright colors. There was probably a melodeon on which Henry's daughters took their music lessons. Factory-made clocks with brass works were becoming popular. Heavy earthenware kitchen pots and bowls were relegated to the cellar. A multiplicity of mass-produced tinware utensils crowded the kitchen: pots, pans, ladles, and buckets, purveyed door to door from ironmongers' wagons. Matches, scissors, needles, thread, and patent medicines were sold by "pack" peddlers.

Kerosene lamps came in; candles went out. White Chimneys' fireplaces were now sheathed with iron and grated because coal-burning superseded log fires. Wood-burning iron cooking ranges had long been in use. So it's likely that the large kitchen fireplace was rarely used and that a range provided adequate heat.

Daguerreotypes of the family were framed for display on tables. Late in the 1850s Henry and Becky sat for large, daguerreotyped portraits. These superb status symbols were meant for walls, amid the array of oil portraits. They clashed awfully. But chances are that Henry couldn't have cared less, for these first photo portraits were very much the rage. Rooms on both floors were covered with unflowered, plain wallpaper; dark blues and beige predominated.

By the 1850s bathtubs of wood became common in the more fashionable homes. The sewing room at the head of the front stairs was probably first converted to a bathroom at this time. No longer was it necessary to sponge-bathe in bedrooms or in the outside washhouse. Hot water was brought in buckets to the second floor. Dirty water was drained from tub to bucket and returned to the ground floor or dumped from a window.

There was still no plumbing. So the outhouse to the rear remained in service. Since flies and mosquitoes could be annoying in summer months, bedsteads were equipped with mosquito netting.

Thus incipient Victorian décor rendered White Chimneys more cluttered, dark, and stuffy. But everything was most contemporary to suit the squire's taste.

In these comforting surroundings Henry Slaymaker lived out his days, dabbling in state and local politics, reading, studying phrenology, overseeing the farm, attending to J.P. duties, and practicing a little law. Only twice did he take fliers in business.

He was one of several founders of an insurance company. In a few years it failed. But not before his barn was consumed by a fire that was seen for miles. His company covered the loss, and a more modern structure was erected. The fire was indubitably accidental. Henry was not the kind to engineer "successful" fires.

The squire next decided to convert the tilt mill (for metal hammering) on the meadow's stream to a wood-turning mill, fit for manufacturing wooden housewares. The boys were put to running it. Business cards and advertising handbills were printed. But a couple of drought-plagued summers dropped water levels so low that the mill was inoperative for long periods. The project was scrubbed.

However tranquil and pleasing Henry found his life as a squire, he remained in need of ready cash. Had he inherited his father's temperament, he would have seized the obvious lifeline. Political pull could surely have brought salvation—with a little bit of luck, even wealth. He had the opportunity to garner political patronage on a national level.

Although not so intimate a friend of James Buchanan as his late brother Jasper, the two had remained good friends for many years after leaving Dickinson College. Possibly there was a hiatus in 1819. Buchanan was then under a cloud in Lancaster. It's probable that very proper Henry joined his peer group in keeping some distance from Buchanan when he drew the ire of powerful ironmaster James Coleman.

James Buchanan had fallen in love with Mr. Coleman's daughter, Ann. Coleman could not see her wed to a poor young lawyer. So he discouraged the affair. It was said that Ann died of a broken heart. Evidence pointed to suicide in Philadelphia, where she had repaired.

Hannah Cochran, writing her son Samuel Slaymaker Cochran at the University of Pennsylvania on December 14, 1819, reported that

after her corpse arrived in Lancaster Mr. Buchanan wrote a note to Mr. Coleman requesting to be permitted to see her corpse and to walk as a mourner but each of his requests were denied which I think must humble him greatly as I believe that her friends now look upon him as her murderer, for previous to her leaving Lancaster she thought that Mr. Buchanan did not treat her with that affection that she expected from the man she was to marry and in consequence of his coolness she wrote him a note telling him she thought it was not regard for her that was his object but her riches—he answered her note politely but never came to an explanation—she then discarded him and afterwards she appeared to be distressed and very low spirited. Her mother persuaded her to go to Philadelphia hoping that would raise her depressed spirits, and they never heard anything from her 'til the express came with the news of her death—but after Mr. Buchanan was denied his request he secluded himself for a few days and then sallied forth as bold as ever. It is now thought that this affair will lessen his consequence in Lancaster as he is the whole conversation of the town. . . .

If Henry's feelings toward James Buchanan were at one with his Aunt Hannah's, they could have been responsible for Buchanan's inattention to an old friend in need of patronage. For unlike others of Henry's friends, Buchanan knew his true financial situation through his work on Boyd affairs. But Buchanan had more important matters on his mind.

After serving in Pennsylvania's legislature, Buchanan planned on retirement. But Ann Coleman's death caused him to reconsider. It was said that out of deference to Ann's memory he vowed never to marry. So he opted for a political career and was elected to the U.S. House of Representatives, where he served from 1821 to 1831. In 1824 he left the dying Federalist Party, became a Democrat, and supported Andrew Jackson. "Old Hickory" rewarded James by appointing him Minister to Russia. He negotiated the first commercial treaty between the United States and Russia.

In 1834 Buchanan was elected to the U.S. Senate. In 1844 he was Pennsylvania's "favorite son" for President but lost the nomination to James K. Polk. He then resigned from the Senate to become Secretary of State under Polk. In this office James Buchanan completed details involved in the annexation of Texas. He helped to defuse the danger-fraught "Oregon Question" with Great Britain.

Buchanan retired to his estate, Wheatland, on the western environs of Lancaster. Again, in 1852, he stood for the Democratic presidential nomination, but Franklin Pierce got the nod. President Pierce appointed him Minister to England. After serving there with distinction, Buchanan finally received the Democratic nomination for President in 1856 and went on to win the election from Republican John C. Frémont.

Had Amos Slaymaker been in Henry's plight, he would have lost no time in importuning Mr. Buchanan. Bygone differences would have been speedily smoothed over and a sinecure obtained.

Henry was probably not too proud to seek help. Rather, it's likely that his political probity prevented his having anything to do with James Buchanan.

They were both Federalists in Dickinson days. With the passing of the Federalists, they became Democrats. Like Buchanan, the Slaymakers were on the party's conservative wing. Then Buchanan joined ranks with that archleveler, Andrew Jackson, while the Slaymakers espoused the aborning and socially conservative Whigs.

If Henry considered Buchanan's move opportunistic, he probably became spitefully disposed toward him by the 1840s. For by virtue of Henry's failure and insecurity, his political thought had lurched to the "Radical Right."

Largely because of the Democrats' ties to ethnic groups—particularly immigrant Irish—the Native American Party evolved, waxing strong in the middle Atlantic states. Many native-born Americans of respectable lineage who had fallen on evil days embraced the American Party. Its platform dovetailed with preconceived rationalizations of their own failings. It was the temper of the times, Henry's kind thought, that brought unstable government resulting in panics and depressions which militated against their betterment. Villains were unenlightened immigrants dominated by the Pope, whose influence was thought by party adherents to be inimical to American views and institutions. "The Americans" wanted political offices barred to such seditious types. The franchise should be restricted. Immigration of seditious types (read Roman Catholics) would be stopped.

Many of the party's chapters operated in secrecy. When supposed members were asked what they were about, the common rejoinder was, "I know nothing." Hence, in popular lexicon, it was dubbed the "Know-Nothing" Party.

The "Know-Nothings'" *modus operandi* must have been as pleasing to Henry as its platform. Those secret meetings in his mansion, where handbills were drawn up and communications with other cells were read and answered, were exciting. Henry was involved, active in saving the Republic! But, as with all else he embraced, the American Party was to come to naught. It was later split asunder by the slavery issue.

Henry was typical of Pennsylvania "Americans." He was opposed to slavery by virtue of the teaching of his church and by the dictates of Pennsylvania law. Since his father's few slaves were considered on virtually the same social level as indentured help, he probably had few qualms about the family's earlier acquiescence in slavekeeping. Anyway, this was long ago.

Hopefully, individual states would outlaw this curse as had Pennsylvania. Prohibition on a national scale was unthinkable. Ironically, his erstwhile friend, James Buchanan, felt the same way.

14

ALTHOUGH HENRY'S FINANCIAL CONDITION failed to improve during the 1850s, it did not worsen appreciably. Subsistence farming sufficed to keep his family, as the saying goes, "in the style to which it was accustomed." But there were few frills and no funds for investment. This was fortunate. For in 1857 came another panic. More affluent acquaintances were wiped out. With nothing to lose, he was able to continue his seemingly secure, idyllic life on ancestral acres as an aging country squire. That he appeared not to be a loser in the Panic of '57 probably enhanced his image. And if there was envy on the part of less fortunate friends, he apparently lost none of them because of it. His correspondence reveals felicitous relationships with family, neighbors, and friends throughout the valley and Lancaster. He seemed philosophic about his accomplishments and/or lack of them. After all, he had held on to his home, farm, village, and status. There were signs that son Samuel Cochran Slaymaker, now a civil engineer, would rebuild the family's fortune on what he, Henry, had been able to salvage.

It was pleasing to ride to Bellevue Church in the handsome phaeton and ponder scriptures and sermons and later converse with the congregation in the churchyard. There were evening session meetings at church during which the moral status of the community and nation were reviewed, new church members queried, and theological pamphlets discussed.

Henry enjoyed helping his sons run the farm. More help was needed because engineer Samuel was frequently away on railroad surveying jobs. Day labor was often unreliable. But it was cheaper than tenant farmers, as long as Henry served as general and Amos F. and/or Samuel as field commanders, who kept a tight rein on his troops of day laborers.

Her letters show Rebecca a solicitous mother. As her children aged, she was anything but strict. Cochran Calvinism had never proscribed merrymaking. Her children were encouraged to attend cotillions, assemblies, and band concerts.

There were languid, peaceful summer days passed by the family at the sprawling white-frame hotel at Ephrata Springs in the hills near Reading. This spa had become one of the seaboard's more fashionable watering places. Here Henry could converse with his intellectual equals in the professions and business. That he was not their peer financially did not matter, even were the fact known, as it probably was not. He could have evidenced an "at home" sort of ease at Ephrata. For Henry and family had become nonpaying guests of the house.

Henry's lovely and vivacious daughter Hannah Cecelia had married the proprietor, Joseph Konigmacher. It was, in the day's lexicon, a "successful marriage." Mr. Konigmacher, considerably older than his bride, had been a onetime dabbler in Democratic politics. James Buchanan had helped him secure jobs.

Thanks to her husband's political connection, Hannah Cecelia frequented Wheatland. Buchanan's niece and hostess, Miss Harriet Lane, must have approved of the friendship. Buchanan always showed deference to Harriet's judgment. He obviously enjoyed the company of Cecelia. He wrote her when he was off on diplomatic assignments—of which more later.

Henry's daughter provided him—at long last—an interest in common with Buchanan. And times had changed. Their views had become less divergent.

For reasons of practical politics Buchanan was not an outspoken opponent of slavery. And he fudged on its extension to new states. Henry, true to the dictates of the Northern wing of his now defunct American Party, was opposed to the institution and the spreading of it. But, as noted, both believed that the issue should be decided by "popular sovereignty" within the states and that it was not a matter for federal intervention.

Then there was their Dickinson College friendship, and James's dealing with Henry's revered late brother, Jasper, along with Buchanan's willingness to run errands in the endless Boyd settlement.

In conversations on the broad verandas of the Ephrata Hotel and in the ordered quietude of Slaymakertown, Henry must have worried over the impending national distempers posed by "Bleeding Kansas." Perhaps by this time he sympathized with President Buchanan, who like so many intellectuals in an executive capacity found hard decisions easier to weigh than to make.

Henry was spared witnessing the inevitable disaster that was Civil War. His failing health gave way, and he died in his mansion on February 8, 1860. South Carolina seceded ten months later.

It can be assumed that the funeral at Bellevue Church was well attended. The Reverend Robert Gamble read scriptures and prayers and delivered the funeral oration. The cortege wound from the sanctuary, down the carriage lane, to the grave site. The Reverend Gamble said a last prayer and ritualistically scattered dirt on the lowered coffin. The dark-clad throng moved toward carriages, taking sad leave of the remains of White Chimneys' second squire, whom the more perceptive and philosophical among them could have categorized as a successful sort of a failure.

During my months of absorption in Henry's affairs I remained unaware of the similarities of our respective squirearchies. Realization came with an otherworldly experience as inexplicable as it was frightening.

I'd had nothing to drink on the night of my confrontation with the shade or dreamed image of my great-great-grandfather. Nor had I ever walked in my sleep before this event or after it. So if sleepwalking was central to it, it was other-directed, as it were, not a phenomenon to be readily accepted on my part.

After leaving Henry's correspondence late on a February night in 1958, I turned in, as usual, with S. W. Fletcher's *Pennsylvania Agriculture and Country Life*. About midnight I cut the light and dozed off.

I seemingly awoke in the front room, downstairs, seated on a Victorian settee. The room was dimly lit. I remember wondering about this, for the lights were off and it was pitch-dark outside.

I arose from the settee with both hands in the pockets of my bathrobe (I'd gone to bed without it) and faced the tall mirror that Amos had built in the forward wall. Henry's image, rather than my own, contemplated me.

Older by far than he appeared in his sister's painting—my only means of recognition—the image certainly was Henry's. The hair was thin and white. Cheeks were sunken. A frock coat was draped loosely over what seemed bony shoulders and a spare frame.

Slowly he raised his right arm. The head nodded slowly, side to side. The arm dropped. He smiled. The teeth were bad, widely separated by dark flecks that evidence decay.

The mirror's image was confusing. The raised hand was startling. The smile scared me.

I was immobilized until this signal's meaning dawned. Then I stumbled to the light switch and turned it. The vision in the mirror was gone. I slumped on the settee and after long rumination slept there for the rest of the night.

I remembered a particularly rough bombing run over Merseburg, Germany, in 1944. Flak blackened the sky and intermittently dimmed the sun's rays through plexiglass above my B-17's radio compartment. Number two engine had just been shot out of commission. Then number four was hit. I glanced at our waist gunner. He stood limply by his gun port, looked at me, and dropped his arms to his sides. The oxygen mask could not hide an expression about his eyes of hopeless resignation. I shook my head in agreement. There seemed no way out. We were convinced that we would go down.

This, it seemed, was the sum of the mirror's image. There had been no way out of captivity for Henry. His mansion had brought him down. It certainly could do the same to me.

Now I realized how greatly my life at White Chimneys paralleled his. We lacked the wherewithal to live in styles befitting our mansion. Yet we refused to admit to the fact, openly. While I can't conceive of our being phonies, in a real sense we were poseurs, bent on playing parts that seemed edifying at first, but which in time became onerous. Both of us sought temporary respite by removing to other scenes where we pondered our plights. Henry had that extended western trip and, in years following, those family vacations at the spa at Ephrata Mountain Springs. I spent a lot of my free time trout fishing and grouse hunting in the Pocono Mountains, and there were frequent sales trips. Henry sought escape, too, in reading the classics. I found a rewarding outlet in writing for outdoor magazines. But after each pleasing diversion our attentions were drawn back to the cares of White Chimneys—skimping, always skimping, in the name of keeping the place afloat.

Psychologically, as well, we traversed twin paths. On taking over we suffered as much from doubting our abilities as from economic insecurity. We compensated by playing rough with some of those about us. Then we got our sea legs and philosophically accepted our lots and improved in temperament.

Bellevue Presbyterian Church probably had a mellowing effect on Henry. I know that it did on me.

Henry had been a founder and contributed $100. His parents, grandparents, and great-grandparents were buried at Leacock. Undoubtedly proud of carrying on the Slaymakers' church-founding tradition, Henry's family went exclusively to "his" Bellevue Church. He broke the family's century-old custom of Leacock burials by instructing that he be interred at Bellevue. His children were confirmed there; my grandfather (who didn't work hard at churchgoing) was a trustee; my father pumped the organ as a boy (10¢ per service), and I went to the Sunday school. So after re-establishing at White Chimneys, attendance there seemed in order.

The small white-plaster building stands as it was built, in what can best be termed rural American-Palladian style. Its broad graveyard borders the main line of the Penn Central Railroad, the same roadbed used by its predecessor, the old Columbia and Philadelphia Railroad. Henry's Railroad Hotel, now a private dwelling, stands close to the tracks at the far west end of the yard, which is dotted about with pine trees.

So much about the church and its surroundings symbolized my atavistic relationship with my great-great-grandfather: the railroad, his hotel, his stained-glass memorial window, the impressive stone shafts above his and Becky's headstones, marked by his children, "Our Father" and "Our Mother."

Bellevue Church reinforced my ambivalent feelings about the future: Could the homestead be held? Should it be, if I was destined to run Henry's course to some sort of tragic end? And what of that image in the mirror? Was it really the shade of Henry observing the helplessness of our states? If so, what purpose was served? Did he mean for me to chuck it all? Or was I becoming so obsessed in ancestor worship that it was all a figment of a subconscious state—say, a hallucination or a nightmare?

Notwithstanding certain most unhallucinatory and undreamlike phenomena about the episode—together with my earlier acceptance of Amos's ghostly influence—I tried to favor the nightmare theory. It seemed more sensible.

Then occurred an event which strongly suggested that hallucinations and dreams could not have been the answer; at least not all of it.

With the pressure of farm and tenant house work it took Lloyd and me more than three years to inventory and clean both garrets. We reserved this seemingly endless job for wet Saturdays.

On a snowy Saturday in 1958 we worked our way into a large stand of cobwebbed wine bottles. On removing the bottles we noted that they stood on what seemed a wooden platform.

"Just like your grandfather," mused Lloyd. "He put some boards under this stuff to keep it free of drafts between the flooring."

But the "boards" turned out to be two large portraits, framed in glass. We hauled them to the front garret's single bare electric bulb. They were twin daguerreotype photos of Henry F. and Rebecca Slaymaker, in old age. There was no mistaking Rebecca. She resembled her earlier portrait by her sister-in-law Hannah Evans. But she was more fleshy. Henry was a shallow, shrunken relic of the young dandy that Hannah saw in the 1812 era.

Then I did a double take: this was precisely the face in the mirror! Yet I'd never seen these daguerreotypes before, even as a boy. Of this I was certain. I evidenced so much surprise and confusion that Lloyd asked, "What's the matter?"

Vaguely, I said something about seeing Henry's likeness before, but never the picture. At first Lloyd understandably made little sense from my remark. Then, as we went about our cleanup, he must have sensed a ghostly implication. That such would come from me surprised him. For always before when he talked of White Chimneys' ghosts, I showed little interest. But now I became an absorbed listener over coffee in the kitchen, to which we immediately descended.

Lloyd's father had told him of three instances of haunting. Before my grandfather's refurbishment of 1907, he had kept tenant farmers in the back of the mansion. One family was petrified by a nocturnal sound of the death rattle emanating from the front bedroom. Tradition held that this was Amos's room. This family left immediately. The next occupants lasted a couple of months. These people were upset by an inexplicable appearance of lighting—weak lighting—with no visible source, again from the front wing. No rooms were specified. Finally, in the 1930s my grandparents' chef refused to stay overnight. Again, the lights. No one else was ever troubled by them.

I charged the death rattle bit to wind-blown house creaks. But there was a fleeting reservation: maybe Amos didn't like tenants in his mansion!

The lighting was something else again. I'd seen it in what I accepted as my nightmare, which now seemed less plausible. For the daguerreotype incident had overtones of that inexplicable but common phenomenon of one's recognizing a place that one has never seen before.

Even if this meeting with Henry was dreamed, I must be pardoned by even the most skeptical of materialists for concluding that said dream was as other-directed as the stares to which Amos's papers gave rise. Perhaps there was a connection. Ectoplasmic theorists might hold that Amos's spiritual desires were strongly enough embedded in his surroundings to influence his successors, especially those so sympathetically attuned to his own wavelength that they would follow his ghostly dictates. Could this have constituted the mansion's holding power? I didn't want to believe so. Yet I continued to exist as though I did. And this gives credence to what I had originally contended against but finally accepted: ectoplasm or no, the mansion was somehow trapping me as it had Amos and Henry.

15

WITH THE DETERIORATION of Henry F. Slaymaker's health during the mid-1850s, his son Samuel Cochran Slaymaker took over his responsibilities. Brother "Fleming" helped, for Samuel was frequently absent. As a budding civil engineer, he was busy job hunting. Continually in need of cash, he sought part-time political sinecures, so there was little time for farm work. Fleming bore a heavy work load, from which he soon tired. While relations between the brothers were always cordial, Fleming —after marrying—settled into one of the tenant houses and practiced law. Later he moved to Lancaster and puttered with minor political jobs for the rest of his days.

Rather than farm himself, Samuel hired a tenant farmer, Mr. Brack-bill. Reduced farm income, Samuel felt, could be more than compensated for through his political jobs and a career in civil engineering.

In 1852 Samuel became acquainted with one of the most noted engineers of the day, John C. Troutwine, whose textbooks were widely used in colleges and universities. Mr. Troutwine was interested in young Slaymaker, became his preceptor, and helped him to land his first position, that of a surveyor of the route of the proposed Phoenixville and Cornwall Railroad.

The short, stout young man with a close-cropped beard who boarded the train at Gap on the morning of May 24, 1852, was no doubt excited at the prospect of carving a niche in the world and seeking that long-awaited fortune.

"Arriving in Philadelphia about 10 o'clock in a heavy shower," he wrote. "Left 3½ o'clock in Reading cars for Phoenixville 28 miles up Schuylkill, beautiful scenery along the river. Passed in sight of Laurel Hill, Valley Forge, Maneyunk, Norristown, Port Kennedy. In the evening visited the Phoenixville Rolling Mills. Among other things saw them rolling railroad iron after night. A beautiful sight, some beautiful places around Phoenixville."

From his vivid descriptions of scenery and wildlife along the line of survey, it's obvious that Samuel enjoyed himself greatly. His party stayed in hotels and boardinghouses; sometimes farmers served them hearty luncheons, including pies and ice cream. Other farmers resented the railroad's crossing their lands and put dogs on them. Rattlesnakes were abundant. Samuel proudly noted in his journal that he killed one.

On Wednesday, July 4, the survey was completed. Samuel spent that night in Philadelphia with his Aunt Susan Cochran. On July 15 he reported: "Took the cars this afternoon at 2 o'clock at 11th and Market Streets. Arrived at home about 6 o'clock in the evening."

Throughout 1853 and 1854 Samuel was commissioned for more

railroad surveys. Between jobs he worked with Brackbill on the farm. Each day's activities were carefully noted in his diaries. He experimented with Mediterranean wheat, started farming tobacco, and went heavily into poultry, which was taken to Lancaster markets in wagons.

Congressman Thaddeus Stevens and Senator Simon Cameron were importuned for part-time political jobs. But his success in landing his first political situation was probably due as much to penmanship as to pull. Samuel's scrivening ability served him well as transcribing clerk in the state's House of Representatives; and later as assistant clerk to Pennsylvania's Board of Revenue Commissioners. In 1855 he was able to land a prestigious appointment: membership on Governor Pollock's staff. With the position went the rank of colonel. Responsibilities were purely ceremonial. He attended some public functions with the Governor and represented him at others.

His engineering sponsor, Mr. Troutwine, was pleased enough with Samuel's abilities to recommend him for a surveying effort of international importance, the laying out of a coast-to-coast railroad through Central America. It was to be called the Honduras Interoceanic Railway. Headquartered in London, it was financed with British money. Mr. Troutwine was chief engineer.

Samuel was one of twenty-six young engineers picked from various countries. Also with the party were Señor D. L. Elverado, Minister to the United States from Honduras; George R. Glidden, Esq., the company's manager in Honduras; Dr. Gustavus Holland, ex-surgeon in the U.S. Army in Mexico; an interpreter; two secretaries, one a specialist in clays; three commissaries; storekeepers, and cooks; labor would be supplied by Indian natives, "Caribs."

Given the international importance of the Honduras Interoceanic Railway, the *New York Times* and New York *Tribune* thoroughly covered the departure of the brig *Favorite* from New York harbor on April 16, 1857. Samuel noted in his diary:

Ordered to be on board the vessel this morning at 11:00 to sail at 12:00 noon, left the harbor at 2½ p.m. . . . took supper, and drew lots for berths. The shores here along either side are lined with beautiful residences. Beautiful view of New York and thousands of lights of various colors adds much to the beauty of the night. Pleasant and jovial party and all lay down well pleased with our first night on our voyage. Coming down among the thousands of vessels we passed the U.S. Steam Frigate "Niagra and Wabash"—large and magnificent war vessel.

Evidently the *Favorite* anchored in the harbor overnight, for early the next morning it passed Staten Island and the Battery, and by 3 P.M. was out of sight of land. Weather turned cold, and there were intermittent gales and snow squalls. The sea was very rough. Samuel was seasick for several days. He commented on whales spouting and on passing the steamer *Black Warrior,* from Havana to New York, which they welcomed with three cheers.

Samuel's day-by-day descriptions of violent, frightening storms and the tedium of being long becalmed on a flat, glassy sea under brassy skies are so vivid as to make one wonder if he had missed his calling.

The brig reached the port of Omoa, Honduras, three weeks later.

This is a town of about 800 inhabitants with the mountains rising over 7,000 feet behind it. At 5 p.m. we came to anchor about 100 yards from the beach. No docks here. Quite a formidable looking fort just at the landing but guns appeared to be all dismantled although the garrison is kept there. Found an American schooner in port about to sail to New Orleans. Dispatched letters to the States by the Captain. . . . Exceedingly pleasant evening. The beach lined with the townpeople and the mountains and shores ringing with the calls of monkeys, parrots, etc.

Samuel was intrigued by the colorful and primitive culture of Honduras. The Spaniards had lost control in 1821; but everywhere their culture was evident: a Roman Catholic mission, the broken-down Spanish fort, and the prevalence of the Spanish language and customs. Native Caribs were of mixed Indian, Negro, and Spanish descent. Samuel wrote on the evening of May 7:

As we walked to the upper part of the town, we found a "Wake" of a child, the body gawdily dressed, was laid out on a table. Some 4 or 5 drummers were at the center of the room and the crowd was encircled around it uttering the most hideous cries. This kept up all night. The drums were logs hollowed out and skins drawn over the ends.

After moving to Puerta Coballo, the party set about making the initial survey of the railway. They slept little the first night because of the clouds of mosquitoes and sand flies.

Friday, May 15:

I was one of a party of four paddling a canoe around a lagoon today putting up flags for triangulating for a topographical map. Very hot! About fifteen miles around. Very tired! Found no drinking water. Refreshed ourselves chewing sugar cane. Where we could see the bottom, saw plenty of fine fish, coral, and quantities of beautiful shells. Paddling a few hundred yards up a river at the head of a lagoon, very wild dark-looking place. The very place where alligators, of which there are, as well, sharks, aplenty in the lagoon.

He was with a party of eight on Saturday, May 16, which established a base line in the lagoon. Samuel's group had to be in water up to their necks nearly all day. The mosquitoes and other insects were devilish both day and night. Samuel noted that at one time when he was in the water, "a shark rose to the top about 40 feet from me. I happened to be prepared with a good pike pole; but fortunately he came no nearer me."

In the evenings, around campfires, they sang to the music of a guitar. They lived amid wild hogs, alligators, baboons, monkeys, and snakes in stifling heat and periodic torrential downpours. Some snakes were "of very bright colors, much resembling barber poles." Their only diversion was occasional dips in the cooling surf.

It soon became obvious that the task was insurmountable. A man died of yellow fever. Engineers began to quit. On Tuesday, June 2, as others came down with yellow fever, Samuel felt that he had had enough. He wrote in his diary:

Rained last night. Very little sleep because of mosquitos, out on the line, leveling. No rest for insects. Tendered my resignation this evening and received an honorable discharge. Salary continued and expense paid upon landing in New York.

Wednesday, June 3:

Making arrangements for going home. Sold many things to the parties staying. Caught an alligator about 2 feet long. Wish I could preserve it to take home. Two p.m., left camp Campana on my return home, paddling down the Rio Charrelicon in a canoe. Very pleasant ride. Stopped all night in a palm hut at the mouth of the river. Slept comparatively comfortable on a palm bed. Had a splendid bath in the surf in the evening.

He went back to Omoa and boarded the *Favorite*, which was taking on mahogany for the return voyage. After loafing and reading Henry James novels in the American consulate for three weeks, Samuel debarked for New York.

On Thursday, July 16, the brig approached Cape Hatteras. A wreck was lying on a bar of reef, directly in the ship's path. With much difficulty the captain managed to clear it.

If a few hours earlier while yet dark, we could scarcely have escaped and if so I would in all probability not now be writing this. Almost certainly it would have struck us. How thankful we ought to be for our deliverance from this danger. Our Captain showed evident signs of fright, turning quite pale and trembling so that he could scarcely give his orders, and indeed it seemed he did not quite know what orders to give. All others appeared calm, from observations.

The voyage ended on July 22:

A little after 4 o'clock we came to anchor in the quarantine grounds. We are in the midst of exciting scenes. Vessels almost in the hundreds around us, bands and music playing on some. Steam boats and excursion boats pass frequently. On one excursion boat we passed, before coming to anchor, quite a crowd were tripping it up in a giddy dance so that the vessel was pitching considerably. Here on either side, both Staten Island and Long Island, were hundreds of splendid residences. Directly on coming to anchor, the boarding officer from the customs house came on board. Soon a reporter from the port from which we sailed came for news of our voyage. About 5 o'clock a physician came on board and quarantined the vessel only three days and gave us a permit to land immediately which we very quickly did, having to leave our baggage until the vessel comes up. We landed through the quarantine gates, immediately made our way to a ferry station, taking the Staten Island Ferry boat to New York and now being landed once more on native soil and comfortably roomed at the Stevens House on Broadway.

Here ends my notes of the ever-memorable engineering excursion to this semi-civilized province of Central America.

While Samuel Cochran Slaymaker surely left his beloved father's funeral in 1860 feeling a keen sense of loss, there is no indication of frustration, the bad state of Henry's affairs notwithstanding. Now as the squire *de jure* as well as *de facto* he was solely responsible for the running of the plantation and the well-being of its mansion's inhabitants.

Besides his bachelor self there were his mother, Rebecca, and his unmarried sister, Isabella Angelica. He hit on a sensible plan for providing them a proper way of life and keeping White Chimneys in the family.

His father, Henry Fleming Slaymaker, died intestate. Since Henry's estate was certain to be in arrears for more than the value of his holdings, a will probably seemed to him redundant. But he gave Samuel to understand that the property was to be his. Hopefully, Samuel would find means to clean up debts and to hang on to White Chimneys.

The late squire's inventory showed $964.05 and debts totaling $4,650, a large portion of which represented Boyd heir claims. Fortunately, there seemed little danger from Boyd heirs. In earlier years Henry's North Carolina lawyer, Andrew Hoyle, had been able to keep them from instituting legal actions. He had written that they "were a poor lot" and easy to handle. By 1860 many were dead and others (and their descendants) had moved west.

Then—as would happen throughout his life—Lady Luck smiled on Samuel. The Civil War broke, and communications with Boyd heirs in the South became impossible. The Boyd issue became a dead letter.

In order to tidy up his financial affairs with the friendliest of creditors, Samuel borrowed $13,769.29 from his rich brother-in-law, Joseph Konigmacher, and bought from his father's estate the White Chimneys property and village. The value was based on 92 acres and 144 perches at $140 per acre. Within two years Samuel was able to free himself of debt, thanks to his highly "successful" marriage to Jane Elizabeth Cameron Redsecker, a dowery-laden young lady and a niece of President Lincoln's Secretary of War, Simon Cameron. Jane, a plump and cheerful young lady from the Donegal area of western Lancaster County, was the daughter of Samuel Redsecker, a well-to-do importer. Jane's relationship —even though distant—to Pennsylvania's political boss, Simon Cameron, could have been beneficial to Samuel if and when he needed help in securing political jobs. Happily, Jane's money lessened the need. Still, the Cameron connection was prestigious enough to enhance the Slaymaker family's image.

The price of Senator Cameron's delivery of Pennsylvania's delegates to Lincoln at the Republican nominating convention in 1860 was a seat in the cabinet: the Treasury, it was rumored. Cameron's reputation for shady dealing was responsible for his being made Secretary of War instead. The rapid buildup of an immense army occasioned logrolling galore between contractors and politicians. Secretary Cameron, perhaps wrongly, became suspected of corrupt practices. Lincoln replaced him with W. H. Seward, and Cameron was appointed Ambassador to Russia.

The Redsecker family and their respected Whitehill and Middleton relatives had roots deep in Colonial Lancaster County. So Jane Redsecker's marriage to Samuel Cochran Slaymaker was a well-attended occasion of note. On May 18, 1862, the old Whitehill-Redsecker mansion grounds were crowded with carriages. Well-dressed ladies and gentlemen debarked and ambled across the shaded lawn and into the mansion's living room, where the Reverend John J. Lane, minister of the Donegal Presbyterian Church, conducted the wedding service.

Colonel Slaymaker and his bride shared White Chimneys with his mother and old-maid sister. Both seem to have hit it off famously with cheery Jane. With an eye toward modernization and a consequent enhancement of the family's status, Samuel immediately set about committing some of Jane's dowery to a major renovation of the mansion.

The stairway in the Francis Jones kitchen was removed. In its place a pantry was built. Beside it a flight of stairs was installed to reach the cellar. The next pantry accommodated the passing of food to the dining room through an aperture cut through the forward wall.

The old kitchen fireplace was boarded over—rather hastily, it seems, since a pot, crane, and andirons were left inside. If ceiling rafters had not been plastered over as yet, they were now. Older, if not the original, flooring was replaced with new pine boarding. A huge cast-iron cooking range was placed before the onetime hearth. In the rear pantry was installed a sink to which water was fed by gravity. A windmill was erected over the well to raise water to the intake pipe. The forward pantry was also used to house ugly, factory-built cupboards of dark walnut in which china and glassware were stored.

The next wing (Amos's first addition) was turned into a commodious dining room. The wall running perpendicularly through the wing

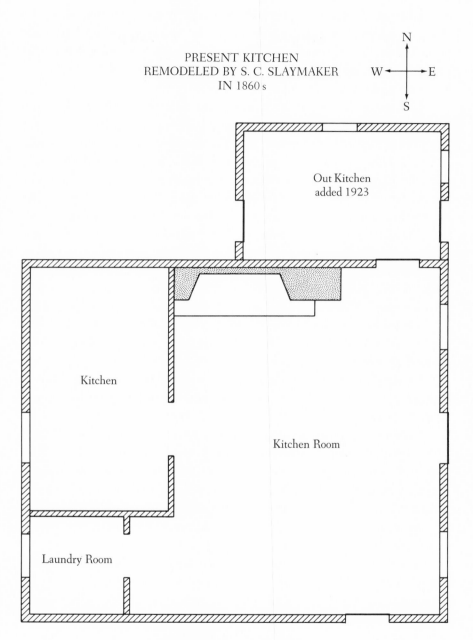

PRESENT KITCHEN
REMODELED BY S. C. SLAYMAKER
IN 1860s

N
W ← → E
S

Out Kitchen
added 1923

Kitchen

Kitchen Room

Laundry Room

(Originally Francis Jones Tavern)

was removed. Ceiling support was provided by two pillars modeled on the same classic motif as those Amos placed in his 1807 mansion to the fore. The original Federal mantels in the now enlarged dining room were removed and relegated to the garret. A contemporary marble mantelpiece for one fireplace was installed.

Samuel made no further architectural changes to the mansion. But he added what he considered an artistic touch to every fireplace in the front house, upstairs and down, save the one in the front room. Facings were set with glossy tiles of green and yellow. The front room fireplace had already been faced with Whitemarsh marble. This, thankfully, was not removed—probably because it would have been too much trouble. Both rooms in the mansion wing were now referred to as "parlors."

The kitchen, dining room, and first parlor were in constant use. The front parlor, reserved for company, was rendered staid and dark by heavy curtains and that newly fashionable dark walnut furniture, upholstered in glossy and prickly horsehair. Carpeting in both parlors became more all-encompassing and flowery. More marble-topped tables appeared. They were set with red plush picture albums, seashells under glass (perhaps some came from Honduras), and bric-a-brac curios. Framed photos replaced daguerreotypes.

Camphene and whale oil lamps were gone; those burning coal oil and kerosene replaced them. Some brass beds were bought. Currier and Ives prints dotted the walls, and wax flowers the mantels.

Samuel was intensely interested in horticulture. Now that he could afford adequate help, a landscaping project was embarked upon. New trees and shrubbery were planted. The flower garden became an expanding mass of brilliant hues, thanks to well-manicured banks of zinnias, petunias, marigolds, geraniums, and nasturtiums. Samuel passed weekends working in the garden. He particularly enjoyed pruning his much-loved rosebushes.

A wooden latticework was erected on the pillars of the front porch, and a trumpet vine grew through it. A new roof was put on the bathhouse, now equipped with a hand-operated clothes-washing machine and wringer. Samuel and his field help took baths here in summer months. In the winter the mansion's onetime second-floor sitting and sewing room—converted earlier to a bathroom—was used for ablutions. It's unlikely that the windmill produced power sufficient to raise water to

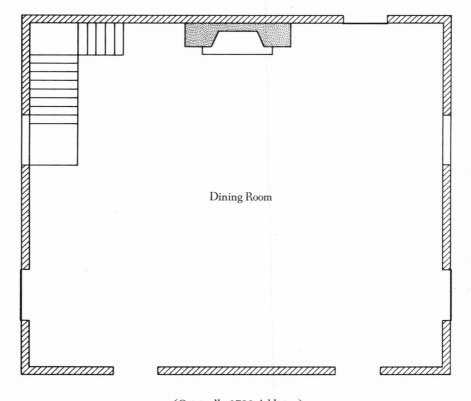

PRESENT DINING ROOM
REMODELED BY S. C. SLAYMAKER
IN 1860 s

N
W ←→ E
S

Dining Room

(Originally 1790 Addition)

the second story. A handsome carriage house was built behind the farmer's house, directly across the turnpike from the mansion. Since the colonel had taken up beekeeping, a "bee house" was set up.

All other outbuildings (the barn, tobacco shed, smokehouse, ice-house, woodshed, and privy) were put in top repair and whitewashed.

A steam plow (a field locomotive) was purchased. It was an excellent labor saver. So was a new McCormick reaper. Crop yields were enhanced by the expanded use of lime as a soil-building adjunct to manure. Samuel also used guano fertilizer and new chemicals made from bones and minerals.

It's small wonder that Colonel Slaymaker's White Chimneys plantation was soon known as a "showplace" farm, which managed to match the criteria set by the most exacting "scientific" gentlemen farmers of the day.

Notwithstanding an increasing number of factory-produced home-making implements, Jane and her sister-in-law Isabella Angelica carried a heavy work load. They helped and supervised hired girls in baking bread and putting up sauerkraut and preserves. While Samuel's clothes were store bought, some of the women's were prepared at home, a task made easier by a new Singer sewing machine. House cleaning meant strenuous work, particularly when it came to beating heavy carpets and drapery. They cooked huge meals. Breakfasts sometimes consisted of hot cakes, sausage, scrapple, and bacon. Lunches of pork, sauerkraut, and dumplings were common. In season, shad and roe were consumed. Evening dinner fare often comprised roasts of beef, pork, or lamb, assorted vegetables, and preserves, topped off with a favorite dish of Samuel's— ice cream. Favored beverages were homemade wines and ciders.

As could be expected, middle-aged Samuel became more stout. So did Jane. But their girths, together with those contented and smug countenances which their portraits reveal, were befitting. For if ever a couple was archetypical of its times, it was the solicitous squire and his adoring wife.

16

AFTER COMPLETING his High Victorian renovation, the Colonel turned back to his favorite work, civil engineering. He lived in an almost constant state of commutation. On becoming assistant engineer in charge of surveys for the Philadelphia and Reading Railroad, he worked on weekdays on location in Chester County and the Pottstown area. He always stayed in the best hotels. On weekends he returned to Slaymakertown by train. Saturdays were spent "in the flower garden" or "about the farm." So well ingrained was farm work that he continued such menial labor as fence repairing and butchering in company with tenant farmer Brackbill.

Without fail his diary entries for all Sundays passed in Slaymakertown read: "Salisbury—to Bellevue Church this a.m." While many people (and local maps) referred to the village as Slaymakertown, the Colonel persisted in using that old, familiar appellative, Salisbury. He usually went to church with his mother, sister, and Jane, to whom he referred in his diary as "Mrs. Slaymaker."

Sometimes on Fridays Jane took the train to Marietta, near Donegal, where she was joined at the Redsecker mansion by Samuel. On Sunday, after the service at Donegal Church, they entrained for Gap. On Monday mornings Samuel went back on his job.

When his work load was heavy, he sometimes remained in the Pottstown office of the Philadelphia and Reading over weekends. On these occasions he never failed to attend the Presbyterian church there. He whiled away free hours attending Republican Party and Masonic meetings. He was a member of Lodge Number 62 in Reading. But his most enjoyable leisure hours were passed on the farm.

There were frequent afternoon teas and prayer meetings in the front parlor. Calls were exchanged with the Duffields, the J. C. Walkers, and the Himes family of the onetime Sign of John Adams tavern property next door. When alone on Saturday evenings the family enjoyed group singing.

His mother, sister, and Jane took turns at the melodeon. They sang such contemporary favorites as "Shall We Gather at the River?" and Stephen Foster's songs. Foster had visited his sister in nearby Paradise some years before. She was married to an Episcopal rector, Edward Buchanan, the brother of James Buchanan. The Slaymakers had made his acquaintance, so his songs were always favorites at White Chimneys. Samuel noted in his diary a couple of songs which seemed incongruous as the favorites that they must have been: "Tenting Tonight" and "Just Before the Battle, Mother."

Samuel was unalterably opposed to the Civil War. He noted frequently to family and friends that he could not bear the thought of "shooting at his own countrymen." Left unmentioned was the fact that he didn't want them shooting at him.

His commitment to holding White Chimneys was as keenly felt as his father's and grandfather's. Samuel was not about to risk losing his inheritance through an untimely end in a war he considered to be unjustified. So he took an alternative common to many in his position. He paid a farmer to serve in his place and evidenced no sense of guilt on losing two close friends in action: a cousin, Captain Jonathan Slaymaker, who fell at Fort Donelson, and General John Reynolds (son of his father's friend, editor John Reynolds), who was killed at Gettysburg.

No better proof of Samuel's sense of rectitude vis-à-vis his Civil War actions—or better, the lack of them—was his retention of the title "Colonel." As noted, it went with his appointment to the Governor's staff in 1855. He served the Governor during one term but kept this incongruous-sounding appellative throughout the war and, indeed, until his dying day.

Colonel Slaymaker seemed as unconcerned with the day-to-day course of the war as with its consequences. The consequences looked bleak, indeed, by late June, 1863.

As a keen student of history (he was a founder of the Lancaster County Historical Society), the Colonel knew that his home had been threatened in the French war, during the Revolution, and in the 1812 war. It's inconceivable that he, like his well-informed peers, was unaware of the almost transparent Confederate plans for concluding the war signaled by General Lee's invasion of Pennsylvania. If Lee succeeded, the homestead would again be imperiled. This became obvious as the invasion progressed and rebel troops embarked on a policy of offering towns the alternatives of ransom or burning. Many citizens in the path of the invasion panicked and left their homes. Yet Colonel Slaymaker seemed unperturbed. His commuting to and from Salisbury and Pottstown continued uninterrupted.

With the Confederate victories at Fredericksburg and Chancellorsville, military ardor in the South peaked and presaged Lee's march to the North. He hoped to break Northern morale, destroy communications and supply lines, capture much-needed supplies, and finally force a negotiated peace.

On June 3 Lee moved his eighty-thousand-man army from Fredericksburg up the Shenandoah Valley corridor toward Pennsylvania. By June 12 Pittsburgh was panicked by newspaper reports that its industrial complex was Lee's objective. "Coal pits will be fired," the papers read. Fortifications were thrown up there, in Harrisburg, and even in Philadelphia.

Governor Curtin called on Pennsylvania's militia on June 16. "The enemy is approaching," his posters screamed. Philadelphia volunteers dragged their feet, and the Governor admonished them.

Between June 23 and 27 Lee advanced on Hagerstown, Maryland, and Carlisle, Pennsylvania. General Jubal Early's forces, under the field command of General John B. Gordon, entered York at 10 A.M., Sunday, June 28, while church bells were ringing. Only two churches opened. When the rebel band struck up "Dixie," their congregations "let out" and joined the staring, dumb-struck crowds on Market Street.

General Gordon ordered the American flag in Center Square pulled down. He told York's citizens that no harm would come to them as long as his soldiers were well treated and provisions and ransom funds of $28,000 were handed over. General Early made a gentlemanly speech in the same vein to town leaders in the courthouse. Meanwhile Carlisle fell, and Hanover was raided and burned.

Railroad facilities there were destroyed, and wire communications with Washington, D.C., were cut. A prime target was Harrisburg's rail network. Skirmishes were taking place at nearby Camp Hill.

The headquarters for defense of Lancaster County released handbills to militia companies headlined: "To the Susquehanna Boys!" Militia units and some Franklin and Marshall College boys were placed at strategic river-crossing points. A body of twelve hundred volunteers containing Philadelphia's famed City Troop crossed the river to Wrightsville on the rebel west shore. There they threw up fortifications. General Gordon moved east from York to engage them. After two cannon shells were lobbed into their positions, the militia took off across the bridge to Columbia. They left one dead behind. The bridge was then set afire, and an immediate rebel crossing was thwarted.

In his postcampaign account General Early reported that he aimed "to get possession of the Columbia bridge and cross my division over the Susquehanna and capture the Pennsylvania Railroad, march upon Lancaster, lay that town under contribution, and then attack Harrisburg in the rear, while it should be attacked in front by the rest of the corps. . . ." He also noted that he planned on sending General Gordon on a raid from Lancaster to Philadelphia.

Had the Lancaster-Philadelphia raid been carried out, hamlets like Slaymakertown on the main route would surely have been laid "under contribution."

General Early's plans were thrown awry by Union General Meade's advance on the Confederate rear near Gettysburg. After that horrendous and climactic battle the gray tide ebbed, and the emergency in Pennsylvania ended. There was a momentary panic a year later when General Early conducted a raid of reprisal on Chambersburg, Pennsylvania. The town refused to come across with a ransom of $100,000 and was summarily burned. Two-thirds of the citizenry became homeless. Fear subsided when the three thousand troops returned to the South.

It might be assumed that one holding the title of "Colonel" would have occupied himself in the emergency by aiding the militia-raising effort. This the Colonel did not do. He stayed on his job with the Philadelphia and Reading Railroad. Undoubtedly, in anticipation of a Confederate victory, the Colonel wished to be on record as a neutral—maybe one with Southern leanings—and had friends who would have come forth to prove the fact. General Early was a gentleman not bent on destruction for its own sake. But there could have been a method in his good manners. His prime aim was the disruption of Union communications. Yet he did not destroy York's depot and rolling stock. He told the town's leaders that this would not serve much purpose. He might well have hoped that the courting of Northern business leaders would speed a negotiated peace.

If such thoughts were entertained by some in the Confederate high command, they could have proved beneficial to the South had her armies destroyed the Union's at Gettysburg. Many Northern men of affairs were bitterly fed up with the war. Samuel was typical of them. A negotiated peace was what they were looking for.

White Chimneys' sole contribution to the Union effort came in the form of bandages. The women had neighbors in to prepare them, after the fashion of sewing bees.

On Friday, August 5, 1864, Samuel wrote: "Mother has taken very sick last night with an apoplectic stroke, and I remained today at home."

Saturday, August 6: "Mother still continues. I am very tired and am almost constantly with Mother."

On Sunday the seventh, for once there was no entry about church. He noted simply: "At Salisbury." On Monday the eighth he wrote: "At Salisbury. Mother continues no better."

The long death watch finally ended on Tuesday, August 9. "At Salisbury. Mother breathed her last at 7 o'clock this morning. Mrs. Shertz, Mrs. Himes, and Mrs. McIlvaine and Mrs. Greenleaf [the new tenant farmer's wife] very kindly attended to everything."

The funeral of Rebecca Slaymaker Cochran Slaymaker, daughter of the first Amos's sister Hannah, widow of Henry F., and mother of Colonel Samuel C., was held at 11 A.M. on Thursday, August 11, in a crowded White Chimneys. Bellevue's Reverend John Elliot conducted the service. A shiny black hearse with matching horses carried Rebecca to Bellevue Church for the last time. She was buried next to her husband, Henry.

Happily, Rebecca had lived long enough to witness the arrival of Samuel and Jane's first child, a daughter and her namesake. "Becky" was born at 3 A.M., May 9, 1864, at the Redsecker mansion and was christened a few weeks later at Donegal Church.

On Monday, April 10, 1865, the Colonel received joyous news. "Spent day in office at Pottstown. Plotting. News of surrender of Lee's rebel army received this morning and the town wild with excitement all day. The shops are all closed and everybody rejoicing. Bands parading the streets with processions following, cannons firing, flags flying, etc. Attended a large jubilee meeting at the Hall [probably Mason's] this evening. There were speeches and music, etc. Rain. . . ."

Wednesday the twelfth: "Working in office all day. Grand illumination of the town tonight in honor of the great Union victory. Dull and raining."

On Saturday, April 15, Samuel was in the office at Pottstown when came shocking and sad news: "Received news of the assassination of President Lincoln last night and his death this morning. Took tea at Mr. MacDonalds. . . ."

On Sunday the sixteenth he "went to the Pottstown Presbyterian

Church and heard a sermon on the death of the President. Dined at the Reverend Mr. Meigs."

Wednesday, April 18, was a "holiday on account of the funeral observances of President Lincoln," but, he wrote, "I worked in office at maps all day. . . ."

He was back in Salisbury on Saturday, April 22, and "walked to the R.R. [at Gap] at 1 p.m. and saw the funeral train of President Lincoln pass."

In the winter of 1866 Jane, pregnant again, removed to the Redsecker mansion. Their first son arrived on March 14, 1866. He was named Samuel Redsecker and, like his sister, was baptized at Donegal Church. Samuel and Jane had two more children: Henry Cochran in 1868, and Anna Cecelia in 1870. Anna lived only three weeks and was buried in the Bellevue churchyard.

While Samuel's family seemed to live congenially with his unmarried sister Isabella Angelica, they were probably happy when she at long last (at forty-eight) married David Agnew and moved with him to Mercersburg, Pennsylvania. Now the mansion was Samuel's in fact, as it always had been in name. But his calling kept him away virtually full time, save on the weekends which he enjoyed so immensely. Often after church in spring and summer months Samuel drove Jane and the children to Gap Hill woodlands, where they searched for wild flowers.

Colonel Slaymaker made almost a score of railroad surveys. None netted him much income. He didn't seem to care and was always eager to accept the challenge of new projects. But Jane's money was draining away, because of the Colonel's proclivity for keeping up with the Joneses. There were also several bad investments and a couple of unpaid loans to cousins.

In the early 1880s much of Colonel Slaymaker's work was in the Lancaster city area. A home was bought there on lovely "Colonial row" on East Orange Street, Number 230. During summer months the family went back to White Chimneys, where Samuel visited on weekends. The farm made a little money under the tenant farmer, Mr. Greenleaf. However, by the early 1890s the Colonel did not have enough to maintain showplace status. By the time of his death in 1894 it was heavily mortgaged.

The Colonel was active in Lancaster's political, social, and civic affairs. He became city engineer and was developing an improved sewer system at the time of his death.

His last diary entry was made on Thursday, February 1, 1894: "Dull raw cold east wind. Strong cold N.W. wind this afternoon and snow squalls. In office [in Lancaster] at maps all forenoon and part of afternoon. Out with Chairman McCompsay looking after new sewer. Had men go in Water Street sewer exploring for size of the Orange Street sewer, etc."

The next entry, February 2, was pasted into his diary by Jane. It's a long clipping from the Lancaster *New Era*'s front page, headlined, "Colonel Slaymaker Dead." It was subtitled: "A fatal stroke of apoplexy. The well-known civil engineer stricken on the street this morning, dying shortly after noon—sketch of a busy career."

Then followed a lengthy account of his family's background and his career. The Democrat *Daily Examiner* of Saturday, February 3, was respectful, but not so lengthy in its treatment of the news as the Republican *New Era*.

The *New Era* reported:

Col. Slaymaker left his home at 230 E. Orange Street this morning in his usual health and started down town. He intended taking the 9:14 train on the Quarryville Railroad to go to a point and make a survey. He passed down West King Street and in front of Hager's store he was observed to totter and would have fallen to the sidewalk had not someone supported him. A coupe was summoned and the partly unconscious form was lifted inside and driven rapidly to Col. Slaymaker's residence. Dr. M. L. Herr was summoned and later Dr. F. A. Muhlenberg. Col. Slaymaker relapsed into deep insensibility and the doctors pronounced it apoplexy. The entire left side was affected, and it was seen that his condition was critical. He never recovered consciousness and shortly before 1:00 he passed away.

Ironically, the Colonel departed this world in financial straits reminiscent of his father's. There was little money and no will. Nor were there any burial instructions. Had he anticipated his passing, Samuel would have probably opted for interment at Bellevue Church. But Lancaster had been the family's home for almost twenty years, and he was a prominent member of that community. So Jane felt constrained to have the funeral and burial there. It was held at 230 East Orange Street on February 5, 1894, and was well attended by his many friends and town notables.

Colonel Slaymaker was buried in Woodward Hill Cemetery, not far from the grave of James Buchanan.

17

PORTRAITS OF THE COLONEL and Jane were painted by Baron Leo Von Osko, an artist very much the rage in Lancaster around the turn of the century. In portraying Jane as a rather austere Victorian lady, the Baron erred. She was really a bubbling, joyful woman: completely open, kindly, and uncomplicated. This I have from those who knew her well, my father and grandparents.

Colonel Slaymaker's likeness more nearly matches the man—a stern and stuffy Victorian squire. That Von Osko hit the mark is borne out by testimony from a couple of aged Lancastrians who remember the Colonel, handed-down tidbits of family gossip, and his own diaries.

In two respects he was like his father, Henry F., and his grandfather, Amos. He was also a prisoner of his plantation. His sole source of motive power, like theirs, was a burning desire to perpetuate White Chimneys within the family. Like them, too, he evidenced a tenacious singleness of purpose in pursuing well-defined objectives. But unlike old Amos—and to a lesser degree Henry F.—there was nothing abrasive about his personality. It was glossed by a patina of refinement that was the hallmark of his mother's family, the Cochrans.

He was very much like his Uncle Samuel Cochran. Scheming tactics on the part of the late surveyor general of the Commonwealth would have been viewed tolerantly by most people. Cultured persons of his sort could do little that was really wrong. So it was with Colonel Slaymaker when it came to his singular behavior during the Civil War.

The Colonel's temperament, then, was a blend of the paramount traits in his father's and mother's bloodlines. He was self-seekingly aggressive—but always circumspectly so. Never acting from desperation, he calmly awaited the main chance, and when it came, he quietly seized it. He was serenely confident of holding White Chimneys. So was I, at long last.

It wasn't that I sensed beyond-the-grave influences exercised by my great-grandfather. A shade of the Colonel's would have been too properly conformist to stoop to the bizarre. And, as noted, haunting was no longer necessary. Already hooked, I was reconciled to remaining so. Actually, I'd become content with my lot. There was no sense of the euphoria experienced during my first months as a squire. Neither did I feel trapped, frustrated, and depressed, as I was throughout the period of my identification with Henry F. I'd become instead contentedly resigned to things as they were and was optimistic about the future.

There was cause for some optimism. My business was garnering better returns. My writing royalties increased. The farm and rental properties —now in top repair—were in the black. Pleasing windfalls these, conducive to feelings as felicitous as those experienced by the Colonel a century before when he engineered the loan from his brother-in-law and achieved security through a successful marriage. His course and mine continued to parallel when, on October 24, 1959, I got remarried.

By the Colonel's definition my marriage was not as successful as his. My grandfather often noted that his father's was "a love match," and that Jane's "money had nothing to do with it." Could be. But her dowery proved very helpful to the Colonel, and he didn't marry until he was thirty-four. I couldn't resist thinking that Jane was worth the wait. Accepting at face value that old saw about some girls with money often being as nice as others with none, I had been seeking to emulate my great-grandfather. But love won out over pragmatism in 1958 when I met Sarah Elizabeth Hazzard.

Sally—or Sal, as she was called—worked in a large New York advertising agency and lived with her mother in a rambling Victorian house in Yonkers, New York. Her father, a White Plains lawyer, had died six months before we met.

Sal was weekending in Lancaster for the christening of a daughter of a cousin, one of my oldest friends. I was to be her blind date for a party. On succeeding weekends, I drove to Yonkers and Sal visited her cousin's family in Lancaster. On a couple of occasions I cooked dinners at White Chimneys—T-bone steaks and German fried potatoes. My two girls, now ten and eight, were often with us. Unbeknownst to me, they regaled Sal with my culinary abilities. When we became engaged in the spring of 1959, Sal's mother asked her how a noncooking career girl like herself could cope in the kitchen.

"Oh," she replied, "I won't have to worry. Sam's a terrific cook." She went on to describe my steaks and potatoes, and added, "Libby and Caroline tell me he makes wonderful Spanish rice!" But it turned out that from the day my bride moved into White Chimneys I haven't so much as shoved a skillet! Sal learned fast. And she was a topnotch typist. I never learned to type. My magazine work was done longhand, and typists were hired.

Sal had less trouble with the cooking than with the portraits. While she sensed no spiritualistic manifestations (I never mentioned mine), the unblinking stares of the portraits was discomforting, particularly when she was alone in the house. But after joining me in researching the papers, she felt progressively more at home with them. Once familiar with the earthly travails and small talk in letters of our predecessors, their portraits became to her—as they had long since been to me—intimate friends.

Prior to Sal's arrival my only expenditures on the mansion were for redecorating. Major cash outlays were lavished on the farm and tenant houses. This budding homemaker was at least deserving of proper kitchen facilities and an efficient heating plant. So budgeting plans were revamped. I blew myself on conversion to an oil burner, a modern kitchen, and a laundry room.

An architect friend designed the kitchen for the north pantry (where I had the old gas range) and the laundry for the south pantry. In repainting, both were blended with the restored Francis Jones room, which continued to serve as an everyday dining room. But Sal soon refurbished the old White Chimneys silver and set the formal dining room (Amos's first addition) for the use of company.

One evening on coming in from work I stood transfixed in the kitchen door. The Empire dining room table (set with silver candelabra) had been freshly polished. Four Wertmüller miniatures were grouped in the southeast corner of the room. Under them was a Hepplewhite drop-

Samuel Redsecker Slaymaker II before present dining room fireplace.
Wertmüller paintings hang above mantel.

leaf table on which stood Faithful's lovely silver teapot. On the Empire
sideboard, beneath an 1800 vintage gilt mirror, was a Federal period
coffee service with matched candlesticks. On the east wall was hung that
charming primitive of White Chimneys, circa 1820, by Hannah Slaymaker Evans.

Throughout following months Sal continually refined the décor by
examining piles of china, cut glass, and silver, stored in cupboards and
boxes in the onetime servants' rooms over the kitchen. This was the only
area I had not had time to investigate thoroughly.

An interesting find was a collection of Export China plates imprinted on the back "S. Redsecker, Importer"—probably a gift from Jane's father. Sal thought the china would go well on the plate rail in the Francis Jones room. I demurred. They were not of an early enough period to match that room's artifacts.

"But," she said, "they do belong in the house. And, anyway, the place has evolved in such a manner that you can't have a pure restoration." She went on to note that the mansion's real charm lay in its mélange of architectural periods, the direct results of almost continuous habitation since the first construction.

I knew this, of course, but must have been too close to the place to grasp possible implications. The plates went on the rail as a constant reminder of Sal's pithy observation. It would lead to an idea destined to rob the mansion of its captivating power.

Nineteen fifty-nine was a red-letter year at White Chimneys for a reason other than the arrival of its new mistress. An Amish farm family was taken on, for the first time.

The Amish sect split from the Mennonites in Switzerland in 1693. Their leader, Jakob Ammann, felt that Mennonites were too worldly. So his followers—the "Amish"—adopted what they believed to be a more stringent, hence more Godly, life style. They eschewed all ways save that of husbandmen.

The first Amish emigrated to Pennsylvania in the middle of the eighteenth century. While Mennonites eventually became bilingual (they now speak English only), the Amish spoke High German and continue to do so. English was used only when necessary.

The Amish have always lived in a world of their own. By virtue of their exclusiveness and the availability of farmland—together with the westward movement of British groups—Amish of the eighteenth and nineteenth centuries generally owned their own farms and rarely hired out as tenants or laborers.

This situation has now changed. In 1945 an acre of prime Lancaster County farmland sold for $189.66. By 1959 it was $494.24 (in 1969 it was $924.35). Thus new land for starting Amish farmers comes very high. And even though they don't use gasoline-propelled farm equipment, the Amish are victims of price inflation. The crowning blow is the school tax. An Amish farmer with one hundred acres pays a school tax of $700. Added to road and per capita taxes, his entire local tax bill comes close to $1,000. Since the Amish insist on their own one-room schoolhouses, they are opposed to the immense public Taj Mahals of brick and glass which they're forced to finance. Then there are state and federal income taxes, which some Amish successfully evade. There's the well-known story of the Amish farmer who said he didn't pay his federal income tax because "once you start you can't stop."

All of which has brought them to tenant farming and, lately, to building and painting contracting, their first moves away from purely agrarian pursuits. Many Amish are migrating to the Midwest and Canada.

Don Ranck strongly advised me to seek an Amish farmer. The Amish custom of intrafamily cooperation ensured growing the maximum amount of tobacco.

One Amos Yoder applied. Preliminary talks between the two of us led to a meeting with his family. On a Saturday morning in December, 1959, Amos, his wife, Barbara, their three small children, and Barbara's father, with two of her brothers, all in neat, black garb, drove into the lane in two buggies. Sal and I met them in the kitchen room and, after introductions, got down to business.

Amos Yoder's father-in-law, Jacob Stoltzfus, led the discussion. A successful patriarch type with a large white beard, Jake owned a farm of 120 acres and had fathered eighteen children.

We agreed on virtually the same arrangement I had with Don. The only hangups were electricity and plumbing. The Amish use neither. But I didn't want these facilities in the farmer's house to deteriorate, and kerosene lamps seemed conducive to fire; "Papa Jake" suggested a sensible solution.

"Now, Samuel," he said, "if you *order* Amos to use electricity and plumbing, he'll just have to tell the bishop that the landlord ordered it."

I said, "O.K., Amos, I order you to use the electricity and plumbing." It was agreed.

We were about to move to another subject, but Amos, who had been quietly intent, interrupted. "Samuel, don't forget to order me to use the electric milking machine, too!"

I quickly obliged.

Arrangements were made for the Amos Yoders to take over from the Don Rancks on the traditional beginning date for Lancaster County farmers' agreements, All Fools' Day, April 1, 1960. Don had a successful sale and entered Millersville State College. He promised to come back to see us and has been as good as his word. On winter weekends the Ranck family sometimes skate on our farm pond. Over the years his advice has been invaluable.

There was still another newcomer who would influence life at White Chimneys.

In 1958 Bellevue Church needed a new minister. I was elected to the Pulpit Committee charged with the responsibility of finding one. The committee drove to Princeton's Theological Seminary to interview candidates. One Samuel Argyle Huffard—a lanky ex-footballer from Philadelphia—suited our fancy and we his. After candidating in the Bellevue pulpit, he accepted the charge and was ordained as the church's nineteenth pastor.

Sam and his new bride, Barbara, moved into the Gap manse in the summer of 1958. On marrying us he turned down a cash honorarium. So I gave him his first fly rod, and we became angling companions.

My research interested Sam. He thought that he was distantly related to "some Boyds in Virginia." Like most ministers he was not overpaid and allowed as how he'd like to reopen the Boyd case and relieve me of the burden that was White Chimneys. The site was a natural for a housing development, he said.

He needled Sal, as well. Jake provided Barbara Yoder with an Amish cleaning woman. Sal had none. Sam never tired of reminding Sal that the squire's wife, at the very least, should be able to "keep up with the Yoders." I broke down and we hired one, two days a week.

Often on winter Saturdays Sam dropped into the tobacco-stripping cellar and entered into friendly theological disputations with Amos. As a postgraduate student of Kierkegaard's Christian existentialism, Sam was well prepared. Buttressed by Sam's philosophizing and a happy marriage, I approached the last stage of my research into White Chimneys' story with enthusiasm surpassing that for earlier eras. After all, I was a witness to some of the story, and as the home's past was blending with contemporary times, my decisions were now central to its future.

PART IV

Contemporary

White Chimneys today

I am quite convinced that we are approaching the end of an era. I don't know quite what will happen to us, but I have faith in our common sense, just as I have faith in our inheritance.

JOHN P. MARQUAND, *The Late George Apley*

18

At the time of Colonel Slaymaker's stroke, his eldest son was at work several blocks away in a tacky red-brick building nestled among warehouses on Water Street. Emblazoned across its front and sides in white paint was "Slaymaker and Barry, Padlock Manufacturers."

Samuel Redsecker Slaymaker was a short, stout, pink-complexioned and redheaded young man of twenty-eight. Stern of mien, he moved swiftly among banging punch presses instructing an employee here, helping to set up a press there. By the flaming furnace in the foundry he checked the work of his molders. When the stunning news of his father's collapse came, he rammed his black derby on his head and charged from the factory for his family's Orange Street home.

He was joined there by his twenty-six-year-old brother, Henry Cochran, and his sister, Rebecca. "Harry," an attractive young man, had come from the bank where he clerked; Rebecca, thirty and very prim, from the public school where she taught. They were at bedside with grieving Jane when the Colonel died.

There was no question about hard-driving Samuel R. taking over as family head. He was his father's favorite. Perhaps the Colonel saw in him qualities lacking in himself which might eventuate in another family fortune. It was understood that "Bud"—his father's nickname for him—would become White Chimneys' new owner and that he must find ways to "have and hold," mortgage-free.

Bud spent the winters of his early years at 230 East Orange Street in Lancaster; summer months were passed in Slaymakertown. There he helped with farm chores, attended Bellevue Church, and, in company with his father, fished neighborhood streams. In Lancaster he attended public school. After graduating from high school he entered Franklin and Marshall College. After two years the family's worsening financial plight necessitated his dropping out and going to work.

The Colonel wangled an engineering situation for Bud on the Pennsylvania Railroad. He rapidly became adept and was assigned to design a large stone railroad bridge spanning the Conestoga. Plainly he had a bright future in engineering. But Bud guessed that big money was not to be made in this field. Although he revered his father, there was a definite predisposition on Bud's part not to emulate him. While the Colonel had been widely respected as a first-rate civil engineer who loved his work, the fact was he never made much money.

The shabby genteel idiom in which he was brought up was galling to Bud. He saw his salvation in the acquisition of money and, as he was later to say, "never working for anyone but myself." Manufacturing seemed the answer. Perhaps Bud's familiarity with railroad switch and signal locks was responsible for his idea to manufacture padlocks. There were few mass producers of padlocks. Most were made individually by skilled locksmiths and were expensive. Bud bided his time while searching for a financial source.

One of his P.R.R. surveys was on the road's main line on the east shore of the Susquehanna River near the hamlet of Highspire, a few miles east of Harrisburg. Bud took meals in a large white farmhouse near the line of survey called the White House. It was owned by one Frederick Cohr, a substantial farmer of German descent. Bud became interested in one of Mr. Cohr's daughters, petite, pretty, and dark-haired Mina Louisa. In following months he made many weekend visits to the White House.

Mina—called Minnie—had a sister, Alice, who was married to a John Barry. After securing a loan from a rich landowning friend of the elder Slaymaker, Bud and John Barry founded in 1888 the padlock manufacturing firm of Slaymaker and Barry in Lancaster. On June 27, 1895, Bud and Minnie were married in the Christian Church in Harrisburg. The couple moved into 230 East Orange with bachelor Harry, spinster Rebecca, and widowed Jane.

Minnie's first years of marriage were trying. Bud was constantly busy at his factory and often took extended sales trips. Jane was kindly disposed to Minnie. So was Harry. But Rebecca disliked the Cohrs' recent-vintage German background. Their fundamentalistic church was not calculated to please her either. It did not matter that Minnie had attended Lebanon Valley College and that her maternal side were Scots-Irish with Colonial roots. Rebecca, a prudish and fanatical student of her family's genealogy, did not approve of the marriage. Her continual collecting of family data (for a genealogical history) magnified Minnie's sense of not belonging.

Rebecca had been graduated from the State Teachers College at Millersville and did graduate work at Columbia University. She taught in various Lancaster area schools but rarely lasted more than a year in each. Bud was greatly annoyed when Rebecca sold two portraits to a Philadelphia art collector.

Whatever the price, Rebecca probably thought it a bargain. For the paintings *were not of her ancestors.* They were of Gustavus Hesselius and his wife, by Gustavus, more valuable by far than any family likenesses. She also sold to the collector Adolph Wertmüller's diary. Both paintings and diary were in turn sold to the state's Hall of the Historical Society in Philadelphia.

During Minnie's first summer at White Chimneys, when she and Jane were house cleaning, they came across a small packet of letters from James Buchanan to the late Colonel's sister, Hannah Cecelia Konigmacher. Jane said that Rebecca had been urging their destruction, that they reflected an "unmentionable relationship." Had it not been for Rebecca's badgering, her mother would probably have never done what she did. In the presence of Minnie, without so much as a glance at their contents, Jane took the letters to the flower garden and burned them.

In addition to helping Rebecca with her genealogical research, bank clerk Harry spent his leisure hours in church and Y.M.C.A. work. The filling of autograph books with signed messages from family and friends held great attraction for Harry. An entry of his father's was typical of the Colonel: "Health, Honor, Happiness, Health to all the World, Honor to those who seek for it, Happiness in our homes. Papa S. C. Slaymaker; 1891."

His brother's lines from Shakespeare reflected an entirely different temperament. Maybe they were meant to jog Harry. Certainly they were prophetic: "There is a tide in the affairs of men which taken at the flood leads on to fortune, neglected—all the voyage of life is bound in shallows and in miseries. Aug. 18, 1891. Your Brother, S. R. Slaymaker."

White Chimneys' new squire would catch the tide and bring the plantation to its balmiest days.

State intestate law dictated that one-third of Colonel Slaymaker's estate go to the widow and that the remaining two-thirds be split among his three children. They turned their shares over to Jane. This was in the nature of a holding operation on the part of Bud, whose arrival as a successful entrepreneur was recognized by all with the sobriquet "S.R."

By 1896 S.R. had acquired sufficient income from the lock firm to buy White Chimneys and its farm and tenant houses from his mother for $8,500. Also, on April 18, 1896, Minnie had her first child. The baby was named after the Colonel, Samuel Cochran Slaymaker II.

As the lock business prospered, additional factory buildings were erected. John Barry was bought out. The firm became Slaymaker Lock Company. By 1905 S.R. was financially able to foot a long-planned-for project, the refurbishing and modernizing of White Chimneys. He aimed to complete the job by 1907, in time for a celebration of Amos Slaymaker's mansion's first century.

A major repair and painting job was embarked upon. Central heating was installed, together with plumbing, electric lights, and telephone. All outbuildings were renovated. Three of the old tenant houses were razed and, as noted, on their sites S.R. built new ones. The family then took up year-round residence at White Chimneys.

S.R. commuted to Lancaster on a trolley line of which he was a founding manager. Little Sam rode with him to the Yeates School in Lancaster, a private Episcopal institution named for Jasper Yeates.

The family of four (Helen was born in 1905) eagerly awaited the day set for White Chimneys' centennial. Engraved invitations with a photo of the mansion were sent to a large guest list.

The Lancaster *Intelligencer Journal* on September 27, 1907, reported:

A DELIGHTFUL RECEPTION GIVEN ON THURSDAY
BY MR. AND MRS. S. R. SLAYMAKER

A Centennial reception, which proved a most delightful affair, was given on Thursday evening by Mr. and Mrs. Samuel R. Slaymaker, at their

Samuel Redsecker Slaymaker I
Painting by John Miller

His wife, Mina Cohr Slaymaker
Painting by John Miller

home, White Chimneys, at Slaymakertown. It was attended by about three hundred persons, coming from the neighborhood, Lancaster and a distance. The occasion of the reception was the one hundredth anniversary of the erection of the Slaymaker home, the beautiful residence which is the object of admiration of the people who pass in the trolley cars. It was built in 1807, by Amos Slaymaker, great-grandfather of Samuel R. Slaymaker. . . . It has remained in the name ever since and has been occupied by a direct line to the present time. A dancing floor and orchestra stand were erected on the lawn and the side porch was extended and covered. The grounds were elaborately lighted with strings of electric lights and Japanese lanterns. The house was also prettily illuminated and was decorated with potted plants, palms and autumn leaves. Music was furnished for the dancing by Stork's orchestra, and refreshments were served by Caterer Eckert. . . .

S.R. anticipated the outbreak of World War I and foresaw an export boom in padlocks when European plants would convert to armaments.

Throughout 1913 he produced at top volume. Locks were stored in warehouses throughout Lancaster. Other plants were "slow" at the time, so his fellow businessmen thought S.R. demented.

When war came in August, 1914, S.R. entrained for New York to visit exporters. His return was graphically described by an old employee: "S.R. got off the trolley at Columbia and West End avenues wearing his derby and carrying a rolled-up umbrella. He walked that fast way of his up the street and came in the shipping room, slapped the derby and umbrella on a packing box and wiped his face with a handkerchief. Then he said: 'All right boys, let 'em go!' "

Warehouses were emptied of padlocks. For days shipments left the P.R.R. depot. Since S.R. had negotiated higher prices, he made a killing. He went the Colonel one better. Once convinced by his father of the futility of war, he set about to profit at the expense of those foolish enough to wage it.

This was the takeoff point in S.R.'s career. He would emerge as one of Pennsylvania's foremost business leaders in fields as diverse as asbestos manufacturing, newspaper publishing, book printing, public utilities, real estate development, banking, transportation, and farm management. (He owned four farms in addition to White Chimneys.)

In 1913 Jane was born; and in 1915, William Frederick, or "Bill." S.R.'s eldest son, Samuel Cochran Slaymaker II, joined the ROTC at Yale. He achieved the rank of captain in the Quartermaster Corps. After duty in stateside encampments he was scheduled for Vladivostok to fight the Bolsheviks. But his call never came, and in 1919 he was mustered out.

Young S.C. II's boyhood years on the farm had been idyllic. With Gap chums he swam and fished in the Pequea, rode horseback in the Welsh Mountains, and started a baseball team that played in the cow pasture. He went to preparatory school at Lawrenceville. Over winter and spring vacations White Chimneys was opened for house parties for his school friends. They danced with Lancaster girls and took madcap rides up and down the Gap hill in S.R.'s Marmon auto, one of the first on the "pike."

After the war S.C. II went to work for the lock company, married a Harrisburg girl, Martha Fletcher, and bought a home in Lancaster.

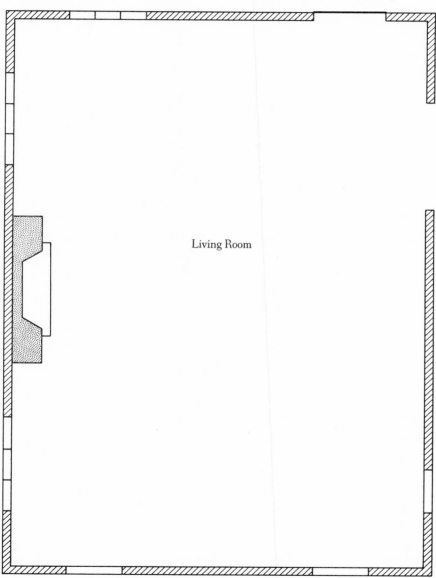

Living Room

S.R. was a rough taskmaster of his eldest son. He refused to permit him to play golf. "Young men who play golf," he said, "never amount to anything."

But he did encourage fox hunting. A singular commentary this on changing times. Today up-and-coming businessmen embrace golfing as a prerequisite to their calling and generally eschew fox hunting as a pastime fit for dilettantes, who, to quote the late U.S. Senator Joseph Grundy, "do nothing but do it well."

S.C. II's training regime paid off. He would take the firm through the depression, expand his father's real estate developments, and become involved in business and church association on a national level.

On January 1, 1923, Martha and S.C.'s first child was born, a son named Samuel Redsecker Slaymaker II. A cable announcing the arrival of his namesake was sent to S.R., then in Europe. He returned with dispatch to find a sign hanging on the baby's bassinet reading: "Don't touch the baby," placed there by a very nervous father.

By the early 1920s S.R. decided that White Chimneys needed a new addition. Three children and a staff of four resident servants required more space. It was fitting, too, that he, as the plantation's most successful squire since Amos, advertise the fact architecturally. So in 1923 a Lancaster architect was retained to convert the rear second floor of the mansion to servants' quarters and to add a west wing.

Viewed from outside, the new addition blended perfectly with the 1807 building. Not so inside, where ad hoc aberrations were born of necessity. Two second-story west windows, for example, became medicine and linen cabinets; another was converted to an inset panel for a portrait.

The entire ground floor of the west wing became a large ballroom. Since the west-facing bedroom of the 1807 wing now had a linen closet instead of a window, a skylight window was installed. It was operated with a long pole with a hook on the end.

While a fireplace was built in the ballroom's west wall, S.R. put none in two new upstairs bedrooms. The new chimney went straight up the west wall. It contributed to a grand total (and a final one!) of five white chimneys.

S.R. put a tennis court on the east lawn. The smokehouse was rebuilt as a playhouse for Jane and Bill. An artificial run, diverted from the pasture's stream, spilled into a waterfall and pool in the west lawn. The barn and tobacco shed were rebuilt, and an additional tobacco shed was erected in the north pasture. A three-car garage and a workshop were built. Tenant houses were generally spruced up.

During the early 1920s S.R.'s family traveled extensively in Europe. Jane and Bill attended a private school in France. S.R. wrote and privately published a book about their tours, *European Holiday*.

While in Italy he got the idea for a flower garden, laid out à la Italia, for White Chimneys. Marble benches and a fountain were purchased and shipped to Gap. The garden, placed in 1925, had the water fountain in its center, concentrically surrounded by four water lily pools and four flower beds. A pergola was built at the northern extremity. Lengthwise, the garden was enclosed with arborvitae hedges.

Before the war, portraits of Minnie and S.R. were painted by a Lancaster artist, John Miller. Baron Von Osko did one of young S.C. II in a sailor suit. After the west wing was added there was wall space sufficient for more paintings. So they were ordered, virtually on a wholesale basis, from Mr. Miller and his artist daughter, Lucy Miller Wellens. Immense paintings in the Sargent style were done of each of the children.

Four of S.R.'s five farms were virtually contiguous, and he numbered them. White Chimneys was "number one"; Duffield Manor, two; Belmont, three; and Avondale (next to the Wilmington Road), number four. Number five was on the Maryland line in the Cedar "barrens." Each farm had a tenant farmer who reported directly to S.R.—usually on Friday evenings in the front parlor of the 1807 wing.

White Chimneys became a summer home after S.R. bought a town house on Lancaster's Duke Street. Built in the mid-nineteenth century by a rich rifle manufacturer, Henry Leaman, the house was an immense Italian Palatinate pile containing four floors and more than twenty-five rooms.

Because of the perpetual nature of life at White Chimneys, its owners did not allow period petrifaction to set in. Perhaps some recognized the earliest furnishings as more aesthetically appealing than those of more recent times. But the inhabitants were not maintaining a museum; rather, at all times, an up-to-date home. This explains the steady

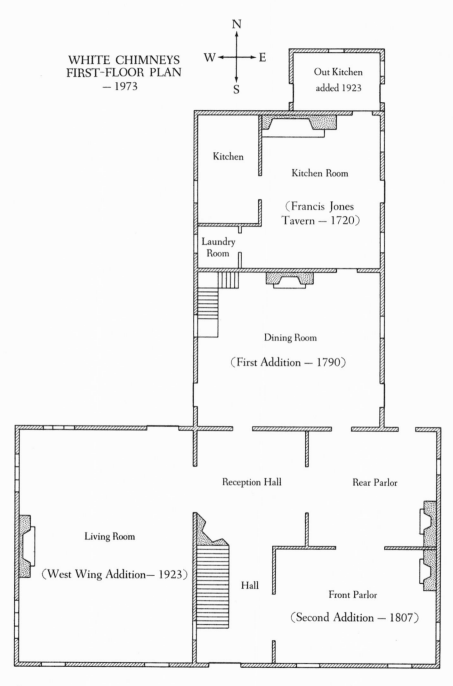

WHITE CHIMNEYS
FIRST-FLOOR PLAN
— 1973

N
W ← → E
S

Out Kitchen
added 1923

Kitchen

Kitchen Room

(Francis Jones
Tavern — 1720)

Laundry
Room

Dining Room

(First Addition — 1790)

Reception Hall

Rear Parlor

Living Room

(West Wing Addition— 1923)

Hall

Front Parlor

(Second Addition — 1807)

relegating of fine early pieces to the rear house and garrets, a process begun by culture-conscious Henry F. and continued by the Colonel, himself certainly a devotee of things aesthetic. Obviously, there were never mass movements. Such usually result in total "cleanouts." Marriage caused some diminution in furnishings. But many pieces were held because of sentiment and their intrinsic worth and beauty. It's likely that at all times early pieces were mixed with the contemporary. For even tycoon S.R.—whose interests lay primarily in fields other than the artistic—kept the odd piecrust table here, a Hepplewhite card table there. Such pieces evoked a sense of permanence which S.R. had learned from the Colonel to revere; and the Colonel, in turn, from Henry F. Still, S.R. could afford to update with quite a heavy hand, and did so.

His new ballroom's ceiling was divided, lengthwise, in three sections, each concavely curving. It and the walls were stuccoed and painted a light yellow. The fireplace was faced with red brick. Three brass chandeliers blended with his new furniture; heavy, dark, and of Moorish design, the whole compared favorably with Palm Beach and Hollywood influences of the twenties.

The new landscaping and garden required an outside staff of four; one was Morris Homsher. When his young son, Lloyd, lost his right arm while working in a factory, S.R. took him on to help his father. The family was put in one of the houses, and Morris became head caretaker.

Against a backdrop reflecting the timeless beauty of the Pequea Valley, life at White Chimneys epitomized the roaring twenties at their most opulent. In the summer of '29, Bill, at fourteen, belted out "Bye, Bye, Blackbird" from his trumpet while Jane's teenage friends—boys in white flannels and girls flapper-skirted—danced in the ballroom. On weekends roadsters jammed the driveway while their young owners played tennis.

On one such afternoon six-year-old S.R. II wandered into the near tobacco shed, where he discovered several teenage boys drinking from an earthen jug. He innocently reported the incident to his grandfather, who was off to the shed in a flash. S.R. tongue-lashed the boys while they trudged dejectedly down the lane to their roadsters. They were drinking applejack. S.R.'s namesake never lived down the story.

Helen's "coming-out" party was a nocturnal lawn spectacular, exceeded in scope only by Jane's a few years later. For Jane's bash the dance floor was built, and the Lucky Strike Orchestra retained.

S.C. II hosted White Chimneys' fox hunts. After crowding the house on early-autumn mornings, red-coated riders were off on the chase across fallow fields and tawny hills. Then followed sumptuous hunt breakfasts during which silver cups were awarded for "the brush." A typical invitation, engraved in red ink, ran:

Mr. and Mrs. S. C. Slaymaker II
request the pleasure of your company
at a Hunt Breakfast
to be held at White Chimneys
Saturday, December tenth, Nineteen Twenty-seven
at eleven a.m.
The fox will be dropped at one p.m.
R.S.V.P. 1024 Marietta Avenue

After Helen and Jane finished at boarding school and had their debuts, they traveled abroad. Then they married, and there were no longer excuses for young people's parties. (Bill was later to hold his own, of which more soon.) But S.R., having come to enjoy these affairs, decided to make excuses for continuing them. He threw prewedding dinner dances for daughters of friends, "Brides Parties," he called them. By the mid-1930s these tapered off. S.R. and Minnie were spending some summers in Maine and winters in Florida. He was then in semiretirement. So on summer weekends Bill took over.

At Lawrenceville and Yale, attractive, fun-loving Bill was as well known for his airplanes as for his fine tenor voice. He traveled with the Yale Glee Club (was a Whiffenpoof) and soloed a plane at sixteen. His Yale crowd repaired to White Chimneys occasionally when his parents vacationed. These get-togethers—something out of the *Decameron*— were never reported to his parents by the staff.

The tenants of Slaymakertown were aghast one afternoon when an inebriated young man, naked but for shorts, shoes, and gartered stockings and a farmer's straw hat, sat a mule backward and rode around the front lawn blowing a trombone. Traffic was backed up to Salisbury Hill and into the Gap.

When a young girl waved a bra from a second-story window and the mule's rider blew frantically on the trombone in her direction, people got out of their cars. Then came a sight that brought tenants scurrying across the highway for a better view. The rider turned himself forward and, still blowing the trombone at the bra-waving girl, urged the mule up the mansion's front steps and onto the porch. Someone opened the door. But others got the mule turned around before damage was done by the rider's efforts to ride down the hallway.

Sometimes Bill landed his plane at the farm. But never when he thought S.R. was there. On one occasion S.R. was in residence and Bill didn't know it.

Bill flew down from New Haven, gave the house a fearful buzzing, and in the process of landing in a hayfield wiped out his landing gear. S.R. bolted into the driveway and watched the entire performance while muttering to Morris and Lloyd Homsher, "Wait'll that damn fool gets in here!"

He gave Bill unshirted hell. The plane's wings were removed, and it was carted to the Lancaster airport on a flatbed truck. Bill never landed at the farm again.

After Bill married in 1939 and went to work for Pratt and Whitney Aircraft in Hartford, Connecticut, White Chimneys' most colorful era drew to a close. When the S.R.'s were there, they still entertained, but sedately, on a small scale. There were small dinner parties for their friends. At the time college professors and businessmen still had common interests. So it was not surprising that S.R. and Minnie often entertained the Franklin and Marshall College president and various of his professors.

S.R.'s teenage grandson, S.R. II, spent the summers of 1938, '39, and '40 at White Chimneys working as a farm hand. His namesake had always been S.R.'s favorite grandchild. In the early 1930s he had taught "little Sam" to fish local streams. Later he kept the west lawn's run stocked with trout, exclusively for the boy. He took him on his tours of the farms, of his Lancaster real estate development, Grand View, always stressing that hard work and a devotion to one's responsibilities were, if not always the touchstones of success, rewards enough in themselves.

By those summers of the late thirties S.R. determined that his eldest grandchild would be the next squire of White Chimneys. He perceived

Samuel Redsecker Slaymaker II at age 16
Painting by Josephine K. Foltz

in the boy a profound love of the place, an interest in its history, and a streak of youthful obstinacy foretelling, with maturity, tenacity—all qualities which bade well for the future perpetuation of White Chimneys within the family.

S.R.'s son and daughter-in-law—S.C. II and Martha—were too wrapped up in Lancaster life to move to Gap. He knew the pitfalls inherent in leaving property split among children. So he took the logical step of willing the plantation and village to his grandson, with a proviso to the effect that if Minnie outlived him, she could hold the property until her death, at which time it would revert to S.R. II.

One hot August day in 1939 when S.R. II was sixteen he came in from the tobacco fields, showered, and dressed for dinner. His grandmother asked him to call S.R., who was walking in the flower garden.

On heading for the garden's east lawn portal the boy was horrified to see his grandfather's upward-turned shoes protruding from a flower bed. He rushed to the spot and found him conscious and angry at having fallen—confused at not being able to speak clearly. He seemed unaware that he had suffered a stroke.

S.R.'s health declined steadily, and he died at 427 North Duke Street on November 28, 1940. The funeral services were held in his crowded Lancaster home. S.R. was buried at Woodward Hill Cemetery next to his parents.

19

S.R.'s CAPTIVITY in the mansion can be likened to that of a penitentiary trusty who eventually makes warden. His desire to possess White Chimneys was so well inculcated by his father that S.R. put its firm acquisition before his first million. And when this came, he was able to practice conspicuous consumption to the extent that—like the trusty inmate turned high and mighty warden—one would have been hard put to remember his former status.

Still, S.R. was as willing a captive as his two predecessors. The big difference lay in his ability to dominate the mansion. They were dominated by it. In this respect he was like its builder, his progenitor, old Amos.

Similar, too, was the nature of their plans for perpetuating the family seat. Both took long shots. Amos gambled on a well-prepared son in desperate financial straits, S.R. on a grandson who had excellent chances of being solvent, but who was only an untried boy.

People who knew him remark about how "farseeing" S.R. was—how wise he was in not leaving the place divided among heirs and how I was "just the right one," etc., etc. But the fact remains that I was very lucky.

At first there was the unstinting interest and support of Lloyd, Don, my parents, Sal, Amos, and that most important ingredient, enhanced wherewithal.

Bittersweet memories were part of my researching of White Chimneys' Golden Age. Its artifacts—now so incongruous—were constantly in view. There was an invitation to the one-hundredth-anniversary party in 1907 and a copy of a poem read on the occasion that seemed too awful to include with this writing. These, along with an invitation to a 1929 fox hunt, were framed and hung in my study. On top of my desk were a couple of fox hunt trophies. Minnie's china closets were full of crystal goblets and finger bowls, Staffordshire and Wedgwood china—superfluous all for most of our dinner guests, who were often served on paper plates around an outdoor grill, hard by Francis Jones's tavern.

Then there were the portraits. Colonial, Federal, and Victorian paintings seemed neat and proper in the restored rear house and 1807 wing. The Sargent types in S.R.'s ballroom, while suitable enough, were simply too overpowering—especially since we had begun to use it as a living room. When, on an afternoon when Sal was alone in the house, a life-size painting of my Aunt Helen and her harp fell with an echoing crash, we decided that something must be done with the ballroom.

We had no desire to destroy the 1920s influence: the curved ceiling, brick fireplace, casement windows, and French door. We did, however, want a proper and restful living room. So we hit on repainting now dingy yellow walls and ceiling with a Williamsburg blue (walls) and eggshell white (ceiling). The red-brick fireplace was blended blue, into the walls. Lloyd and I built and painted floor-to-ceiling bookcases covering the entire west wall flanking the fireplace. We carpeted the oak flooring with a 10-by-18-foot Oriental rug donated by my parents.

Prior to Sal's arrival Lloyd and I had little time for the flower garden. It had come to look for all the world like one out of a Tennessee Williams novel. Pipes feeding the fountain and water lily pools had long since decayed. We ordered repairs for the fountain pipes but did away with the pools by filling them in and seeding grass. Arborvitae hedges— now half dead—were replaced with privet. Lloyd painted the pergola. Four rectangular flower beds now encircled the fountain. The pergola dominated the north end; two boxwood bushes, the south entrance; and lengthwise, privet hedge provided north-south borders. The result was a less constricted, more pristine garden which Sal and Lloyd found manageable. Perennial arrangements consisted of daffodils, tulips, iris, roses, day lilies, and phlox.

The artificial pool and run in the west lawn were forever filling with silt. So we bulldozed both.

Our functionalizing of hallmarks of long-gone opulence that were S.R.'s west wing and formal garden tended to mitigate wistful nostalgia on my part. At last the place was—to use an overworked word—a more relevant abode, one befitting our way of life, which by the early 1960s had taken a turn to outgoing jollity. At its new mistress's behest the squire emerged further from his shell and became involved in community life in Lancaster as well as Gap. We entertained friends at dinner parties. Large Christmas gatherings were held for our families. There were Memorial Day and Fourth of July cookouts, after which Gap's traditional parades were witnessed with the Reverend Huffard's family from the front lawn of the manse. Occasionally, we socialized in Lancaster, and I began to take on civic chores there. Sal joined the premier women's club of the Pequea Valley, the Mary Ferree Society, dedicated to perpetuating the memory of the indomitable lady pioneer.

On August 31, 1960, our first child arrived: a girl, Susan Frances. At long last, after three daughters and my becoming reconciled to being the last of the line, a boy arrived on June 28, 1963. He was baptized at Bellevue Church and named Samuel Cochran Slaymaker III, after my father and the Colonel. Like their much-loved older sisters, Libby and Caroline, the children were befriended by area youngsters, particularly the Reverend Huffard's offspring and the youngest Walkers.

In 1857, J. C. Walker founded his grist mill in Gap and was soon successful enough to become a banker. A first customer was Colonel S. C. Slaymaker. The mill and bank continued in the Walker family and, like my predecessors, I deal with both. On those first summer weekends in the late 1950s, when my Libby and Caroline visited, we often swam in Colonel "Pete" Walker's pool and picnicked on the broad lawns of his home, Henry F. Slaymaker's onetime Railroad Hotel. Our children personified a friendship spanning five generations.

Conversation in the Sign of John Adams home of the Clinton Himes Martins also yielded descriptions of the property in the 1890s.

Clint's aged mother, Sarah Himes Martin, an old friend of my grand-mother, vividly described Slaymakertown, the Colonel and Jane's socials, their children's hay rides and sleighing parties. Her grandson, James David Clinton Himes Martin IV, Peter David Walker, and Libby and Caroline comprised a preteen foursome dubbed by the Reverend Sam Huffard "the Gap 400."

Judge Henry Slaymaker's Mt. Pleasant home is now owned, al-though not lived in, by my lawyer, a fishing and hunting crony, Ralph Eby. His family have been large landowners since the eighteenth-century days of his pioneer ancestor, Mennonite Peter Eby.

Mt. Pleasant is on the Gap-Strasburg Road (the onetime Great Conestoga) and is so situated on Eby lands that it could be conveniently detached, as it were, and sold. I allowed as to how it might be nice if someday I bought and restored it. The attorney bellowed, "You don't need another house." To which rejoinder I hastily agreed. Nevertheless, the idea still persists, especially when I go in the empty place and feel the same nostalgia expressed by Judge Henry's ailing daughter, Lydia.

Leacock Church is nearby on the old Philadelphia Pike (the pre-vious King's Highway). Slaymakers from Mathias's generation through Amos's lie here in "Slaymaker Row." Revolutionary War markers and flags are placed by the headstones of Leacock VII Battalion veterans. While the stones are badly weathered (the eulogistic poem on Henry's is almost illegible), Leacock Church is beautifully preserved as a historic shrine. Services are held on special occasions.

Mathias Slaymaker's first church, Pequea Presbyterian, is in use, but there is no trace of the Reverend Robert Smith's Latin School.

Cochranville is still a hamlet on Route 41 to Wilmington, Delaware (the old Newport turnpike). Samuel Cochran's mansion is a private dwelling unspoiled and in excellent repair. But it was difficult for me to see it as Samuel did: a self-sufficient plantation set in Chester County's rolling, verdant hills. For much of the land has been built upon, and the mansion's grandeur has been fatally compromised.

Such, happily, is not the case with Jasper Yeates's Belmont planta-tion. It went out of the Yeates family in the mid-nineteenth century. In 1932 my grandfather bought the home and its 125 acres for his daughter, my Aunt Jane, who lives in Pittsburgh. Her farmer, Glen Miller, and his family now reside there. One of Belmont's most interesting features is a hearth inlaid with Delft tile. Legend has it that President Washington received the tile from the Netherlands Ambassador. Not wanting to keep the gift, he turned it over to Judge Yeates for his then planned-for mansion. Before the hearth facing was completely "tiled," the set obviously ran out, because the job was never completed!

Many were the summer evenings that I fly-fished for bass on our farm pond and watched the sun sink behind the slope topped by Belmont. At sunset on summer evenings like these the plump jurist and the spare squire could have been seen pacing that wide piazza while discussing new farming methods, politics, and their families.

Duffield Manor is a comfortable white-plaster farmhouse directly opposite White Chimneys, to the south of Slaymakertown. It was the seat of a remarkable family who settled there just after the Revolution. Three successive generations boasted nationally known Presbyterian divines. Dr. William B. Duffield was Amos's doctor from 1792 to 1820. Like the Cochrans, several of the family married Slaymakers. Just before World War I my grandfather bought the farm and house (one hundred acres). It was sold at my grandmother's death. The new Amish owner moved in just before my arrival in Gap.

This continuing association with families, homes, and landmarks having roots deep in areas of my research reinforced a willingness to remain the mansion's captive. I was like the model prisoner who, on being faced with the possibility of parole, chooses to "stay on the inside." Sal, as a newcomer, was still enamored with a novel and pleasing way of life. But she became progressively aware of its inconveniences and perceived harbingers of strictures on marital bliss, particularly in the form of tenant houses. These dawned like thunder in 1966 when Clint Martin decided to sell all of the old Sign of John Adams property except the building and its immediate environs. Twenty-five acres, Amos Slaymaker's old stage barn, a tenant house, and garage were to be sold. He came to me before putting the properties on the market.

The prospect of restoring virtually the same boundaries obtaining at the time of the Yeates-Slaymaker split in 1795 was exciting. But when I broached the subject to Sal, it was plain that a Lizzie Borden type of ax murder was in the offing.

I was almost out of hock and would have been were it not for continuing tenant house repairs. Still, we were able to take vacations in the Poconos and, as the hackneyed saying goes, "live a little." So acquiring another tenant house was more than Sal could bear. Lawyer Ralph repeated his injunction about houses to the effect that there were two things I didn't need: another house and another divorce, and that acquisition of the first might lead to the second. But, be it remembered, I was a successful salesman. The purchase was made and the domicile preserved.

Back to the bank I went, but happily so—proof positive that if Amos had haunted me into captivity in his mansion, he had been eminently successful. So successful, indeed, that the need for occult influences no longer existed. And there were none, ever again.

While Sal hated the tenant houses, she was a friend and confidant of their renters. Their children played with ours; and as they said in Amos Slaymaker's day, "harmony prevailed." We had no tenant turnovers for five years.

Particularly, Sal was popular with the Yoders and their Stoltzfus in-laws.

The following lines are written with the approbation of Barbara Yoder, since we have long since buried the hatchet.

Amos Yoder is possessed of a fine sense of humor, born of an almost latitudinarian acceptance of "English" ways. (The Amish refer to the non-"plain" as "English.") Barbara is more strict in outlook. We had our wrangles when Amish custom clashed with English farm management practices.

During a late spring, Amos got behind in his plowing. It was incumbent that he get caught up, and fast, since planting would be delayed to the detriment of our crops. I arranged to rent a tractor and Lloyd offered to plow, thus getting Amos off the hook. Barbara castigated me mightily. When I went ahead, notwithstanding, she insisted that we remove the tractor's tires (some Amish will permit tractors if tires are removed). This I refused to do.

"You, Sam, will go to hell for this!" she shouted, waving her finger in my face. I said that I might end up there, but that if I did, it wouldn't be because of the tractor. I shouted, "I'll see you down there for being bullheaded!"

For the first time I succumbed to Slaymakertown's longtime virus. Barbara and I "weren't speaking" for several days, much to the tenants' delight. Then Sal brought us together again. But not for long.

On a lovely morning a couple of weeks later we awoke to the sounds of exploding rifle bullets. I ran to our bedroom window and was horrified to see flames and smoke erupting beside the farmer's house across the highway. Colonel Slaymaker's old carriage house was burning down. Amos had some 22-caliber rifle ammunition inside. I threw on a bathrobe and raced across the road as the Gap Fire Company trucks arrived. Oblivious of exploding cartridges, we gathered around the structure, now totally enveloped in flames while the fire fighters vainly tried to save it. It was a total loss.

It turned out that Barbara, on kindling her wood stove to heat washing water in the carriage house, had accidentally set it on fire. This, after I'd urged her since the Yoders' arrival to use an already installed electric heater!

I blew up to the extent that our farm agreement was on the verge of being voided. Then, as the carriage house sank to cherry-red embers, Patriarch Jake embraced me, apologized on his daughter's behalf, and assured me that in the future when I "ordered" Barbara to use a facility, he personally would back her up with the bishop. Jake assured me that his family would help in raising a new building. This delighted the insurance company—and me. For we had hit the company so hard of late that I feared for our future insurability. Only two weeks before, the mansion had caught fire.

On Saturday morning, March 6, 1965, Sal and the children were in Gap shopping. I was reviewing barn repairs with Amos and Lloyd. On coming out of the barn we saw dirty brown smoke pouring from the mansion's chimneys. I ran to the kitchen. It was full of smoke and the phone was dead. We dashed across the highway to Lloyd's house to call the Gap Fire Company. The trucks arrived in scant minutes.

The blaze in cellar beams was persistent and caused heavy smoke, which made it difficult to extinguish. The firemen had to wear masks. In an hour they succeeded in controlling the fire and soon stopped it.

A bad wire had caused the fire, which burned through the floor of the first room in the front house adjoining the dining room. The resulting hole was a foot from an Empire papier-mâché table. Miraculously, it was not impaired. Other than the flooring, nothing was burned. But smoke damage was heavy. Had the fire occurred at night, the mansion and ourselves would probably have been destroyed.

We moved into my parents' home in Lancaster for ten days. On returning and for months afterward, we smelled the acrid scent of smoke. The insurance company covered everything except the inevitable locking of the barn after the horse has been stolen: to wit, new wiring for the entire house and a fire alarm system.

As the earlier squire's deliberations and actions affected my own—through my identification with theirs—so S.R.'s philosophy began to rub off on me; more markedly than was the case with our predecessors, because I had reverential remembrances of my grandfather in addition to some of his correspondence and various published biographies. It was high time. I had been too long controlled by White Chimneys. It seemed incumbent that—like the first S.R.—the second must needs hit on a way to dominate the place on his own terms.

The times and to some degree previously made business commitments precluded my setting about to make a million. Another way would have to be found. With the excitement of the challenge came a dawning realization that I was reverting to type. As a purposeful setter and meeter of deadlines, I had been very much like S.R. I, a fact noted by those in the business who remembered him. We even looked alike, they said. The mellowing effect of my research and squiring years spiked by a rekindled sense of direction just might, I thought, result in a wiser head, fit to solve the problem of White Chimneys' future.

It was time for stocktaking. I began by reviewing my life as it related to the farm from the days of my earliest recollections.

I can dimly remember sitting on the rear seat of my parents' green Cadillac touring car while they stood in the lane nearby and discussed with S.R. and Minnie my Great-aunt Rebecca and Great-uncle Harry. "Becky" had died a couple of years before; Harry, having contracted tuberculosis, had been placed in a sanatorium.

Another tableau of the late 1920s made a stronger impression. I can see quite clearly a distinguished elderly lady standing in the formal garden conversing with Minnie and S.R. She was "cousin" Mary Cameron, Senator Simon Cameron's granddaughter. I had been feeding goldfish in the lily pad pools, accompanied by my ninety-year-old black nanny, "Nana," who was born a slave in the South and had come to Colonel Slaymaker's household as a young woman. She had cared for S.R. I, S.C. II, and me, when I visited the farm. Nana led me around the fountain to greet Miss Mary Cameron.

"Master Sammy," Miss Mary said, "come here and I'll tell you a story."

We walked to the pergola, where she sat in a rocker and took me on her lap. She said that when she was about my age she was staying with her grandfather in Washington when President Lincoln came to call. He almost frightened her, being so tall and stern-looking. Mr. Lincoln must have sensed the little girl's feeling, for Miss Mary said something like "He leaned over, picked me up, stood me on the piano, and remarked, 'Now, Missy Mary, I can get a better look at you.'" She remembered feeling much better and laughing.

I have no memories of the applejack incident which occurred about the same time, but as noted, I've never been permitted to forget that it happened.

Perhaps these two initial memories of White Chimneys—disconnected as they were—are lasting, because the first reflects realization of the fact of death; the second, an emerging reverence for things historical. Recollections of following years came more clearly and began to assume a pattern.

My sister, Ann Louise (born in 1925), and I grew up in our parents' Lancaster home. On the ending of our school years we came to the farm as guests of Minnie and S.R. Summers came to mean, literally, fun and games. I was blissfully unaware of the ravages of the Great Depression. While I vaguely remember my father's concern about layoffs in the business, nothing—particularly at White Chimneys—seemed to change. S.R.'s varied interests suffered, but his aversion to "stock market gambling" had stood him in good stead when came the crash of '29.

With my Aunt Helen's children, Helena and Jack Mitchell, Ann and I, along with the farmers' and tenants' children, played hide-and-seek in the evenings. Throughout long, hot days we sailed boats on the west lawn's pool, flew model airplanes from the top of the silo, swam in the pasture stream, and rode the hay wagons. Rainy days were spent in the playhouse.

The coronation of King George VI in 1937 prompted Jack Mitchell, aged ten, to declare himself "King John of Pequea." He reigned from a throne in the playhouse. Levees, replete with lemonade and crackers, were held there, and he dubbed us all with titles.

One of Amos Slaymaker's old stagecoaches was stored in the main tobacco shed. It had been reconditioned after World War I for use in local parades. The farmer hitched it with horses, and King John rode in triumph from the tobacco shed to the playhouse (waving all the way), where my sister crowned his wigged head with a brass flower pot.

We took postcoronation drinks of lemonade on the east lawn. Festivities were cut short, however, by the arrival of Uncle Bill. He and a couple of his flying Yale friends had been at an "air meet" in Wilmington. Since S.R. was in residence, they *drove* up for the night and arrived feeling a bit high.

Bill stared incredulously at the scenario before the playhouse, bolted over, and tore away King John's robe. I went in the house with Bill and heard him say to Minnie, "That damn fool is out on the lawn with a brass pot on his head and my good counterpane dragging on the grass!"

I enjoyed this visit of Bill's because of an incident which I—as opposed to the younger children—could appreciate since, at fourteen, I knew the "facts of life."

Minnie's old-maid companion, Evie (the retired art teacher), had been receiving visits for a couple of years from a septuagenarian gentleman caller. When she primped for his calls, Bill ribbed her unmercifully, much to the delight of my grandparents. On this particular evening Evie's gentleman caller, Henry, arrived bearing a gift-wrapped package. We were all on the front porch where Minnie, S.R., and Evie were rocking.

Evie, blushing as red as her lipstick, opened the package and displayed a pair of shoes, suitably as large as proverbial canal boats. I can see Bill now, leaning against a pillar, saying, "Hey, Evie, what the hell did you have to do for Henry to get those shoes!"

S.R. rarely laughed loudly. But at this he did so lengthily, much to Evie's and Henry's embarrassment.

After the King's disrobing we turned to a more red-bloodedly American area of make-believe. In the rear of the barn was an ancient Conestoga wagon. It might well have been in the family since Colonial times. The wagon, too, was reconditioned for parade use. We got it out and staged pioneer-Indian battles around it. Both the wagon and the coach were sold by Minnie after S.R.'s death. The coach ended up in Hollywood, the wagon in a museum.

Far and away my favorite activity over these summers was fishing with my grandfather. S.R. drove us with picnic lunches to the glassy riffles of the Octoraro Creek, where we caught smallmouth bass. Sunfish were sought in the more placid Pequea and Mill creeks. S.R. always enjoyed bringing in a basket of fish for the next morning's breakfast.

On one occasion when we had empty creels and he was unhappy, we drove by some boys trailing a heavy stringer of sunfish. S.R. stopped the car, backed up, and offered the boys one dollar for their fish. Wide-eyed and happy, they came across.

"Don't tell anyone," S.R. warned, "where and how we caught these fish."

When S.R. stocked the pool and run with trout, he told me that "these are fish deserving of flies." He had fly-fished with the Colonel in the Pocono Mountains when, as a boy, he accompanied his father on railroad surveys. S.R. gave me basic instructions and I became a fly angler.

Now, years later, as an outdoor writer, a fly tier, and an activist in trout conservation work, I recall that fish-buying incident and wonder what S.R. would think about my returning most of my catches to the water so as to provide sport for other anglers. Were he here now, he would surely think me foolish. This prompts me to wonder how he would take to my writing about *l'affaire* Boyd. On reflection I'm convinced that with a little effort I could sell him on my rationale in both cases.

In the fall of 1937 I was sent to board at the Lawrenceville School in New Jersey. During succeeding summers my life of fun and games on the farm was forgone for one of labor in the wheat, tobacco, and hay fields. I didn't need the encouragement given by my father and grand-father. There was the desire to body-build in order to improve my athletic standing at school. At this time my grandfather began to take me on his rounds and to talk about my taking over someday.

The younger children's activities—so much a part of mine only a summer before—seemed irrelevant. On rainy days when they frolicked in the playhouse (Ann and Helena sometimes donned their great-great-grandmother Rebecca Cochran Slaymaker's wedding dress), I explored the garrets and talked with S.R. Only on Sundays did we youngsters perform in concert. As always, we went to the Bellevue Sunday school, where Minnie taught and donated Bibles to the senior class each year.

My last boyhood summer at White Chimneys was that of 1940. I listened avidly to radio reports of the Battle of Britain. Always air-minded, I now became obsessed with becoming an airman and joining the fray.

During one of the bacchanalian weekend frolics in which my school friends indulged in New York, I decided in 1941, at age eighteen, to make the move.

A plain-clothes committee was recruiting Americans for the Royal Canadian Air Force in the Waldorf-Astoria Hotel. That the Canadian Aviation Bureau endeavored to operate within U.S. neutrality laws did not deter "America Firsters" from picketing the hotel. I clearly remember alighting from a cab in a new Chesterfield coat, facing the pickets indecisively for a few seconds, and then bolting through the front entrance.

Application was made, and I was put on a waiting list. Then came Pearl Harbor. I was advised to join the U.S. Army Air Forces. Applicants were so backed up that I had to cool my heels in the lock company's tool room for almost a year.

After receiving my wings at Yuma, Arizona, as a radio operator and aerial gunner I was assigned to a B-17 bomber group of the Eighth Air Force in England. My tour in England was responsible for a most crucial turning point in my young life. As is so often the case, it was due to happenstance.

History was always my favorite subject in school. So I spent leaves sightseeing. Much free time was available, because nonflying time was virtually our own. I was stationed near Cambridge and spent a couple of days there in the autumn of 1944.

Through a chance meeting with the master of Corpus Christi College, who knew my school's headmaster, I received an invitation to study there after the war—contingent, of course, on its being won and my living through it.

I came home from my tour of missions with the usual Eighth Air Force combat decorations and my appetite for warfare more than sated. After V-J Day I took up the master of Corpus's offer, flew to England, and entered the college as an undergraduate "reading" history in the Easter term, 1946.

To live and study and imbibe with friends in quarters that have served such purposes for six hundred years is to inspire more than that euphemistic something called a "sense of history." Such surroundings can provide, in simple terms, an unquenchable desire for the hard work required of aspiring scholars. Thus, when my supervisor heard me read my first paper and remarked that it "read like a rather bad American movie script," I took no offense. In school years I would have. But thanks to the Cambridge atmosphere, I dug in and taught myself to write.

I "went down" from Cambridge with second-class honors after the spring term in 1947, returned to the States, and settled into the real world of marriage and raising and supporting a family. At first business seemed unenthusing. Then our sales manager was smitten by a stroke of genius. He thought me just the one to fill a vacant territory—a most unpromising one—West Virginia.

I was put on the road, enjoyed the experience greatly, and was successful. Selling success led to my being picked to train new salesmen; later to handle key accounts, which meant more traveling. All the while my marriage was foundering. The breakup came in mid-July, 1955. My grandmother died on August first.

It was during these difficult days that the lawyers badgered me about selling White Chimneys. They probably felt that with the Duffield Manor and Avondale farms going on the block a clean sweep was in order. I don't blame them now. For with the divorce, White Chimneys' future didn't look at all promising. But I wasn't so tolerant then. After one of these sessions I angrily stomped from their offices, got into my car, and began that drive down Route 30, the onetime Philadelphia-Lancaster Turnpike, toward Slaymakertown.

20

I CAME TO SEE these fond remembrances of White Chimneys summers as crucial to its later rehabilitation. For the early attachment to the place which they epitomized led directly to my urge, in 1955, to dig out its true story and to make it a continuing one. On doing this I discovered the real significance of White Chimneys. It had escaped my predecessors, a fact proved by their general lack of interest in and knowledge of the contents of the old family papers. They bore out the truth of the well-worn saw about truth being stranger than fiction.

Familial mobility is and has been a distinctive fact of American life, an exception proving the rule being this family's presence in one locale for more than 250 years. Moreover, for almost two centuries Slaymakers evolved under one roof. Their hoarded paintings, artifacts, and architectural aberrations mirror a microcosmic saga of the nation itself.

Significant were the neatly compacted life spans of the family's heads. Each fell within American history's commonly accepted "station breaks." Mathias lived in the Early Colonial period; the first Henry's career spanned the later Colonial, as his son Amos's did the Federal. Henry F. and Colonel S.C. were respectively early and late Victorians, while S.R., my father, and I were and are of modern times.

Our ongoing home, then, represented a phenomenon unusual enough to merit public attention.

Given my occupation (sales promotion) and our location (in the heart of the nation's number one tourist area), it's obvious that salvation lay in riding the tourist boom. My first local historical writings and their attendant publicity led to occasional house tours. Historical, patriotic, and educational groups requested them, and I obliged, gratis. With the explosion of Amish tourism in the mid-1960s, eastern Lancaster County in general, and U.S. 30 east in particular, became garish studies in phony Pennsylvania Dutch honky-tonkism.

A taste-conscious promoter and friend felt the need of an attraction that did not smack of the "Dutch Country," something symptomatic of the area's varied cultural background, the better to blunt mounting criticism of the tourist industry's alleged prostitution of the Amish. White Chimneys was singled out as the answer.

The idea intrigued me. But first we needed a theme which would epitomize the home's singularity. There are many ancient family seats containing indigenous paintings and antiques. How was White Chimneys "different"?

Previously noted were Sal's comments—on her discovery of the Redsecker china—to the effect that the real charm of the place lay in its mélange of periods, its architectural aberrations which precluded restoration to any given era. Earlier, too, I commented on feeling relieved that the dining room's marble Victorian mantel had not been replaced by one of the twin originals which I found in the garret. In light of Sal's observation, the marble mantel—ugly though it was—typified this architectural mix of periods. So did the colored tiles in the front house's fireplaces, the Hollywood-Spanish influence lent the ballroom, together with Federal mantels and columns throughout Amos's wings.

Unlike many old homes which are in themselves "period pieces," this one reflected *each* American architectural era as completely as its paintings, papers, antiques, and artifacts. White Chimneys, then, could accurately be termed a "House of American History."

While pondering the possibilities of escape through tourism, we were faced with the prospect of an experience as exciting as it was strangely coincidental.

Mentioned earlier was the fact that one of the artist Wertmüller's subjects was Revolutionary France's first Minister to the United States, Edmond Genêt. Instead of returning to the dangerous uncertainties of France's Reign of Terror, "Citizen" Genêt remained in America. He married the daughter of New York Governor George Clinton and settled along the Hudson.

The last Genêt of his line is a lady who is a contemporary of mine

Federal: front parlor of
1807 wing. Mirror reflects
portraits of Rebecca
Cochran and Henry
Fleming Slaymaker

House of many mansions: entrance hall
to White Chimneys, as it looks today

Federal: rear parlor, from reception hall.
Portrait of Faithful Richardson Slaymaker
above mantel.

Colonial: present-day
kitchen—original Francis
Jones Tavern

Contemporary: 1923 west wing, with Sarah Hazzard Slaymaker
and ninth-generation children,
Susan Frances and Samuel Cochran Slaymaker III

and a lifelong friend, Nancy Genet. Nancy and her mother, Mrs. A. Rivers Genet, are owners of Wertmüller's *Citizen Genêt*. That both of us owned Wertmüllers—which in America are scarce—was coincidental. More so were Nancy's efforts to interest her employer in White Chimneys. Nancy was an editor of *Life* magazine. Were *Life* to do a piece on the home, it would dovetail with my idea of establishing its validity as a landmark, now on a national level.

Life's editors were as intrigued with the home's reflecting all eras of American history as they were with the fact that our family lived in a veritable museum. It was determined that these phenomena merited a picture story of the home's evolution. Editor Muriel Hall was put in charge. The photographer was Nina Leen.

Two years after the project was undertaken, the August 25, 1967, issue of *Life* appeared with a thirteen-page feature piece titled "Houseful of Our History," an exquisite rendition in color photography of the home's story, beginning with Francis Jones's and Mathias Slaymaker's cabins and ending with Sal working in the flower garden.

I was in Seattle, Washington, on business when this issue of *Life* appeared. Sal was deluged with phone calls from family, friends, and pitchmen. She started to put the latter types through to my motel. The first got me out of bed late at night by exploding, "My God, mister, you people got more coverage than ancient Greece!"

He went on about being an account executive in a Manhattan ad agency who had a mouth-wash client. "Jesus, what a view for a commercial—that garden and meadow scene's a beaut," etc., etc.

Not having that kind of promoting in mind, I hastily signed him off. Later another adman phoned. He, representing an aftershave lotion company, saw the formal garden—with the water fountain and pergola as backdrops—"just perfect" for a film clip of a couple loving it up to the greater glory of the aftershave lotion.

I phoned Sal and requested a cutoff. She spared me five more calls, from a Philadelphia tour promoter to a Sunday supplement free-lance seeking an inside story on how *Life* did the job.

For months the property was besieged by tourists. Cars slowed, and many stopped by the lawn. Others were driven in the back lane. Some people peeked in windows. A few knocked on the front door and asked admittance. When I could, I talked with them.

This interest was to be expected. That it would taper off (some are still at it) was also understandable. So there was no need to rush an "opening." It would have been crudely unrealistic to try to merchandise the *Life* piece. Its effects would have had only flash-in-the-pan longevity. It was enough that the home was now properly established as a landmark that would appeal to growing numbers of the more discriminating lovers of Americana.

Planning a project that would be adducive yet enlightening would take time. Meanwhile, on the theory that nothing succeeds like success, I decided to await additional opportunities to undergird the home's distinctiveness. They seemed sure to arise and did, in the form of articles in regional publications and art reviews. The Pennsylvania Historical and Museum Commission placed a large descriptive marker in front of the house. The manuscript collection was lent to the Commission for microfilming.

As a result of the publicity we were visited by celebrities—Mrs. John Eisenhower, Phil Harris, Curt Gowdy, Lord Snowden, and that eminent British authority on America, Sir Denis Brogan.

We treasure memories of these big-name visits. They were fun and inflated our egos. But their import went deeper. In a sense they justified my garret decision of years before.

For me—to parody nurse Edith Cavell on patriotism—restoration "was not enough." Had I restored for my personal satisfaction, I would have been like a painter who refused to show or a writer who eschews publishing. The completed effort, I'd come to believe, should be shared and enjoyed by others. VIP interest proved that the game had been worth the candle. We genuinely had something for the public's edification. It only remained to set a date for opening up.

A benumbing wind blustered about the auction shed in Intercourse, Pennsylvania, on the afternoon of February 5, 1972. Roughly a hundred souls crowded the auctioneer's platform. There were many dark-garbed plain folk, a scattering of blue-jeaned long-hair types, some earnest-looking businessmen, and a clutch of tweedy matrons whose tanned, weather-beaten visages bespoke a Palm Beach winter. One of the ladies had just bid successfully on a battered spool bed and a brass four-poster. There was little to interest most bidders in the remaining pile of musty pillows, threadbare comforters, and picture frames—some mildewed, most containing New Testament scenes.

As the crowd drifted toward the concessionaire for steaming soup and coffee the auctioneer cried: "Now for the big one, a large tobacco shed on the Slaymakers' White Chimneys farm!"

Here *was* a switch! From whatnot junk to a farm building! "And in top repair, too," he continued.

"Come up here, Mr. Slaymaker, and tell 'em about it."

Amish farmers became intent and edged closer to the stand as I attested to the tobacco shed's fine condition.

The auctioneer opened at $1,000. No takers. Then two Amishmen began bidding $350, $400, $500, $600, until the shed was finally "knocked down" at $670, roughly its cost when S.R. had it built back in the 1920s.

Still, it was a good deal for me and the white-bearded patriarch purchaser. A new shed could cost him at least $2,000. I no longer needed it. Our farm buildings were to be painted in July. There was no sense in painting what we couldn't use, and were it not painted, it would clash awfully with the buildings that were, not to mention that the building would require insurance, taxes, and eventually repairs. At no expense I was able to get rid of it for its cost. Such arrangements usually call for buyers to dismantle buildings at their own expense. In the case of the Amish no money is involved because, like barn raisings, removals and reconstruction are community efforts.

When a landowner sells a building or a major piece of equipment at such a typical Lancaster County auction, his neighbors often interpret the move as a harbinger of an eventual sellout. That ours assumed as much was soon obvious.

"The talk is," Lloyd said, "that you're getting tired of the place, and you'll be selling out in bits and pieces."

We both laughed because the opposite was the case. We were making the farm more adaptable to future conditions. As a redundant ballroom had been converted to a family room with a 21-inch color TV set to facilitate modern living, so the farm was in the first stage of transformation. The sale of the tobacco shed signaled our move to an expanded steer-fattening operation in which the preponderance of acreage will be in corn and only a few acres will remain in tobacco—just enough to fill our remaining shed.

The move seems a sensible one. The U.S. per capita consumption of beef two decades ago was 62.2 pounds. Today it's 117, and an end to the rise is not in sight, as long as this consumption is concomitant with increasing incomes. Tobacco is as difficult to grow as corn is easy. So while we'll always want some tobacco for a cash crop, in the long run conversion to corn as our basic commodity will make for a more economic operation in the future. What of the future?

It's been five years now since we decided on opening up for tourists, but we haven't got around to doing so. This will be a difficult move to make. While I'm not one to live in the past, I admit to enjoying life with mementos of White Chimneys' bygone years. I can't go up and down the front stairs without seeing the rack by the front door where stand Amos Slaymaker's walking sticks—his Lafayette-head cane and two of Simon Cameron's: a gold-headed one and another which he whittled from a tree limb. In the kitchen hangs our prized letter of 1777 from George Washington to General John Cochran.

In the kitchen, too, is the framed letter from Hannah Cochran to her son concerning the Ann Coleman–James Buchanan affair and a bill to Amos Slaymaker for a slave. In the upstairs hallway are framed stock certificates, bills of sales, and deeds from Amos's halcyon years. Together with the antiques these documents—only a bare fraction of the entire manuscript collection— bear testimony to an American *Cavalcade* which should be shared with lovers of U.S. history. Since the *Cavalcade* continues and we're part of it, however, I feel a lingering urge to keep on keeping on, thus savoring our possessions in solitary, as it were. Hence the delay in opening up. But I know that my state of ambivalence will pass. And I'll be glad when it does, for our plans can perpetuate the plantation for the next squire.

Libby recently graduated from college and is teaching in a New York City girls' school. Caroline is studying ballet in Philadelphia. Their interests and probable future marriages will preclude all but occasional visits here. Sue, at twelve, feels uncomfortable with friends who dwell in less pretentious houses and would rather live in a ranch house.

Samuel Cochran Slaymaker III, nine, is the logical future squire;

hopefully, though, one who will operate within the self-denying though safe strictures which I plan for him, namely an incorporated tourist operation.

On writing these lines I permit myself a wry smile. In a sense we're still captives of our mansion. But now we've got the upper hand, the better to ensure White Chimneys' permanence as a houseful of American history throughout years to come.

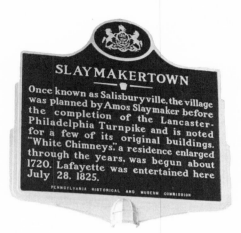

Slaymakertown marker in front of White Chimneys

Epilogue—Monday, July 24, 1972

ON RETURNING from the office this evening I could not help recalling that summer day in 1955 when I drove this same Route 30 and, with feelings reminiscent of an approaching ether sleep, became White Chimneys' fifth squire. Extreme trepidation on that drive was felt as keenly as contentedness on this one. My felicitous state owed entirely to the renewing experience that was researching and writing this book. Hopefully, I'll be pardoned a bit of introspection—born of reflection—beginning when I rounded Salisbury Hill and looked down on Slaymakertown.

I remembered that in 1955 the mansion had just been painted, an effort that was to it what a face-lifting is to an aging dowager. This evening the mansion's exterior (painted last year) had no deteriorating interior to hide. It signified a well-kept home, just as the barn and tobacco shed, which had received double coats early this month, epitomized a well-ordered farm.

After being greeted by the family I felt impelled to walk alone up the back lane to the top of the hill. It's wheat-threshing time, and Amos

Yoder rented a threshing machine from an Amish neighbor. The entire Yoder family and four helping neighbors were feeding lemon-colored wheat sheaves into the clanking, puffing steam thresher on the south slope.

On reaching the hilltop I gazed on eight-foot-tall stands of corn glistening emerald under a copper-colored sunset. Half-grown tobacco plants looked crisp and promising. A cooling clover-scented breeze— welcome after almost two weeks of record-breaking heat—played across hay strips in the north waterway. How improved was the state of the slopes over what they had been when Don Ranck showed them to me seventeen years ago!

Old area landmarks were as comforting as the lush cropland was pleasing. Bellevue Church, Duffield Manor, and the neat, compact tenant houses reflected a light gold glow from the sinking sun behind the highway atop Salisbury Hill. That damned cluttered highway! This particular segment, known as "death highway," has one of the highest fatality rates of any combined three- and four-lane road in the country. Its average daily traffic rate in July, 1971, was 17,588 vehicles, making it one of the nation's most heavily traveled highways.

The view beyond the tourist traps bordering the road is depressing, too. Thanks to ever-rising land taxes, farms are becoming building lots and this part of the "Garden Spot" is being engulfed by a creeping mauve and chartreuse fungus of split-level similitude.

I forced forgetfulness on the subject by being thankful for small blessings. The first Salisbury township zoning meeting was held in White Chimneys in 1971. And, happily, there's now a move afoot to assesss farmland at lower rates. So the highway is beyond redemption. At least there is good reason to believe that the beauty of outlying areas of the Pequea Valley can be preserved. The zoning meeting, our plans for the mansion's future, the revamped farming operation epitomized that afore-mentioned renewing process.

Early in my research I was impressed by the fact that none of the squires excelled in statecraft and the arts. They seemed forever occupied with the mundane, day-to-day pressures of staying afloat and those born of the pursuit of wealth. I thought of them as a money-grubbing lot and wished that at least one squire had unscrambled priorities and put the common weal, if not ahead of, at least on a plane with perpetuation of his plantation. But none could do so because in varying degrees they were its captives. As such, fealty was due it at the expense of all else.

Later I began to find this not all bad. Perhaps it was for the best. After all, the family's tenacious hold on its property *has* resulted in this singular home. Here is a collective contribution surpassing in value any others which might have been made individually in the name of human betterment. If they did not contribute to the arts, they were at least connoisseurs enough to collect and to hoard. Had they not done so, their home could never have reflected the story of the United States, writ small.

Important also was the fact that they were producers. Each contributed through commerce and industry to his country's gross national product. A pedestrian observation, this, but some must produce the wherewithal so that "public servants" can serve.

Of the lot, of course, my grandfather was the best producer. His grateful family revered him as such. But I owed him a special debt of gratitude, the magnitude of which increased as I became aware of his struggle to master his inheritance and preserve it, out of respect for his forebears. Certainly *he* did not think them an ordinary lot. It seemed unbecoming for me to do so. It was then that I began to reassess the collective contribution of the squires, found it good, and became inspired to plan a future for the place that would be deserving of its past.

These were presumptuous ruminations—even for a country squire surveying his acres from a hilltop at sunset. But they came naturally. For I'd devoted many years to breathing new life into the old white elephant—years which might have been much less trying had the experience been forgone. But deep down I now know that my decision of '55 had been the right one.

The sun had sunk behind Salisbury Hill, leaving the sky over Jasper Yeates's Belmont with salmon-pink tints reflected clearly in the still farm pond toward which the threshing party was repairing for an evening swim. I began to walk downhill to the mansion and the study where I would write this epilogue.

On doing so now I feel a lingering sense of embarrassment. Somehow it seems improper to be so self-satisfied. I remind myself that such an outlook is altogether proper. After all, it goes with my calling, and I don't feel up to fighting it.

Index

White Chimneys (*cont'd*)
180, 183; restoration after 1956, 23–26, 47–48, 119–122, 165–170, 188, *see also under* Slaymaker, Samuel R., II; Samuel C.'s management, 151–156, 162–164; Samuel R. in, 173, 176–178, 180–181, 183–187; silver, 166–167; tilt mill, 76, 135–136; tobacco shed sold, 206; as tourist attraction, 201, 204–205, 207, 208; Victorian period remodeling, 25–26, 47, 111, 134–135, 152, 154–155; water supply, 152, 154, 176
Whitehill, James, 87
Whitehill family, 152
Willard, Simon, Jr., 75

Winder, General, 86
Wolfe, Gen. James, 32
Woodhull, Rev. John, 37–38, 40
World War I, 177–178
World War II, 198–199
Wrightsville, 159

Yale, 178, 184
Yeates, Jasper, 33, 35, 36, 45, 55–59, 61, 62, 71, 75, 76, 80, 107, 176, 190–191, 211
Yeates School, 176
Yoder, Amos, 169–170, 192–193, 209–211
Yoder, Barbara, 169–170, 192–193
York, 159, 160

73 74 75 76 77 10 9 8 7 6 5 4 3 2 1